FOOTHOLDS

FOOTHOLDS

Understanding the Shifting Family
and Sexual Tensions in Our Culture

PHILIP SLATER

Edited by Wendy Slater Palmer

BEACON PRESS   *Boston*

Copyright © 1977 by Philip Slater

Originally published as a Dutton paperback.
Reprinted by arrangement with E. P. Dutton & Co., Inc.

Beacon Press books are published under the auspices
of the Unitarian Universalist Association

Published simultaneously in Canada by
Fitzhenry & Whiteside Limited, Toronto

All rights reserved

Printed in the United States of America

(hardcover)   9   8   7   6   5   4   3   2   1

Chapters 7 and 5 of this book are revised and abridged
versions of chapters 2 and 4, respectively, of *The Temporary
Society,* copyright © 1968 by Warren G. Bennis and Philip E.
Slater. (Courtesy of Harper & Row.)

Library of Congress Cataloging in Publication Data

Slater, Philip Elliott.
    Footholds.
    Bibliography: p.
    Includes index.
    1. Sex customs—United States.   2. Sex role.
3. Family—United States.   I. Title.
[HQ18.U5S57   1977b]   301.41   77–12124
ISBN 0–8070–4160–2

To Alex Palmer

CONTENTS

Editor's Note ix

1. Sex in America 1
2. Kicking the Domestic Habit 12
3. Identification: Personal and Positional 20
4. Parental Roles 27
5. Some Effects of Transience 36
6. Democracy and Grandparents 43
7. Changing the Family 48
8. The Family in Ancient Greece 68
9. Traits of Warlike Cultures 90
10. Civilization, Narcissism, and Sexual Repression 96
11. Short Circuits in Social Life 114
12. Emotional Priorities 141
13. Dualities 155
14. The Fish Commission and the Water Problem 170
15. Pleasure, Healing, and Conflict 175
Appendix A 193
Appendix B 197
Notes 203
Bibliography 210
Index 219

EDITOR'S NOTE

Footholds was designed to pull together under one roof a series of scattered but related observations about family process, sex roles, and social change. At the same time we wanted to create a readable book rather than a collection of unrelated articles, written for different audiences. My task was to extract those ideas that seemed most important, tie them together, and make them stylistically consistent.

The articles on which *Footholds* was based were selected by the author. Some are previously unpublished; others have appeared in professional journals and were inaccessible to most readers. Chapter 15 is completely new and unedited; I feel it brings together many of the themes of *Footholds*.

My goal in editing the articles was to turn them into chapters, into unified parts of a whole. Many related ideas and themes were scattered through the articles. I tried to bring these themes into sharper focus and to weave them into a coherent book. I also tried to make the material more personal and easier to identify with.

The actual editing process involved repeated readings of the articles so that I could preserve the content as well as the style and language of the author. I cut out the parts of each chapter that were distracting to me: sociological jargon, some academic debate, and references to psychoanalytic literature. Trying to represent most readers, I kept what was interesting and meaningful to me. I also updated some articles, translating them into more readable language and cutting ideas that have become clichés since original publication dates. My work was mainly condensing, summarizing and clarifying, occasionally adding a thought. Some of the changes in the articles reflect changes in our culture which needed to be recognized and some reflect the changes and growth of the author, with whom I collaborated often. But the most important task, and the most difficult, was trying to link chapters, to highlight similar themes as they emerged in varying contexts. I believe the flow of thought is uninterrupted by the beginning and ending of each chapter.

I also have a more personal reaction to *Footholds*. I enjoyed working closely with my father and discovering how his ideas and theories have developed. As I worked on the manuscript I was drawn into the material, which stimulated introspection as well as family discussion. Much of the book has spoken to me directly about my cultural origins and ways I relate in family and professional situations. I also enjoyed being able to bring to bear on the manuscript my experiences and insights as a woman.

WENDY SLATER PALMER

Haverhill, Mass.
June, 1976

Chapter 1

SEX IN AMERICA

Americans talk a lot about "adequacy" in relation to sex. This use of an engineering term—adequacy—in reference to an act of pleasure exemplifies the American gift for turning everything into a task. Even more curious is the fact that the criteria of "adequacy" are not the same for men and women. For men "adequacy" is usually focused on erection; for women, on orgasm. A man tends to be defined as "adequate" to the degree that he is able to bring a woman to orgasm, preferably through the use of his penis. ("Look, Ma, no hands!") A woman, however, tends to be defined as "adequate" to the degree to which she is able to "achieve" orgasm rapidly through the same method. Thus, a woman gets defined as sexually "adequate" insofar as she can make the man feel that *he* is sexually "adequate." Since it was men, by and large, who attached competitive rules to an act of pleasure and then loaded the dice in their own favor, one wonders what they had at stake.

Note that by these definitions a man was considered "adequate" when he could delay orgasm, while a woman was considered "adequate" when she could accelerate it. We live in a highly scheduled, clock-oriented society, and it seems to be important to us that people arrive at the same place at the same time. Sex is no exception, and the onus for not reaching orgasm together has typically fallen on the woman, who was stigmatized, in good bureau-

1

cratic tradition, as being "late." (Only in the most extreme case
would a man be blamed for being "early.") In recent decades men
have increasingly accepted a patriarchal responsibility for "getting
her there on time," but the "problem" to be solved was feminine
"slowness."

In the last decade our physiological sophistication has increased,
but definitions are slow to change. It's recognized that women
come just as fast as men, given direct clitoral stimulation (perhaps
psychoanalysts can explain how men managed for so long to ignore
the obvious fact that during oral sex women regularly reach
orgasm as fast as men do), but the idea that "fast is good" is still
prevalent.

Suppose we were to say not that "it takes a woman longer to
reach orgasm during intercourse than it does a man" but that "a
woman can delay orgasm longer than a man." Our view of the
matter would be totally transformed. But if we are going to use
terms as absurd as "adequacy" in relation to pleasure at all, this
seems to me the more reasonable statement. We are talking about
the "ability" to tolerate and sustain pleasurable stimulation without
release: The simple fact is that women can absorb and tolerate
more pleasure than men can and are hence more "adequate" to
the "business" of enjoyment. They may not have acquired this
strength voluntarily, and historically a good deal too much strain
has been put on it, yet it's a strength nonetheless, and has important consequences.

MEN, WOMEN, AND TASTE

I have always been fascinated that women seem to be far more
capable of being attracted to a homely male than vice versa. Why
is it that a homely woman is so much more likely to be disqualified
as a sexual partner? And why are so many men in our society only
attracted to young, thin, long-legged, large-breasted, made-up and
deodorized women? Does the fact that men are so easily turned
off—by age, weight, and sundry other departures from some narrow *Playboy* ideal—mean that they really don't like women much?
Is their heterosexual desire so weak that only some weirdly spe-

cialized feminine image can flog it into being? Why is it that women can be turned on by men who are old or ugly? Are they sexier than men? Less squeamish and fastidious? Or do they really like men more than men like women?

Psychiatrists ténd to respond to such observations by talking vaguely about latent homosexuality. Yet many male homosexuals can only be aroused by *men* who are young or exceptionally good-looking. Reaching the age of 30 can be as great a disaster for a gay male as for a straight woman. Men, whether gay or straight, seem far more finicky about physical attractiveness than either lesbians or straight women. This is another way of saying that women are more easily turned on than men, that they can take their sex with fewer condiments.

A SHORT HISTORY OF LABELS

This statement flies in the face of the Victorian belief that men are "more sexual" than women, but this idea had a relatively brief history, largely limited to the Western world. Historically and cross-culturally it has been women who were portrayed as the sexual, earthy beings, with men viewed as more restrained, controlled, spiritual, and less susceptible to the demands of the flesh. Women have usually been seen as the source of evil and have appeared frequently in folklore and literature as sexually insatiable creatures, undermining the efforts of men to pursue chaste and lofty enterprises.

Men throughout history have devoted a surprising amount of energy to the construction of a feminine ideal. These ideals have varied from culture to culture, but they share a large area of agreement: Women should be sexually accessible but not sexually demanding, docile and servile yet not totally uninteresting. The contradictions are worked out in different ways. Sometimes, as in Victorian England and America, the anxiety over woman's sexuality led to an ideal that was utterly chaste, it being left to un-ideal women to gratify men's sexual needs. More often the contradiction is resolved by emphasizing the passivity of the feminine role (always willing but never asking). The ideal woman is sometimes encouraged to develop pleasing little skills that will make her interesting to the male without threatening his vanity, but in some instances it is stated flatly that the ideal woman should be an ignorant booby. On one issue all writers are in complete agreement: The ideal woman exists only for men. "She must be enduringly and incorruptibly good," says Ruskin, "the centre of order, the balm of distress," providing a shelter that will protect the hard-working man from his troubles and knowing only enough to sympathize with his interests.

It is difficult to read these documents—whether Greek, Chinese, Moslem, English, or American—without sensing the profound pathology that lies beneath them: the obsessional detail, the exhausting struggle to resolve ambivalence by controlling and constricting another person's behavior, the inability to recognize that a completely accommodating individual can only be a nonperson, a robot. One suspects that these lectures are really misdirected: Intended, perhaps, for the frantic, seductive, demanding, and overpowering mothers of their authors, they are delivered instead to their wives, who, thereby constricted and constrained, frantically transfer their seductive demands and overpowering needs on to their sons, thus continuing the cycle.

Women rarely write such documents, perhaps because fathers, as a rule, are less omnipresent in the life of a small child than are mothers. In any case, women seem to have been able to take men pretty much as they found them. They may have tried to make improvements on a given man, they may have longed for some perfect Prince Charming, but by and large they have not wasted paper writing perseverative, nit-picking treatises on how the ideal male should behave in the daily fulfillment of his role. By contrast, men seem always to be saying that if only women could manage to walk this or that psychological tightrope, *then* men would be attracted to and feel safe with them.

All this suggests that men feel at a severe sexual disadvantage with women. They want them passive, docile, exciting, yet undemanding. A man, it seems, has difficulty feeling like a man if a woman approaches him as a free, independent, fully sexual being.

It is as if he felt handicapped in sexual encounters and needed to create a comparable handicap for the woman.

Perhaps men *have* become sexually handicapped relative to women—not just in the physiological sense of having a more finite capacity for repetition but culturally, in the sense of having evolved a social role that limits their capacity for physical pleasure. In all civilized societies men have sacrificed a part of their eroticism to the pursuit of wealth, status, and power, and then harassed their womenfolk in a variety of ways to compensate for the feelings of sexual inferiority that this sacrifice engendered.

Work and sex are natural enemies, and the more personal commitment the work generates, the more inroads it makes into erotic life. Vacations release eroticism in most people, and work that can be utterly forgotten when the five o'clock whistle blows has little dampening impact. But for the ambitious careerist, as John Cuber and Peggy Harroff found in their study of successful executives, government officials, and professionals, eroticism tends to become perfunctory, a release rather than a pastime.[1] Clearly if pleasure is something to be caught on the fly in the interstices of effortful striving, then the quicker it is done with, the better.

Men tend to define themselves by their jobs—a man is a banker or lawyer first, a person second—and it is difficult for someone who thinks this way to invest himself totally in a love relationship. Even leaving time and energy aside, a man devoting his life to successful achievement is unlikely to want to spend hours in leisurely lovemaking.

It used to be said that love was only a part of a man's life, the whole of a woman's. Leaving aside the political intent of this sentiment (to keep women in their place), it expresses a historical reality. Men have invested in professions a part of the energy and interest that women devote to love relationships. Eroticism thereby became a woman's domain into which a man entered in some sense as a dilettante.

It is primarily men in literate societies who have made the kind of emotional commitment to work that tends to encroach on the sexual impulse. The result of this commitment has been the amassing of wealth and power and the establishment of political dominance over women. But this political dominance has been bought at the price of accepting a sexual handicap. The history of sexual mores in civilized societies is a chronicle of the efforts of men to use their political advantage to rectify their sexual disadvantages.

The most common form of harassment has been through sexual restrictions. Such restrictions (premarital virginity and marital fidelity being the most common) have almost invariably been applied exclusively to women and have succeeded to some extent in warping, crippling, and blocking their sexual spontaneity. The limitation of this approach, however, is expressed in the frequency with which themes of feminine infidelity, wickedness, and sexual insatiability appear in the literature of such societies.

Nineteenth-century Europe produced a more subtle and insidious form of sexual control. Men began to succeed in imposing on women a feminine ideal stripped of sexual impulse. Reversing the usual idea of the spiritual male opposed to the carnal female, they made allowances for the "animal nature" of men and denied that any respectable woman had such a thing. This was a more powerful device since it served to cripple feminine sexuality at its core. Its transparent absurdity, however, made it vulnerable to social reform.

Ironically, the efforts of psychoanalysts to achieve such reform produced what was by far the most powerful technique yet devised for giving women a sexual handicap comparable to that borne by men. This was the dictum that mature female sexuality should be centered in the vagina and de-emphasize the clitoris, a magnificent double bind inasmuch as the clitoris is the center of erotic sensation. The researches of Masters and Johnson undermined this dogma by discovering what women had known all along: That in ordinary circumstances, there is no such thing as an orgasm that does not involve the clitoris. Two generations of women had condemned themselves and felt guilty and inadequate because of a man's fantasy about how their bodies should function. Thus the psychiatric profession was for some years able to achieve psychically the same goal sought by certain primitive tribes that limit the sexuality of their women by cutting away the clitoris at puberty.

Whoever makes the labels holds the power, and all these devices have been invented by men. Each has served in one way or another to cause women to doubt their natural sexual impulses, and this limitation on feminine sexuality has in turn served to make men feel more competent in the sexual sphere.

ORGASMS AND PRODUCTIVITY

Discussions of sexuality in America have centered on the orgasm rather than on pleasure in general. This seems to be another example of our tendency to focus on the *product* of any activity at the expense of the *process*. It may seem odd to refer to an orgasm as a product, but this is the tone taken in such discussions. Most sex manuals give the impression that the partners in lovemaking are performing some sort of task; by dint of a great cooperative effort and technical skill (primarily the man's) an orgasm (primarily the woman's) is ultimately produced. The bigger the orgasm, the more "successful" the performance.

This thought pattern owes much to the masculine preoccupation with technical mastery. Women in popular sexual literature become manipulable mechanical objects—like pianos ("it's amazing what sounds he can get out of that instrument") or objects of earthmoving equipment. ("He can excavate a swimming pool in just four minutes.") Even more pronounced is the competitive note in writers such as Lawrence and Mailer who often make it seem as if lovemaking were a game in which the first person to reach a climax loses.

The emphasis on orgasm also reveals a vestigial puritanism, for the term "climax" expresses not only the idea of a peak, or zenith, but also the idea of termination or completion. Discussions of the sexual act in our society are thus overwhelmingly concerned with how it *ends*. Leisurely pleasure seeking is brushed aside, as all acts and all thoughts are directed toward the creation of a "successful" finale. The better (i.e., the bigger) the climax, the more enjoyable the whole encounter is retrospectively defined as having been.

This ensures against too much pleasure obtained in the here and now since one is always concentrating on the future goal. In such a system you can only find out how much you're enjoying yourself after it's all over (just as many Americans traveling abroad don't know what they've experienced until they've had their film developed.)

Eastern love manuals, although rather mechanical and obsessional in their own ways, direct far more attention to the sensations of the moment. The preoccupation in Western sexual literature with orgasm seems to be a natural extension of the Protestant work ethic in which nothing is to be enjoyed for its own sake except striving.

The antithetical attitude would be to view orgasm as a delightful interruption in an otherwise continuous process of generating pleasurable sensations. This would transform our ways of thinking about sex. We would no longer use the orgasm as a kind of unit of lovemaking, as in "we made love three times that day." (Cf. "we played nine holes of golf," "I have two cars," "I caught seven fish," "he's worth five million dollars.") The impulse to quantify sex would be sharply diminished and along with it the tendency to infuse pleasure seeking with ideas of achievement and competition. Affectionate caresses exchanged in passing would not be so rigidly differentiated from those interludes culminating in orgasm.

Women already espouse this view to a much greater degree than men: Witness the complaint of many women that their husbands never caress them except in bed. The reason they assign to this behavior, however—"he's only interested in sex, in my body, not in me"—misses the point. A man who behaves this way is not interested in sex, either; he is interested only in releasing tension. Far from enjoying pleasurable stimulation, he cannot tolerate it beyond a very minimal level and wants it to end as rapidly as possible within the limits of sexual etiquette and competent "performance."

This desire for release from tension, for escape from stimulation, lies at the root of our cultural preoccupation with orgasm. In a society like ours, which perpetually bombards its participants with bizarre and dissonant stimuli—both sexual and nonsexual—tension release is at a premium. It is this confused and jangling stimulation, together with the absence of simple and meaningful rhythms in our daily lives, that makes Americans long for orgasmic release and shun any casual pleasure-seeking that does not culminate in rapid tension discharge. What pop novelist today could make a living writing about casual dalliance instead of earth-shattering orgasms?

But it is men who suffer most from this need for tension release since it is men who have specialized most acutely in sacrificing feelings in the service of ambition—postponing gratification, maintaining a stiff upper lip, avoiding body contact, keeping emotional distance. Women often express the feeling in the midst of intense lovemaking that they want it never to end, want it to go on forever. I wonder how many men are capable of sustaining such a sentiment, are able to imagine themselves enjoying endless inputs of acute pleasurable stimulation?

The emphasis in popular sexual literature on the ecstatic agony thus caters primarily to men. A favorite theme, for example, is that of the inhibited or resistant woman forced by overwhelming sexual arousal into unexpected and explosive orgasm. This sadomasochistic fantasy has two roots. First, it expresses the common masculine wish for some kind of superpotency: One glance and she falls writhing to the ground, one stroke and she explodes in ecstasy. Second, it involves an identification with the woman herself. For since it is men who control and suppress their feelings it is men who experience the most intense yearning to have those controls burst so that the bottled feelings can be released. But since this yearning endangers the whole edifice of our ambition-crazed culture, it cannot be allowed direct expression and is projected onto women. Women, after all, are assigned the role of emotional specialists in our society; they are supposed to do the crying, screaming, clinging, and so on, not only for themselves but for the men in the family as well. ("It would break your mother's heart if you went away.") The fantasy of the woman propelled into orgasm against her will is just another expression of this general tendency of men to give women the job of releasing masculine tensions vicariously. Indeed, part of the sexual hangups suffered by women spring from having to play out this fantasy for men. Many women feel inadequate when they are not consumed with passion at the first approach of their lover and guilty that they have thereby injured his vanity.

TOWARD A TASK-FREE EROTICISM

It seems reasonable that when sexual gratification is plentiful, orgasm need not be the goal of every erotic encounter from the start but is a possible outcome arising naturally as the lovemaking proceeds. In a comfortable sexual setting, in other words, some lovemaking is nonorgasmic. This assumes more leisure time than most people have available and a constancy of physical contact that most Americans would find unpalatable. But it serves as a useful contrast to established thinking on the matter, which is obsessively goal-oriented.

I want to stress that this should not be considered some sort of ideal. The last thing I want to do is to add another "should" to our already overburdened sexual mores. The removal of Victorian restraints from sexual life in America will have been in vain if they are merely replaced by a series of sexual grading systems. The notion of sexual "adequacy" seems to have had as poisonous an effect on the American psyche as did simple Puritan prohibitions, and the contributions of psychiatry, however well-intended and often insightful, have merely added to the confusion. Psychoanalysts have demanded that orgasms in women be "vaginal," have ranked orgasms in terms of degree of total bodily involvement, have demanded that sex be fantasy-free (which has the amusing effect of consigning all sexual intercourse performed with procreation in mind to the realm of perversion), and so on. All these efforts to establish medical grading systems for different kinds of sexual behavior seem to have had the unfortunate effect of increasing the sexual pathology against which they were directed.

From a detached, physiological viewpoint the "goal" of the human orgasm is the maintenance of some kind of balance around pleasurable stimulation. Some degree of tension and excitement is prerequisite to life, but a degree of release is necessary for internal order and serenity. The fantasy of complete discharge—of the perfect, ultimate orgasm—is fundamentally a death fantasy. People we view as particularly "alive" are those capable of sustaining a lot of pleasurable stimulation without discharging it or blunting their senses; but a person *unable* to discharge often seems nervous and jumpy. These styles are sometimes difficult to distinguish in practice, and by the same token, a person with a low level of tolerance for stimulation may appear either serene or dead. What is most important to recognize is that this balance differs for each person, and no one else can decide for that person the appropriate balance to be maintained or the best way of obtaining it.

But this is, as I said, a cold physiological view of the matter. From a merely human viewpoint an orgasm is simply something that happens involuntarily when pleasure peaks, and probably the less cognitive messing about with it we do, the better.

Chapter 2

KICKING THE DOMESTIC HABIT

During the 1960s I once gave a course on the "generation gap" to a group of middle-class, middle-aged women. Since I was also teaching a group of undergraduates concerned with the same issues, I thought it might be interesting to bring the two groups together. Their backgrounds were so similar—ethnically, socially, educationally—that they could have been mothers and daughters.

During one session a few of the older women launched a rather vicious attack on some of the students who were discussing their personal lives. The other women made little attempt to stop this, although several of them later expressed distress over it. The more the women attacked, the more open and self-revealing the students became; and the more the students opened up, the more they were attacked.

The students were very depressed by this encounter. Even though they assumed that the attacks were motivated mostly by jealousy (envy of their sexual freedom in particular), the students were afraid that their own radically different life styles would not prevent them from falling into the same pattern at the same age. Most of the students seemed to fear marriage, but they felt themselves and their friends drifting helplessly into it—either out of some vague insecurity, or as the natural culmination of a prolonged serious relationship, or for convenience (since our society is, after all, structured around marriage).

They saw little in marriage that was appealing. Most of the students felt that their parents were trapped in unhappy and destructive relationships, and they wanted to avoid this experience at all costs. They also feared life-style changes. They imagined themselves 20 years hence, bored and isolated, preoccupied with material things, hating and envying young people as they were hated and envied now.

I felt these young women's fears were well-founded. A woman who does not maintain a fierce and dogged foothold in the job market may find herself slipping helplessly into old cultural patterns. Isolated, deprived of social and personal stimulation, she may feel pressure to make a career out of child rearing. And at that point it is difficult to escape the clutches of a culture that encourages living beyond one's means and "sacrificing" for the children.

Despite their anger and envy the older women of the group competed in asserting contentment with their situations—and it cannot be denied that their lives *were* richer than those of many women their age. They had great resources—personal as well as material—and they had made adaptations that were difficult to fault. But a well-appointed prison is still a prison, and a healthy prisoner who uses her time to good advantage is still a prisoner.

For most college women graduation means abandoning the very real community life that school provides. By "community" I mean a group of people spending most of their waking hours in the same place and engaged in a common enterprise. A "community life" exists when one can go daily to a given location at a given time and count on seeing most of the people one wants to see. This effortlessness is central to my point. A large high school, university, or corporation is not in itself a community, but it may contain a number of small communities that assemble automatically; no one has to bring them together.

Before industrialization most people lived a community life. To be deprived of it was a punishment, an exile. For a woman today, graduation itself can be exile, a permanent end to community life.

If she is married and not working, her community may not extend past the walls of her own house.

Of course, she will have friends, neighbors, and family. She may participate in local activities; she may join clubs and work for causes. But none of these associations are automatic. The relationships are separate and fragmented; the activities are usually diluted by the need to be watching small children or to make arrangements for them. Her various friends may not be part of the same group and may not even know each other.

Furthermore, there is no outside structure supporting these relationships; she must maintain them herself. There is no spot where everyone hangs out; people must be called and invited over. Pregraduation social life may be effortless, but postgraduation social life takes work.

This system of more formalized entertaining minimizes the sense of shared activity on which good times so often depend, and maximizes anxiety over achievement and the mechanical dreariness of obligatory social occasions to a point at which even close friendships can seem hardly worth the effort.

Most men retain some community life in their jobs; so do working women, within the limits of the inferior jobs available to most of them. But a woman who accepts only the domestic role may lose all remnants of community life and find it virtually impossible to recreate one within the confines of conventional living arrangements.

The kind of clutter a woman creates to fill this vacuum depends on the kind of person she is. If she is gregarious and extroverted, she will suffer less because she will be able to surround herself with people and thus seem to be participating in something, belonging to something.

Some women will try to create a community *within* the household by raising a large family, but this works only for the children, not for her. Most women just look around, see that they are in a little prison, and try to improve the cell by making it larger or better appointed. Whole lives may be spent trying to fill this emptiness with possessions.

Throughout the ages women have played the role of domestic in

their own home without protest. But isolation was rarely a par[t]
the picture. (Pioneer women are often cited as models, but they
are poor examples because they had a tendency to die a lot.)
Wherever domesticity seems to have worked well for women,
they have had considerable community life, a variety of group activities, a reasonable amount of mobility, and a sharing of household and child-rearing responsibilities with other adults. The idea
of expecting the average mother to spend most of her time alone
with her children in a small house or apartment is a relatively
modern invention and a rather fiendish one at that. Men may
engage in work that is as stultifying and tedious as domestic work,
but usually they do not have to do it alone.

The process through which a woman drifts into her prison is
gradual and subtle. She and her husband may begin by sharing
household chores, especially if they have lived together before
marrying. But if the wife does not work, as time goes by she finds
usually that his job and his need for mobility begin to take prece-
dence while she assumes most of the domestic tasks. As she becomes increasingly isolated in her home, she begins to demand
more from the house itself. This heightens financial pressures and
pushes her husband into a more aggressive career role, which in
turn permits him to demand even more mobility and freedom
from domestic responsibility. And the pattern is established.

The clincher, of course, comes when children are born. The
wife may welcome them. (She is supposed to, in any case.) But a
child, after all, is not a full-time toy, and by the time a woman
becomes aware of the futility of trying to build a whole existence
around baby tending, she finds that she has made decisions that
push her deeper into her prison. Perhaps she thinks that a back
yard would save her pushing a stroller to the park, or perhaps she
worries about good schools. As a result, the family buys a house in
the suburbs. Her husband has to drive to work, but he, at least,
can get out.

I suspect that if this way of life is to be changed, only women
can do it. Most men are too enmeshed in the system to understand how it works and too comfortable in it to want to change it.
But if women were to stop colluding in the division of labor that

now exists, men would be forced to begin to work *with* them in changing the process that creates this division. If women were to stop suppressing their own curiosity and ambition, men would be forced to stop suppressing their own emotionality and humanity.

We're beginning to realize that the temperamental traits assigned to men and women in a given society are completely arbitrary. In some societies men are supposed to be emotional and flighty and women stoical and down-to-earth; in others the reverse is supposed to be true. In some societies men are supposed to be more sexual, in others, women. In some societies men are supposed to be the vainer sex, in others, women.

But no matter how the traits are assigned in a given society, it is always assumed that these male and female attitudes are biologically based. Yet in raising children parents are very careful to see that these supposedly biological characteristics are drummed into them. We say that a boy or a girl "instinctively" acts in such and such a way, but our actions indicate merely that we feel he or she *should* act that way.

By reinforcing certain behavior, men try to "keep women in their place." If a woman does not act according to our cultural stereotype, she may be accused of being "unfeminine." Male logic, for example, gives us the following syllogism: Women are not logical; this woman is logical; therefore, this woman is not really a woman.

Feminine unity has provided the major solution to this oppression. Many women, however, are shamed out of it—shamed into isolation and powerlessness and forced to accept a male definition of their essential nature. To the question, "How can I avoid the pitfalls that women of my parents' generation fell into?" the answer of the women's movement has been: "Don't let them hang you separately."

Yet many women are unable to apply this suggestion to their own lives. "Why should I view the man I love as an enemy?" they ask. Is any relationship more important than the one between a man and a woman? Don't both the man and the woman subordinate all other relationships to it?

Yes, they do. But the man hedges. Often with the best intentions, he winds up having it both ways: He has a couple affiliation and a male affiliation, while women usually abandon their loyalty to other females to a far greater extent. However many friends a nonworking wife may have, she does not have a community life. Her husband has. Furthermore, if her husband changes his affiliations—leaves his job or is transferred to another city—she often must change hers also, whether she wants to or not.

This imbalance does not occur because men are malevolent or unjust but because the culture prescribes it. The most loving and devoted husband must leave each morning for work; he must invest a lot of energy in a community system from which his wife is excluded. If he is sensitive to her needs, he feels guilty, but he doesn't know quite how to help.

The wife, on the other hand, sees that her husband's role of breadwinner gives him satisfaction. If she feels guilty that her domestic role isn't fulfilling her enough, she may decide that perhaps she should make an even bigger commitment by having children. Her husband is likely to support the idea with some relief. ("Kids will give her something to do—they'll be company for her.")

Now everything is "even"—he has his job, she has the children. He has a community life, she has someone to take care of. She is not only committed, she is in over her head, completely dependent on the marriage for everything in her life.

Marriage, in other words, can be a very unequal bargain. But as long as men and women are assigned markedly different roles in our society, every marriage will be a contract between Romeo and Juliet, between a Montague and a Capulet. Women considering marriage don't like to think this way—nor do men, for that matter. But men can afford to have a more romantic view because it is Juliet who gives up her family name, who ceases to be a Capulet, while Romeo continues to be a Montague.

Women are taught to compete with each other for men, even to sacrifice their friendships. Men are less apt to do this—more likely to preserve close friendships even at some cost to their marriages. Men are also more willing to discuss their marital discontents with friends. But for women—especially middle-class women—the need to confide is often hampered by a competitive need to prove that "my marriage is happier than yours." There is a very simple reason for this: A man talking to another man tends to think of himself as an individual, while a woman talking to another woman is more likely to think of herself as a member of a marriage.

These attitudes, of course, are changing. Young women seem to care more about their friendships than they used to; they seem less willing to sacrifice a friendship to "get a man." And even though Women's Liberation groups have been subjected to end- less ridicule by men, it is through participation in such groups that an increasing number of women are rediscovering themselves as individuals. For centuries women have endured their common problems in needless isolation. When people cannot share their problems and experiences they feel uncertain, confused, lethargic; while the discovery of their common fate often produces intense feelings of relief, bursts of energy, and a sense of purpose.

There is nothing inherently wrong with a division of labor as such. But a division of labor that forces people into emotionally crippling sex roles can have only unfortunate social consequences in the long run. Some of these consequences are highly visible today: The mechanical and dehumanizing society we live in could have been created only by beings who had delegated the expres- sion of feelings to others.

A reasonable bargain between a man and a woman who intend to commit themselves to each other should necessitate guarantees against isolation and immobility, refusal to accept the role of do- mestic, and insistence on equal job priorities. But even these changes are not enough. The superiority of women rests in the fact that, unlike men, they have not learned to deaden their feelings. Job equality should not be simply a matter of women moving in a "male" direction but should also force men to stop using work as a justification for life-destroying activities.

People have always said jokingly that if women ran the world, they could hardly do a worse job than men have done—that there would be fewer wars, less ecological destruction. This is a joke no longer. The homes people live in and the planet people live on should be the equal concerns of everyone. When women are responsible for the home alone and men for the planet alone, both do a terrible job. For the home includes the planet and the planet the home.

Our planet suffers from being run by people who ignore their own needs for intimacy and hence the needs of everyone else. Our homes suffer from being run by those who are ignorant of their interdependence on all other homes. The division of labor by sex helps people forget the connection between the fumes they create and the fumes they inhale. If this kind of connection were re-established, we would inhabit a more humane environment, one in which both men and women could live richer lives.

Chapter 3

IDENTIFICATION: PERSONAL AND POSITIONAL

When a child adopts the personality traits, values, and attitudes of a parent, including the parent's view of the child, I call the process "personal identification." It is motivated primarily by the child's love and admiration for the parent. The child is saying in effect: "I want to be like you. If I were, I would have you with me all the time, and I would love myself as much as I love you. Therefore, I will incorporate your qualities and values, and will view and judge myself through your eyes."

"Positional identification" involves merely a fantasy of putting oneself into the other's position and acting out the appropriate role. It is motivated not by love but by envy and fear. The child who identifies with a parent in this way is saying, in effect: "I wish I were in your shoes. If I were, I wouldn't be in the unpleasant position I am in now. Perhaps if I act like you, I will achieve your more favorable status." This situational improvement is of two kinds: (1) "I will be strong and powerful rather than weak and helpless"; and (2) "Mother (or Father) will love me instead of you."

The all-or-nothing quality of these two desires betrays their unconscious basis. In neither case is there any need to love the parents or to internalize their values. Both types of positional identification require the destruction and replacement of the other— not necessary in personal identification.

20

Historically, psychoanalysts have been concerned with positional identification, while social psychologists have been busy carrying out research on personal identification. The result has been utter confusion.

"It is easy," according to Freud, "to state in a formula the distinction between an identification with the father and the choice of the father as an object. In the first case one's father is what one would like to *be,* and in the second he is what one would like to *have.*" [1] This formula has a pleasing simplicity but has led theorists to exaggerate the distinction to the point of assuming a negative relationship between the two. Certainly there is no contradiction between identification and "object choice" in the minds of children. The self-conscious hypermasculinity of young boys, for example, is challenged by mere feminine contact, as if association with girls would be feminizing by contagion; the boy who violates this cross-sex taboo is often teased by being called by the name of the girl he is enamored of, as if by liking her he had identified himself with her. Other forms of identification, on the other hand, may lack any positive regard, and this is the basis of the distinction I'm making here.

Personal identification, in other words, may be defined as identification based on and combined with love of the other, positional identification as identification based purely on fear and envy of the other. Personal identification *includes* "object choice" while positional identification *excludes* it.

Freud died dissatisfied with his identification theory [2] and left the door open for clarification. Yet the psychoanalytic definition that has come down to us is almost entirely positional. This creates much confusion since psychoanalysts connect identification with the internalization of parental values, a process associated exclusively with personal identification—studies have found repeatedly that internalization is enhanced by warm and affectionate rather than frustrating parents. [3]

Anna Freud tries particularly hard to relate positional identification and internalization. Discussing a child who plays dentist after having been hurt by a dentist, she notes that "there was no actual impersonation of the dentist. The child was identifying himself not with the person of the aggressor but with his aggression." [4] Yet it was not the viewpoint of the dentist that was adopted but the immensely more favorable power position in which he stood relative to the frightened child. This view is shared by Nevitt Sanford, who argues that positional types of identification do not produce any lasting internalized structures in the personality.[5] I would argue that positional identification tends to occur only insofar as personal identification fails.

My definition of positional identification makes no mention of adopting characteristics of the model because in general we would associate this with personal identification. An exception to this rule would be traits expressing directly or symbolically the position desired by the identifier. In psychoanalytic therapy, for example, positional identification might appear in the form of an imitation of some nervous mannerism of the therapist, expressing the desire of the patient to be in the superior status position of the therapist, whose tics do not have to be analyzed and interpreted.

In positional identification, then, only a few characteristics of the model will be adopted—those that symbolize the model's desired position—but these will be very literally copied, as in Freud's example of the sergeant who imitates the way the general clears his throat and spits.[6] In personal identification a wide range of characteristics of the model will be adopted, but with substantial modifications, since, as Sanford says, the individual "puts his own stamp" on them.[7] In the first case a few symbols are swallowed whole and left undigested; in the second a broader viewpoint is selectively adopted and resynthesized.

Jerome Kagan suggests that models will be identified with to the degree they command desired goals of the subject.[8] Insofar as these desired goals are inherent in the personality of the model, the identification is personal, while insofar as they represent the model's situation, the identification is positional. It might be argued that aggressiveness and hostility—traits associated with positional identification—could be viewed as "inherent in the personality of the model" and thus contradict this distinction. But it is not hostility that is desired in identification with an aggressor (it may already be amply present) but the freedom to express it without fear.

What has been said thus far suggests that while personal identification occurs in response to parental warmth and affection, positional identification is more likely to result from the absence of these qualities. This distinction removes the apparent discrepancy between Otto Fenichel's dictum that identification (positional) is a function of "frustrating" parental behavior [9] and studies showing that identification (personal) increases with gratifying parental behavior and decreases with parental punitiveness.[10] As Mowrer observes, drawing a distinction similar to the one made here, the frustration in personal cases "arises from a sense of helplessness and loneliness: The parent or parent-person is *absent*, and the infant wishes he were *present*. In the other case, the frustration arises rather from interference and punishment: The parent or parent-person is *present*, and the infant wishes he were *absent*." [11]

Thus far I have made no distinction between paternal and maternal identification. Yet Fenichel's dictum is actually stated in terms of "which parent" the child identifies with. This assumes that identification is an all-or-none proposition, and that identification with one parent prevents identification with the other—assumptions that can't be justified by research findings, clinical experience, or even conceptual elegance. When measured independently paternal and maternal personal identification are strongly and positively correlated. When measured in either-or terms, the child identifies with whichever parent is seen as more warm and supportive.[12]

The either-or view of parental identification has led to confusion whenever an attempt has been made to correlate identification with measures of emotional health. When a preferential measure is used, there is no correlation. When paternal and maternal identification are measured independently, emotional health increases as identification with *either* parent increases—a result that contradicts the psychoanalytic theory that cross-sex identification is maladaptive. The apparent contradiction arises from the fact that the measures used are measures of personal identification, while the sexual and emotional difficulties postulated for cross-sex parental identification pertain solely to positional identification. There is nothing in the description of personal identification given above that implies any kind of sex typing.[13]

This is not to say there is no significant qualitative difference between maternal and paternal identification. Such a difference is proposed by Talcott Parsons, who sees the development of the child as a series of identifications, with maternal identification being the first for both sexes,[14] due to the greater contact between mother and child during the early years. It is also implicit in the findings of some researchers that identification with the father depends on the mother's attitude toward the father. From this viewpoint it is difficult to see how paternal identification could take place at all without a substantial degree of prior maternal identification. At the same time, a satisfying sexual development is impossible unless the child of either sex can acquire some understanding of and appreciation for "masculine" as well as "feminine" attitudes, interests, and characteristics, however these are defined by the culture. This will occur if the father (or some substitute) is warm and affectionate and provides an effective source of emotional support for the child. It is less likely to occur if the father is too harsh, too withdrawn, or too ineffectual to provide such support.[15]

POSITIONAL FANTASIES

Logically, positional identification with both parents is impossible. One cannot destroy and replace the father in order to possess the mother and then turn around and destroy the mother to possess the father. But the greatest appeal of fantasy is its ability to exist without logic. In the unconscious, total contradictions can exist side by side. There is no subtle way to integrate ambivalences and contradictions. As in dreams, the opposing ideas are simply presented one after the other in their raw form.

Since maternal and paternal personal identification are correlated, and since positional identification arises when personal identification fails, we would in fact expect these twin positional fantasies to often occur together. Insofar as there is a lack of warmth and affection in the family, the child will both demand it from everyone and feel resentful of everyone. The greater the deficit, the more uncompromising both of these contradictory feelings will become. This is perhaps another way of saying that the central discomfort of the Oedipal situation for the child is being excluded from a loving relationship.

Freud seemed to be aware of this problem. In *The Ego and the Id* he speaks of the "complete Oedipus complex" in these terms: "A boy has not merely an ambivalent attitude towards his father and an affectionate object-relation towards his mother, but at the same time he also behaves like a girl and displays an affectionate feminine attitude to his father and a corresponding hostility and jealousy towards his mother." He further states that "it is advisable in general, and quite especially where neurotics are concerned, to assume the existence of the complete Oedipus complex." As this complex "dissolves, the four trends of which it consists will group themselves in such a way as to produce a father-identification and a mother-identification," which together constitute the ego-ideal.[16] In other words, the twin positional fantasies will be exchanged for a personal identification with both parents.

The idea that cross-sex parental identification is associated with homosexuality—a notion basic to psychoanalytic theory—leads to manifest absurdities. Studies have found, for example, that the mothers of homosexual males are "masculine," dominant, and aggressive. Yet Symonds, referring to this correlation, goes on to say that the homosexual male "identifies" with his mother and "takes on feminine ways." Perhaps a great deal of confusion would be eliminated if we recognize that positional fantasies do not involve any realistic adoption of parental characteristics. Furthermore, there is considerable evidence that cross-sex *personal* identification actually facilitates heterosexuality. It seems to make very little difference for sex-role adoption which parent the child identifies with most. Furthermore, Brodbeck found that cross-sex identification actually increases with age.[17]

The ability to relate to the opposite sex is a function not only of one's own sexual role but also of an ability to accept, emotionally, the complementary role. This is made more difficult by the fact that in many cultures the sexes, especially as children, are segregated in their activities, so that most of the sex role learning must take place in the family. Without this empathy, apparent acceptance of the "appropriate" sex role may go together with hatred and fear of the opposite sex, as in patriarchal Greece of the classical period.

Chapter 4

PARENTAL ROLES

Sociologists often argue that role specialization between parents is essential to the growth of a healthy personality in the child because it facilitates the child's identification with the same-sex parent. They maintain that in the "normal" family, roles are sharply specialized, with more of the demanding or disciplinary functions being performed by the father and more of the expressive or nurturing functions by the mother.

There are many problems with these theories. First, they imply a rigidity and compartmentalism to human behavior that typifies the university more than the give and take of family life. Second, they pay little attention to the fact that different cultural systems demand different family arrangements. An unspecialized family system, for example, in which parental roles are shared is more suited to today's mobile, fluctuating society and better prepares children to live in that society.

Actually, in many cultures one parent, usually the mother, is both more nurturant and more demanding. Thus, on the South Pacific island of Pukapuka,

the child is mainly cared for by its mother. The father has no specific duties to perform. He is sympathetic and lavish in his affection for his child, caring for it, however, only when it is

27

necessary or convenient . . . authority over the infant is largely
focused in the mother. Love, dependence and affection on the
other hand tend to diffuse themselves among many members of
or visitors to the household.[1]

But suppose the parents *are* strongly specialized along traditional Victorian lines, and suppose a child wants something and
fears it might be denied. He or she will probably go to the mother
for it. If the mother grants the child what the father would have
denied, does the father nonetheless support her? Are the parents
in an unspoken coalition? The notion of collaborative specialization
in child rearing assumes that there is no relationship between
one's personality and one's parental role. But if the father is a disciplinarian it isn't simply because he feels it is something that *he*
should do, but because he thinks it is something that *should be
done* to the child, in which case he will not support the mother's
indulgence at all but will instead probably accuse her of subverting
his authority or "spoiling" the child. The maintenance of a "coalition" under conditions of sharp specialization assumes that the specialized parents *will never interact with the child at the same time*,
since it would obviously be impossible to do so and still support
each other. This type of coalition is therefore primarily relevant to
the large and formal upper-class households of an earlier era,
when mother, father, and child were rarely together at one time.
It was easy under those circumstances to "agree" that the child
going from room to room and from parent to parent should encounter different responses to the same behavior, and that when
all were together, the mother should place herself in a totally subordinate position. But in the less formal, more intimate middle-
class household of today, any such arrangement would be laugh-
able. Major differences between parents in beliefs about what is
"good" for the child can no longer be masked by drawing a kind of
38th parallel between the front and the back of the house.

SPECIALIZATION AND IDENTIFICATION

In the last chapter we made a distinction between "personal" and
"positional" identification, the former based on a desire to assimi-

late the valued personal qualities of a loved person, the latter based on a desire to assume the position or role of an envied or hated person. It is to "personal" identification that this section is devoted.

The traditional theory behind the relationship between role specialization and identification is clearly stated by Talcott Parsons. "If the boy is to 'identify' with his father in the sense of sex-role categorization there must be a discrimination in role terms between the two parents." [2] For the sake of simplicity, let us follow Parsons' example and concentrate on the identification of the male child with the father.

Since Parsons has defined the role of the father as being "more denying and demanding," we would expect identification to be a function of the father's strictness. That being "denying" is inherently paternal is extremely problematical in view of research findings. In one study, 87 percent of adolescent boys saw their fathers as more rewarding than their mothers. [3] Furthermore, studies have shown that (1) chronic punitiveness seems actually to impede identification, while nurturance seems to facilitate it, (2) boys identify most strongly with whichever parent is least extreme in the performance of his or her sex role, and (3) the more denying and strict the father and the more supportive and lenient the mother, the more the son identifies with the mother. [4] These findings suggest that when the father confines himself to denying and demanding behavior, he may actually be inhibiting the son's identification with him.

Parsons also points out that the child forms several identifications, the first being with the mother. Only after this identification is formed does the child develop identification with the father. If the parents are highly specialized, and particularly if the father is primarily a source of frustration for the child, this transition will be a difficult one. The only inducement for the child to identify with the father would be to please the mother. A major aspect of identification is adopting the viewpoint of the other toward oneself. The importance of paternal identification is that it makes possible the development of a *generalized* self-image from the perceived viewpoints of the two parents. Forming a second identification, in other words, is analogous to the advantage of binocular vision—it provides depth and distance. Now, if the parents' attitudes toward the child are reasonably similar, such generalization is possible. But if they clash, the child can only empathize momentarily with first one and then the other, but cannot easily form a generalized self-concept from the conflicting perceptions.

Many studies also show a strong negative relationship between sharp parental role specialization and the emotional health of the child, using conventional psychological tests.[5] One cannot, of course, generalize such findings beyond the American middle class. In extended families, for example, the effects of sharp specialization between the parents is diluted by the presence of parental substitutes. Our own society is unusual because it concentrates the child-rearing process in the nuclear family.

ROLE SPECIALIZATION AND MARITAL DIVISION OF LABOR

Elizabeth Bott studied the relationship between the division of labor in marital couples and the kind of social network in which they found themselves. She distinguished between "loose-knit networks," in which friends, neighbors, and relatives of the couple tended not to know each other, and "close-knit networks," in which the people known by a couple tended also to interact with each other. She found that couples in close-knit networks expected husbands and wives to have a rigid division of labor and placed little emphasis on shared interests and joint recreation. Since both partners could get help outside the family—wives from their relatives and husbands from their friends—a rigid division of labor between husband and wife was possible. Successful sexual relations were not considered important to a happy marriage.[6]

In contrast, families in loose-knit networks had a less rigid division of labor. They placed much more emphasis on shared activities, recreation, and successful sexual relations. They were more concerned about the "right" way to bring up their children and were more aware that the people they knew had a great variety of opinions on child rearing. They often were worried about which course they themselves should follow with their children.[7]

Note that Bott associates this lack of specialization with marital solidarity. She suggests that couples who cannot rely on a stable and supportive external social context must develop a more intimate relationship with each other. This is achieved through an increase in shared, joint activities and labors. It would seem that the sharper the division of marital roles in a society, the greater the degree of sex segregation that will occur in the training of children for these roles. For while some segregation of the sexes in childhood groups may be universal, the degree and duration of such segregation may have important consequences. In some societies it becomes something of a Frankenstein monster, inasmuch as the individual who has spent most of his or her youth in same-sex groups only feels at ease in same-sex groups as an adult. This creates much stress for marital relationships.

Decreased role specialization is particularly marked in families in which one partner works for an organization whose offices are widely distributed, so that advancement requires frequent changes of residence; or when such advancement necessitates the formation of new relationships at each status level. David Reisman and Howard Roseborough refer to the "young married proto-executives" who "become very adept at pulling up stakes, and at being at home everywhere and nowhere," [8] and the academic world is very similar. It would seem, then, that couples will tend to decrease role specialization whenever the family must be independent of external social relationships.

Although it is difficult to generalize from animal behavior to human, J. P. Scott implies that this relationship extends to the other primates when he contrasts the relative lack of sex role differentiation among the gibbons, who live in isolated nuclear families, with the strong specialization among baboons, who show extended social groupings. [9]

The degree of specialization, furthermore, may vary within the couple over time as well as from couple to couple. Decreased specialization typically occurs whenever a family is removed from its usual social context, such as during a vacation or a change in residence.

The lack of specialization of parental roles can be a useful preparation for this kind of transient adult life because it teaches the child at an early age that her human sources of gratification are more or less interchangeable. But there may also be a particularly strong need for parents in these isolated families to place on the child emotional demands that had previously been directed outside the nuclear family. In this case, sharp parental role specialization would negatively affect the emotional adjustment of the child, who would be torn between the demands of one parent and the affectionate permissiveness of the other. In a more connected family, the peripheral members tend to balance parental inconsistencies and offer other models with which the child can identify. Parental specialization is healthful for the child only when the parents are relatively distant and formal, with many of their emotional needs being met outside the nuclear family.

But apart from emotional health, is there any more universal effect of parental role specialization on the child, one that might be functional in some social contexts and dysfunctional in others? For example, does parental role specialization help foster a personality trait that is maladaptive for children growing up in a fluid social environment but necessary for life in a stable one?

One possibility is suggested by a study of the Gusii in Kenya. Among the Gusii, who tend to violate cultural norms when authority figures are absent, the father is an unaffectionate and punitive disciplinarian, while the mother tends to specialize in the nurturing role, using the threat of paternal punishment as her principal means of control. "The child thus learns to fear the father's painful ministrations and to avoid them by being obedient and performing his tasks; but he does not internalize the father's evaluation of his behavior." [10]

It is not difficult to see why this is so. To the extent that the father is nonrewarding, he will tend to appear as an alien ruler to the child. His demands will be met only when he is present, but when he isn't and can't exert his authority, nothing is to be gained by obedience. To the extent that he *is* rewarding, however, much is to be gained by being a "good boy or girl" even when the father is away. In other words, the internalization of parental values tends to occur when nurturance and discipline come from the same source. This point, which seems to be fairly well established today, is stressed by Eleanor Maccoby. She cites Solomon's work with dogs, noting that "punishment by a stranger, or a person who has been primarily cold and restrictive toward the animal in puppyhood, does not seem to last very well in its effects when the trainer's back is turned" and even goes so far as to recommend that "if nurturant caretaking is divided between two people . . . then discipline should be similarly divided." [11] This will not occur in a sharply specialized family.

Similarity between parental roles also tends to ease one of the major strains on the mobile nuclear family: The potentially fragile relationship between child and father due to the latter's absence from the home during most of the day. For as the burden of child rearing became increasingly concentrated in the nuclear family, the father became even less available to share the burden. Hence in the mobile nuclear family there has been a great deal of pressure to soften and familiarize the paternal role. The specialized disciplinarian of immobile and extended families is the representative of a like-minded community of persons well known to the child. If the son does not fully internalize his father's values, he at least develops a sense of respect for them as a consequence of their apparent universality. If the father is too extreme in his role, furthermore, there are substitute males with whom the son can form a more complete and adequate relationship.

In the isolated mobile family, however, the father does not represent a known community of adults, and there are no permanent substitutes. The father who attempts a specialized disciplinarian role becomes an alien intruder to his children. This state of affairs, while tolerable in the "connected" family, is severely disruptive in the isolated nuclear family. When large numbers of individuals spend their lives in shifting loose-knit networks, social control cannot be based on external sanctions. The need, then, is for a family structure that promotes the internalization of parental values. In a society with a more stable social structure a high degree of internalization is unnecessary to ensure social control because the society has a complex system of *external* controls.

Perhaps the most dramatic expression of the difference between the two systems is that while in the unspecialized family a great deal of effort is devoted to bringing the father closer to the children (often through his adoption of a tolerant, easygoing, playmate role), in the specialized family one of the principal mechanisms used to handle hostility is distancing the father from his children. This is effected not only by the general aloofness of the father in his disciplinary function but also by the mediator role played by the mother—a role that generally purports to be self-dissolving but that usually proves to be self-perpetuating. In the most extreme case the father may play a kind of scapegoat role. If an individual is always nonrewarding, it is easy for him to become the recipient of the hostile feelings aroused by others.

This is particularly likely to occur in a highly patriarchal family system in which the mother may compensate for her inferior status and power in the society at large by using her strategic position as mediator to control family relationships. By a combination of public endorsement and private subversion of the father's authority she indicates to the child that the father is the source of all discomfort and she the source of all good. It should be clear that internalization of paternal values under such circumstances is rather unlikely. The German hausfrau who supports the father's disciplinary measures in his presence and then hustles the child off to the kitchen for candy and sympathy is making a sharp distinction between public behavior in the presence of authorities and what one may do and feel privately in their absence.

This point is sometimes misunderstood. It is assumed that because a mediator attempts to prevent conflict by separation, she will ultimately be able to establish solidarity and thus eliminate the need for her existence. But just as insulation keeps out heat as well as cold, so distance forestalls affection as well as hostility. As Simmel once pointed out, "Although a bridge connects two banks, it also makes the distance between them measurable." [12] When the mother teaches her child how to please and placate the father, how to "deal with" and occasionally "get around" him, she is creating a gap between father and child that will operate effectively even in her absence, since the two will always feel a little strange with each other. This perhaps accounts for the brittleness of paternal identification in the German family—a brittleness brilliantly manipulated by Hitler. For the mother's teaching, while it establishes the superior power and status of the father and sets him up as a person worthy of imitation, does not really permit the child enough closeness to the father, or the father enough affectionate behavior toward the child, for a full internalization of paternal values to take place. Instead, she teaches the child her own role of submission, placation, and deception, thus causing an identification with herself. The yearning for a powerful authority, which helped give rise to the Nazi era, may be seen as an attempt to complete the semi-identification with the father while at the same time maintaining identification with the submissive mother.

The mechanism of the maternal mediator, adequate in a family system that has many father substitutes, is worse than useless in a system desperately bent on intensifying the intimacy of the child-father relationship.

Ambivalence toward a parent, in this case the father, is a difficult emotional state for human beings to handle. Often they are able to cope with it only through rigid and awkward mechanisms. In other words, if the individual cannot find direct ways of expressing his or her feelings, the ambivalence is likely to reappear in the form of social customs.

Now it's easy for sociologists to see how human emotions are neutralized with distancing mechanisms, as in the case of the maternal mediator. Sociologists are fascinated with institutional forms such as parental role specialization, joking relationships, and puberty rites precisely because they are simple and crude enough for us to understand. It may be that the more highly specialized family is simply too unsophisticated a structure for a technologically advanced industrial society such as ours. Because it is dependent on a stable social context, it creates a rigid family system, unable to adapt to changing social patterns. It is in part this very rigidity that aids us in studying its structure, while the mechanics of the more unspecialized family remain somewhat obscure.

That greater attention has been devoted to the specialized family pattern is therefore natural and appropriate. The rapidity of social change, both subtle and violent, in our own era raises the fascinating possibility that a clear understanding of the functions of emergent as well as decadent institutions might enable us to anticipate the family patterns of tomorrow.

Chapter 5

SOME EFFECTS OF TRANSIENCE

We live in the most mobile society that has ever existed. It is true that there have been many societies that continually moved from place to place. But these nomadic tribes moved as a group and usually over a fixed route. They carried their possessions, their relationships, their entire way of life along with them, unchanged. In most cases, even the land did not really change since every part of the route was re-encountered at predictable intervals. Nomadic tribes are just as rooted to the land as a peasant farmer, but to a corridor instead of a site.

Mobility in modern society is quite another matter. Here individuals or family units are plucked out of their social context and transplanted. They may never live in the same place twice. While they may stay within the same society (and even these boundaries may weaken in the future), they must form new relationships, adapt to a new physical environment, new norms, and so on. Those who remain behind must repair the social fissure that the transients have created.

The effects of mobility on our culture have been profound. George Pierson has argued with great force that most of what is distinctively American can be traced to it. Optimism, conservatism, other-directedness, individualism, egalitarianism, superficiality, identity diffusion, gregariousness, alienation, homogeneity, money-mindedness, loneliness, nostalgia, anxiety, conformity, activity, achievement orientation, pragmatism, love of novelty, materialism, youth worship—all these real or imagined qualities bear some relationship to the tendency of modern Americans to uproot themselves frequently.[1] Constant moving about tends to detach the individual from enduring and significant relationships. But the difficulty of continually forming new bonds and breaking old ones can be eased by learning to speed up the process of making friends —developing an informality, an easy friendliness, a capacity for ready, if superficial, ties.

Human beings are all equipped with the same emotional repertoire, the same basic needs, the same basic defenses. Out of these evolve more idiosyncratic patterns that we call personality or shared patterns we call culture. These differences help maintain boundaries between individuals and between groups, but at the cost of some violence to the emotional life of the individual. My body may tell me, as a human being, to respond in a given way to a punch in the nose, a sexual stimulus, a loss, or a rejection, but I may have learned, as a member of a specific culture or as one playing a special role within that culture, not to react in this human way but in some way that defines me "uniquely."

To be more individual, in other words, is to be less human, more of a social artifact. One person learns to lose the capacity to respond with love, another person with anger, another with jealousy, another with tears, and so on. This process of emotional crippling we call personality development. Its effect is to create a kind of emotional specialization between people. In a permanent group the alienation that comes from a man's specialized response system is eased by his contact with other specialists, who express his needs and feelings for him as he does for them. In a culture in which a man cannot weep, his women may weep for him. If he is a group jester, there will be some dour compatriot to feel gloomy for him, and so on. And where the group as a whole warps human feeling in a given direction, defining its differentness from other groups, his similarity with those around him relieves his sense of alienation from his feelings.

When a man loses a permanent role in a permanent group, his

specialization becomes pointless and somewhat burdensome. He becomes a part in search of a whole, feeling unlike others and therefore alone and lost but having no sense of himself as a separate entity firmly fixed in a pattern of other such entities. In a society that places a value on individualism, this inability to experience oneself leads paradoxically to a cry for *more* uniqueness, more eccentricity, more individuation, thus increasing the symptoms.

The solution to this problem, to put it bluntly, is the obliteration of differences by increasing uniformity and sameness among people. But uniformity could only be tolerated if people were all transformed into full human beings rather than remaining specialized semipersons as we are now. Fantasies of uniformity have always assumed that all humans would affect some specialized posture: the gregarious suburbanite, the submissive peasant, the Prussian officer. We imagine with horror everyone being forced to assume some narrow role now played by only a few. But such a uniformity would not work since (1) it would retain the same constraints under which we now suffer without providing the assurance that others will express the stunted sides of ourselves; and (2) the advantages of a social division of labor would be lost, and the society as a whole would suffer from the loss of variety, the lack of human resources. Attempts to evolve this kind of uniformity may be (and are being) made, but a society so structured will fail. A viable society needs a great variety of contradictory human responses. If members of that society are to be limited in the ways they can respond, then each must be limited in different ways; otherwise generalized shortages will (and do) arise. On the other hand, if a society is to function with uniform participants, each one must be individually complex and comprehensive in his or her available responses. Each must have the capacity to be introverted *and* extroverted, controlled *and* spontaneous, independent *and* dependent, gregarious *and* seclusive, loving *and* hostile, strong *and* weak, and so on.

This is, of course, utopian. Human beings will never attain this degree of humanness; nor, happily, will complete uniformity ever be achieved. I am merely saying that if uniformity is the goal, specialization and incompleteness must be avoided. Less variety from person to person requires more variety within each person. The individual will be more changeable, less predictable from moment to moment and from situation to situation, less able to play the same tune all his or her life long.

Now if one must make and break relationships rapidly, then it becomes increasingly important that people be as interchangeable as possible, like the motel. An American today can travel almost anywhere in the country, stop at a motel, and find himself in an entirely familiar environment. He would, indeed, be hard put to distinguish one from another. As relationships become increasingly temporary, the need to establish such instant familiarity will correspondingly increase.

But people are not motels. We have already pointed out the necessity for an enrichment of the individual before interchangeability can exist. Transience also makes it more necessary to take people as we find them—to relate immediately, intensely, and without traditional social props, rituals, and distancing mechanisms. Distance is provided by transience itself, and the old patterns of gamesmanship, of extended, gradual, and incomplete unmasking, become inappropriate. By the time the individual reaches his "here is the real me" flourish, he finds himself alone again. It has often been observed that encounter groups are adapted to a transient world since they emphasize openness, feedback, immediacy, communication at a feeling level, the here and now, more awareness of and ability to express deeper feelings, and so on. Members of such groups often express surprise and chagrin at their capacity to respond warmly to people they would in other situations have regarded with indifference, fear, or contempt. After the initial shock has worn off, the old preferences are rediscovered, but there remains a sense of how often opportunities for significant relationships are wasted by casual stereotyping.

Another effect of transience is the development of more flexible moral patterns. Mobility and change rule out the effectiveness of any permanent system of social control. *External* controls depend on the permanent presence of the individual in the same social unit, a condition that has largely vanished from the civilized world. Even *internalized controls of a fixed kind* rapidly become irrelevant to a changing social environment. Our society has long required, and obtained, a system of internalized controls that incorporates moral relativism—what David Riesman has called "other-direction." [2] The individual must both be capable of self-restraint and, at the same time, recognize that groups vary in what they consider desirable and undesirable social behavior. He or she must be acutely sensitive and responsive to group norms, while recognizing the arbitrariness, particularity, and limited relevance of all moral rules.

This idea is offensive to many and generated a whole tradition of angry nostalgia among postwar critics of American society. But the "inner-directed" individual is like a wind-up toy, programmed at birth to display a limited range of responses in all situations regardless of environmental variation, and while this may well be considered heroic, it is, like all heroic traits, excessively simple-minded.

Greater complexity is also required at the marital level. Two married persons in a stable and permanent social context need seek little from each other. Psychological and interpersonal needs can be satisfied in a variety of other relationships—kin, neighborhood, friendship. In many societies and subcultures, deeply entrenched patterns of sex segregation make intimate communication between the sexes difficult or impossible; men and women literally live in different worlds. Wherever this stability begins to break down, husband and wife tend to increase their emotional demands on each other. The transition from working-class to middle-class status and from "urban village" to suburban environments often brings about a loosening of social relationships and is therefore usually associated, as we have seen, with an increase in the intensity and intimacy of the marriage and a decrease in role specialization. [3]

Sociologists have generally argued, with good reason, that higher income, education, and other attributes of middle-class standing are stabilizing forces for marriage. But we could also anticipate that the greater burden placed on the marriage by the reduction of other intimate and lasting relationships would increase marital discord. In a nonmobile society, one expects of marriage only a degree of compatibility. Spouses are not asked to be lovers, friends, and mutual therapists. But it is increasingly true of our own society that the marital bond is the closest, deepest, most important, and supposedly the most enduring relationship of one's life. Therefore, it is increasingly likely to fall short of the demands placed upon it and to be dissolved. As emotional alternatives are removed, the limitations of a marriage become less and less tolerable. The social ties of modern Americans are becoming so transitory that a permanent point of reference seems essential, and this perhaps accounts for the heroic effort made in our society— through marriage manuals, counselors, psychotherapists, magazine articles, and so on—to find ways of enabling the marriage relationship to bear the enormous emotional burdens placed upon it.

The most obvious strain in a transient society is produced by each partner having a career. This means that at any moment competing job requirements or opportunities threaten to separate the couple geographically. This is an increasing problem in a world in which more and more professional couples are appearing. Unless one or the other is willing to assume subordinate status, it is often difficult for the couple both to find desirable positions in the same community.

Yet the decline in the specialization of marital roles constitutes a powerful force for feminine equality, and a mobile society must either tolerate the pull of competing careers or the push of feminine discontent. For decades our society chose the latter, and one result has been an exaggerated investment of feminine energy and ambition into the child-rearing process. While the social costs of either solution are high, it is difficult to envision a more serious social risk than that which results from children having to validate their mothers' competence through their own successes, creativity, and mental health.

The "problem" of the working mother is often discussed as if the mother's presence in the home were an unqualified blessing. Child rearing, however, has never been, throughout history, either a full-time or a one-person task, but rather the adjunct of an otherwise full life. The children, meanwhile, have been their own heroes, not merely the central character in their mother's drama. No one ever asks the victims of our American pattern whether they might not have preferred to see a little less of their mothers and let both mother and child win their own rewards.

Chapter 6

DEMOCRACY AND GRANDPARENTS

There are many conflicts in our feelings toward old people in American society, and these conflicts tend to introduce a sharp tone of artificiality into our relations with them. We are ashamed of our negative feelings and try to mask them and hide them from ourselves, assuming a pose of respect and interest that we often do not feel. Our position is somewhat like that of a hypochondriacal man greeting an old and dear friend who has contracted a loathsome, highly contagious disease. He finds it impossible to behave honestly because he can bear neither his friend's condition nor his own reaction to it.

Our ideas about old age are inherited from two contradictory traditions. On the one hand, we have the classical Greek view that aging is an unmitigated misfortune. That attitude is best expressed by the seventh-century poet, Mimnermos of Kolophon, who said: "Brief is the fruit of youth, no longer than the daily spread of the sunlight over the earth; but when that springtime of life is passed, then verily to die is better than to live, for many are the ills that invade the heart."

On the other hand, we find the Middle Eastern view that old age is the summit of life. This view permeates the Old Testament and characterizes the Middle East even today. Age brings prestige not only in the family but in the community, where it almost auto-

43

matically confers political influence. The well-known title "sheik" originally meant simply "old man." Great age is also viewed as a sign of innate virtue and divine blessing, and it is probably for this reason that such extravagant ages were assigned to the early Biblical patriarchs. The ancient Hebrews believed that the wicked die young, while the Greeks not only said, "Whom the gods *love* die young," but invented two or three myths to prove it.[1]

On the surface it might seem that our attitudes are entirely derived from the Greek. We worship youth and scorn old age, which in our society confers no dignity but only losses. Yet we feel some guilt over this. We even try to deny the existence of old age by using words like "aging," which is as if to say: "Old age is such a depressing state that we must never admit that anyone has finally entered it—even a person in his eighties is only moving toward it."

An artificiality of this kind always increases distance between people. This dishonesty—this unwillingness to accept our own negative attitudes toward old age—does far more to make old people feel isolated and alienated than do the attitudes themselves. In many societies the aged are valued far less than in ours; indeed, they are assigned the lowest possible status. Yet interaction between the young and old is free and comfortable within that context. The loss of status causes suffering, discontent, and a sense of loss, but everyone at least knows what the problem is and can talk about it. The young can commiserate with the old and the old with each other.

But how can the young commiserate with the old when we dare not admit to ourselves that old age is a misfortune, when it is taboo even to speak of decline and deterioration and approaching death to those experiencing it? Would it not, perhaps, be better to engage in frank condolences than to pretend, as the young often do, that nothing is happening or changing, that no misfortune has taken place, and that retirement, failing health, and abandoned activities and relationships are occasion for bland and superficial cheerfulness?

Positive or negative attitudes toward old age and the aged don't occur randomly but are based on the social, economic, and political characteristics of the society in which the attitudes prevail. If we are to resolve our ambivalence in this area, we must first get a clearer notion of the meaning of old age for a given society.

It seems obvious, for example, that the aged will be valued and deferred to in a society in which they perform some important function. In a primitive society in which there is no written language but rather a fixed body of knowledge that must be transmitted orally, old people are the experts, and other members of the tribe will be more dependent on them. In our society, most of the knowledge acquired by old people, no matter how wise and experienced, is obsolete and irrelevant—the techniques and skills we spend our lives acquiring become of purely historical interest in a decade or two.

From a study of the aged in 71 "primitive" societies, Leo Simmons compiled an extensive list of the social and environmental characteristics of each and the specific treatment of the aged in each.[2] The treatment of the aged ranged from the most profound respect and reverence to callous rejection, abandonment, and deprivation. In some societies the aged are even killed rather than allowed to die of starvation and exposure. Simmons found that the prestige of the aged in a given society is dependent on the number of important functions they perform in that society.

Examining Simmons's data, we find that societies in which the elderly have high prestige are generally authoritarian, collectivistic, and static—usually governed by monarchs or chiefs. They have hereditary castes or classes, and all the important decisions are made by the society or the extended family, not by the individual.

In societies in which the aged have low prestige, on the other hand, government is by general assembly or some other democratic system. Individualism is prevalent and highly valued, and able people can improve their social and economic position. This comes closest to being a description of our own society as most people would like it to be.

A positive orientation toward the aged cannot be based on some artificial attempt to reverse the prestige structure of our society. A society that values change and freedom and is suspicious of authority and tradition, impatient of restriction, and hungry for new

ideas and ways of doing things is never going to welcome old age
or accord high prestige to the elderly. Youth-worship is inherent
in a democratic society such as ours, and if we want to improve the
welfare of the aged in the society, we can only do so by recognizing that for an American old age is a misfortune. The aged American does not, for the most part, have an important role to play in
our society.

It might be useful to reduce some of the guilt aroused by com-
parisons with societies in which the elderly are revered and admired, for guilt is a great source of good intentions destructively
executed. In fact, if we examine the data more closely we find that
attitude differences between "age-oriented" and "youth-oriented"
societies are often exaggerated. In many societies that are tradi-
tionally believed to show great deference to the elderly, only the
most intelligent and able ones are respected (just as they are in
our own society), while the less capable are shown no respect at
all. In others, the aged are valued and admired only until they
begin to show signs of weakness, incapacity, illness, or senility, at
which point an abrupt change takes place and they are treated
harshly and rejected. Only continuing usefulness or continuing
power through the control of property will enable them to maintain their position.

Still other societies have achieved the reputation of age deference solely by written records containing admonitions to the
young to defer to their elders—data that we could just as easily interpret as revealing a lack rather than a prevalence of respect.
Such admonitions may be found in all societies, including our
own.

Finally, in many societies the notion of the "golden years" reveals itself as a myth; with the elderly complaining bitterly that
while in their youth they respected the aged and looked forward to
the time when they themselves would be old, they now find it a
difficult and unpleasant condition. As one old Hopi woman said,
"See how we suffer. It is foolish to look forward to such a time." [3]

The aged have always been closely associated with sorcery in
the minds of people (witches and wizards are almost always old)
partly because of the association between age and knowledge and

partly because old age is a period of life that the young have never experienced and that, therefore, seems strange and uncanny. Perhaps it also serves to counteract the increasing frustration of the dependency of the young: If the aged are not old, impotent, and passive but actually old, omnipotent, and active, then the young need not fear having to face life alone and unprotected. Finally, the fewer stimuli sent out by a person, the easier it is to project on to that person. In practice, this seems to be particularly true of hostile impulses, which are often attributed to passive, silent persons. Whatever resentments are roused by the parent's decline are disowned, and instead of it being the child who feels malevolent and who has suddenly acquired an unwanted power over the parent's destiny, it is the old person who has acquired malign and magical powers.

Although in modern urban societies the belief in sorcery has somewhat declined, our attitudes about hospitalization are of the same order. The fear of magical contagion, for example, may often underlie the intense need to isolate and insulate the aging parents in a hospital, and the mysterious collapses of patients following hospitalization greatly resembles the equally mysterious collapses and deaths of sorcery victims in primitive societies, where there seems to be something fatal in knowing that one is hated and plotted against. All of this may seem far removed from the everyday world of families and hospitals, but magical thinking and responses did not disappear with the practice of magic. The notion that a problem will disappear if you put someone in a hospital is an excellent example of magical thinking, one of the most pervasive in our society.

Chapter 7

CHANGING THE FAMILY

Evolution (biological as well as cultural) proceeds in a kind of leapfrog fashion: Bold new advances don't usually occur in those groups in the vanguard of development. The advanced cultures and advantaged groups are too embroiled in their success to be available for new departures. It is those societies with nothing to lose by change—nothing invested in today—that can exploit the radically new opportunity.

Democracy, then, is a device for speeding up evolution, since it makes the uncommitted more available and powerful. Unfortunately, however, as we raise the position of any group in a society, they thereby *acquire* a vested interest in the status quo. Without the democratic *family*, democracy would be a self-extinguishing mechanism.

By the "democratic family" I simply mean a family system in which there is little social distance between parent and child, the exercise of parental authority is relatively mild, and the child is not a mere parental possession but has independent legal status. It is, in other words, the system that presently exists in our own middle class and toward which most of the Western world seems to be moving.

Now the young are, by their very nature, uncommitted. They constitute the only group that can perpetually renew its lack of

48

commitment as its older members are siphoned off into the ranks of the committed. The only status quo in which youth as a whole acquires a vested interest is the democratic family itself. The democratic family assigns high status to a group that has no commitment to any specific item in the culture other than its accent on youth. It thus maximizes the possibility for exploitation of new opportunities.

An interesting forerunner of the democratic family is primogeniture. This is a compromise institution that realizes many of the advantages of both the democratic and authoritarian family systems. The eldest son exploits existing conditions, while the younger, who has no vested interest in the status quo, provides the raw material for social change. This is enhanced if the younger son is given some kind of special status, as in Japan. William Goode comments that younger sons in Japan are more indulged and allowed more freedom since "in Japanese folk wisdom, it is the younger sons who are the innovators." [1]

The democratic family extends this approach to all children in the family. It assumes that children may adapt better to their environment than did their parents, and that therefore their parents cannot take for granted the superiority of their own knowledge, perceptions, attitudes, and skills. Thus it not only causes but can only exist under conditions of chronic change. The democratic family is based on an expectation that tomorrow will be different from today, and that there is, hence, some ambiguity as to how to socialize the child. "Socialization for what?" is its fundamental question.

The democratic family is a key link in the circular chain of change. By raising the status of the child, lessening the social distance between child and parent, and reducing parental authority, the child's susceptibility to the social environment is increased, while susceptibility to tradition is decreased. But the democratic family is a result as well as a cause of change acceleration, for any increase in the rate of social change tends also to increase the parents' doubt about their own values and customs and to make them view their children as better adapted to the world they will grow into than the parents themselves. [2]

But how is such a cycle set in motion in the first place? The most likely answer is that some sudden external, accidental, but overwhelming change in the social environment produces what Norman Ryder calls an "experiential chasm" between parents and children. Such chasms serve to invalidate parental authority and parental wisdom, for the parents have not even experienced the change in the same way, at the same time of life.

In most cases such events—an unprecedented climatic disaster, for example, or an invasion of unfamiliar warrior nomads—are temporary disturbances. They are somehow integrated into a new pattern, which is just as stable and enduring as the old. Parental authority is invalidated only for that generation that was unable to anticipate the crisis, and it soon re-establishes itself. But what if the community or society receives several such shocks in succession? Change then becomes an expectation, tradition irrelevant, and the democratic family obtains a foothold. As Ryder observes: "The products of earlier education become debris that chokes off later growth," and major environmental changes enhance the importance of such growth.[3] Two examples will serve to illustrate the role of environmental disturbances in transforming parental wisdom into "debris."

THE JEWISH IMMIGRANT

My first example is the impact of immigration on the family system of the shtetl, the small Jewish communities of Eastern Europe. It illustrates again the advantageous position of the uncommitted under conditions of rapid social change.

Any persecuted minority group must in some way cope with the fact that its position impairs the traditional male role. Protecting and providing may not be universal masculine attributes, but when the larger community in which the minority is embedded defines the role in this way, the minority-group males will tend to appear less adequate. For Eastern European Jews living in the shtetl, an interesting if only partly successful solution to this dilemma emerged from centuries of persecution. Masculine status was attached to learning—a learning that was essential to the core of the culture but rather irrelevant to issues not tied to human relationships within that culture. It was an ingenious solution, making a virtue of a necessity and creating a practicality (i.e., the moral and legal problems created by the confrontation of ancient laws and current realities) where none had existed. The man with the highest status was not only the most learned but also the most withdrawn from worldly activities and most insulated from daily contact with the hostile majority. The learned man did not concern himself with the business of making a living and protecting his family from harm. These more practical issues were left to his wife and to God, which in practice often meant gentile police, firemen, and soldiers. It was the woman who managed and often earned the money, who bought and sold, who bargained with peasants and spoke the local language, acting as a buffer against the world for her sheltered husband.[4]

The women could not carry so great a share of the burdens of life and still be altogether comfortable with the submissive feminine ideal. They were conscious of the extent to which they were mothers to their husbands, although their protest was limited to irony (such as referring to the husband as "my breadwinner").[5]

For the common people this pattern was less marked. There was less sexual segregation, a less rigid sexual division of labor, and a tendency toward freer choice in marriage.[6] When it came to emigration, then, it would be the common people and the women who would have least to lose in terms of status, who would be best adapted to transact successfully the difficulties of the journey, and who would find themselves most at home in the new environment. The knowledge and skills of the learned Jew would be essentially useless unless and until he could be transplanted into a complete new ghetto. But the more permeable nature of the new society, which both demanded and offered new occupational roles, upset the old balance and made the position of the learned Jew somewhat difficult to re-establish. The ideal of learning became diluted with practicality, so that status went to the doctor or lawyer. The brittle patriarchy collapsed.

Thus it was those least committed to the old cultural pattern who were best able to seize and mold a new pattern under new conditions. For Jews emigrating from the shtetl the availability of the uncommitted was accidental. The democratic family system translates such accidents into certainty by insulating the young from the committed, minimizing the prestige of adults, and building segregated worlds of childhood and adolescence.

THE MANUS

My second example involves a democratic family system where we would least expect it—in a remote New Guinea island inhabited by nonliterate Melanesians. We don't know how such a system ever emerged in such an unlikely place; the causes are lost forever in unrecorded history.

The Manus were first studied by Margaret Mead in 1928, when she commented at length on the contrast between their permissive child-rearing practices and the prudish, materialistic, ascetic, industrious, business-oriented quality of adult life, a combination similar to our own culture. She returned to the Manus in 1953 "because I had heard that they had changed more remarkably and more drastically than any other of the peoples of the Pacific." [7]

Although adult males were engaged in "unremitting labor" directed toward the accumulation of property, these same fathers made no demands whatever on their children, outside of prudery and respect for property. They were not taught anything about the complexities of adult life. "Property, morality, and security for the next generation" were the concerns of the adults, but the children did as they pleased, bullying and tyrannizing over their parents. Obedience and deference were unknown, and children ate and slept and played when and where they wished despite their parents' futile pleading. They lived in their own world, a cooperative, sharing one that had no relationship to the competitive, property-centered world of the adults. Yet when they reached adolescence, they moved painfully from this happy, irresponsible existence on to the bottom rung of the adult economic ladder, partaking in the adult quarrels they had treated with such indifference, abandoning their world of friendship for one in which friendliness detached from economic considerations was almost impossible.[8]

Between Mead's first and second visits a cataclysmic environmental change occurred: During World War II more than a million Americans occupied the Admiralty Islands. The Manus, who prior to this time had encountered only small groups of colonial rulers, had an opportunity to experience (in a dazzling if somewhat distorted form) Western culture to the full. In response to this experience the Manus consciously and deliberately discarded the bulk of their old culture, particularly its more inconvenient and burdensome aspects, and adopted a new one. They destroyed their household "ghosts," relocated their village, abolished taboos and avoidances, rearranged their economic system, and (against the resistance of the colonial authorities) tried to establish broader political cooperation.[9]

The Manus in 1928 were in no way less primitive or superstitious than their neighbors, although their culture was unique in its insulation of children from adult life. In their "New Way" they drew upon the social patterns of their childhood peer groups as well as their experiences with an alien culture. This child-adult discontinuity provided a ready-made lever for change. The Manus' willingness to protect children from the burdens of the present was easily translated into the idea that the children constitute the best hope for a better future society.[10] The fact that the Manus of 1928 did not provide their children with an education that would become "debris" gave their society an advantage over other Pacific cultures.

This idea helps us to understand the "cargo cult" phenomenon, which has occurred so frequently since World War II. Its usual form is a kind of religious frenzy that sweeps over an area, sparked by a prophet who persuades people to destroy all their possessions to make room for the Second Coming of American cargo ships bringing all the trappings of Western culture. Westerners typically look upon it with indulgent condescension as another example of how primitive irrationality can lead to disaster. If our argument is correct, however, the cargo-cult response is a rational act of commitment to change. It takes a bit of frenzy to reject one's whole way of life in favor of a distant and uncertain possibility. But if the change is desired, the first necessary act is the destruction of the "debris that chokes off later growth." This destruction is unwise in the sense that the ships will not come. But it is sociologically wise in that such areas have placed themselves in a state of psychological readiness for the Western culture that they ardently desire. As Mead points out, it is easier to embrace a new culture in its entirety—since it is a meaningful, integrated whole—than to try to splice two cultures together. Substituting clothes for grass skirts (to use Mead's own example) without introducing soap and chairs produces dirt and disease; without sewing machines, starch, and irons, it creates a society of ragamuffins; without closets, it produces huts that are cluttered with hanging clothes, and so on.[11] The cargo cultists seem at some level to have recognized a truth that has eluded Western colonialists for centuries. Only their wish to embrace Western culture can be called irrational. Once this goal is accepted, the steps they have taken toward it are the only ones that are both rational and possible for them. They have freed themselves from commitment to the past.

The democratic family, by insulating childhood from adult tradition, achieves the same effect.

THE AMERICAN FAMILY

The best example of how a democratic family system comes into being is found in our own history. Here four historical forces served to produce and sustain a family pattern that was unintended and is still under attack, although it is far too firmly entrenched to be dislodged by anything short of a world cataclysm. Each of these four forces—the transplantation of the original settlers, the Western frontier, the great immigrations of the nineteenth and early twentieth centuries, and the profound technological changes of the past one hundred years—drove an experiential chasm between parent and child that eroded the authoritarian family pattern prevailing in Europe.

Some people imagine the democratic family to be of very recent origin, emerging full-blown from Victorian patriarchy. There is no evidence, however, that an authoritarian family system ever existed on American soil as a widespread social pattern. Individual authoritarian families and small groups and subcultures always have and always will exist. Moralists have been advocating parental severity since the first boat landed. But as nearly as we can tell, the democratic family began to prevail throughout the American colonies within a generation or two following the first settlements and, as we shall see, has never been seriously challenged.

We would expect that whenever and wherever the rate of change slows, the democratic family should decay and a more authoritarian pattern emerge. What seem unique to the American situation are the forces that have successfully and repeatedly reversed this process. Despite the efforts of Puritan moralists, the continual replenishment of American life with European families (with European assumptions), and the gradual aging and stabilizing of the society, the authoritarian family has been repeatedly uprooted whenever it threatened to take hold.

The First Settlers The beginnings of the democratic family in the United States can be located in the experiential chasm between the first generation of native-born settlers and their European-born parents. To the European-born settler, for example, the forest never ceased to be a dangerous and magical place, filled with supernatural beings of malevolent intent. But to the native-born child it was simply the back yard, a comfortable and interesting place in which to run about. The example may seem trivial, but it is one of many such differences.

Most writers stress the role of economic factors in bringing about the democratization of the American family—the dependence of the male on wife and children for survival in the wilderness. But similar dependence can be found elsewhere without the democratic family, and while it may be one condition, it clearly cannot be the only one. What seems crucial is the irrelevance of most parental knowledge for the successful adaptation of the child, often accompanied by explicit parental hopes for the child's social mobility. Indeed, who could teach the other more about living in the wilderness, parent or child?

The Frontier What was true for the first settlers remained true on the Western frontier as long as it existed. As the terrain changed, the qualities necessary for successful adaptation changed, and the child continued to teach the parent the ways of the world.

This is perhaps the real basis for Frederick Jackson Turner's argument that the frontier was a perennial democratizing force in American society.[12] While there were other springs to the democratic impulse, the frontier was a major source of radical democracy as long as it survived. Above all, it helped maintain the democratic family as a dominant form in American life. As Arthur Calhoun observed, " 'For the children' was the motto of many a pioneer, who endured the wilderness hardships that the next generation might have a better chance." [13]

But did the democratic family atrophy in the East with the passage of time and increasing stabilization? If we use the reports of foreign visitors, then we must conclude that the American family has *always* been egalitarian, permissive, and child-oriented relative to its European counterparts.[14] At every period in American history statements are made by foreign visitors that American children are treated as equals and friends by their parents, that they are never punished or disciplined, that their parents indulge them and are constantly concerned about their needs and wishes, that they are allowed to intrude on adult activities, and so on. Even the restrained de Tocqueville was moved to remark that in America "the family, in the Roman and aristocratic signification of the word, does not exist." [15]

The Authoritarian Family Myth Throughout Calhoun's history of the American family, he speaks of the decay of authoritarianism in the parent-child relationship as if it occurred anew in each generation. Yet, these distinctions receive little emphasis in the reports of travelers and the complaints of natives. The mildness of parental authority and the independence and omnipresence of children are attributed by foreigners to all classes and regions. But the curious tendency for native Americans to perceive this chronic condition as a new phenomenon deserves brief attention. For example, in the 1830s and 1840s—the supposed heyday of the belief in "breaking the will"—an educational journal comments on the *new* "cult of childhood" as something duplicated only in the classical age; a physician attacks the "growing view" that punishment is unnecessary in child rearing; and a man complains that he grew up in an age when the child was nothing and reached maturity in a period when childhood was everything. Calhoun comments in 1900 on the decline of moral tales in children's literature, notes that because of the absence of a nursery the children are allowed to "tear all over the house," and suggests that "the best American homes have come to center in the child." These comments, however, are interspersed with quotations drawn from the 1860s that refer to the same phenomena. Finally, we note with interest that "one reason Americans are not strenuous in discipline is that coercion is supposed to break the will and hinder self-expression"—an attitude that we usually attribute to Freud's influence and that is supposed to have first made its appearance in the 1930s. Actually, it is mentioned as a parental motive by travelers throughout the eighteenth and nineteenth centuries, usually accompanied by the equally familiar argument that such a policy results in the American child's becoming a dictator in the home.[16]

Apparently, then, there have not been any gross changes in parental-authority patterns in America during the past three centuries. Clergymen and physicians may have exerted authoritarian pressures at one time or another, and the emergence of large family fortunes and pseudoaristocratic traditions may have given a toehold to familial authoritarianism in the more settled sections of the country during the nineteenth century. But even if so, the trend was not strong enough to cause so much as a ripple in the stream of foreign commentary on the American family. If there was an authoritarian threat it did not succeed, but was soon overwhelmed by new pressures for change and forced to take refuge, like the losing tribe in some ancient invasion, in whatever small and undesired corners were left to it by the victors. The myth of the authoritarian family of yore has probably never lacked for a few real-life models here and there, but fundamentally it merely expresses the fact that a child is unaware of living in a child-oriented household while a parent is sharply cognizant of it, and can therefore easily imagine a change to have occurred.

The Puritan Dilemma The Puritan family is usually regarded as the foundation of the old-fashioned American family. A great deal of nonsense has been written, and even more assumed, about this chapter in American history. The worst error has been to equate the aspirations and rules of a few leaders with the practices of the population at large. We have no evidence to indicate that the Puritan fathers were any more successful in imposing an authoritarian family system than they were in abolishing the casual sexual customs of the rank-and-file colonist. Complaints about the rebelliousness and disrespectfulness of youth and the generality of fornication and adultery are equally pervasive throughout the early Colonial period, and while there is no reason to assume that the actual behavior in either category was more conspicuous than in our own era, there is equally little reason for assuming it to have been less so.[17] Puritan efforts to legislate family relationships had the unintended consequence of contributing to the democratization of the family, a process that is of the utmost relevance to the comparable efforts of the revolutionary governments of the twentieth century.

We know, of course, that the manifest intent of the Puritan leaders was quite different, that their image of the proper family was a highly authoritarian and patriarchal one. God was viewed as an absolute ruler, and the Fifth Commandment was to be the governing principle of all human relationships, with the father receiving respect, submission, and obedience from wife, children, and servants alike. Independence and initiative, far from being encouraged, were seen as sinful.[18]

I believe, however, that any group that intervenes between parent and child and attempts to regulate and modify the parent-child relationship *will have a democratizing impact on that relationship regardless of its intent.* For however much the state or community may wish to inculcate obedience and submission in the child, its intervention betrays (1) a lack of confidence in the parents, and (2) an overwhelming interest in the future development of the child—in other words, a child-centered orientation.

Edmund Morgan places great emphasis on Puritan intervention in the parent-child relationship. He points out the many regulations protecting family members from each other, the great concern that children be properly educated, and the willingness to remove the child from the family should the parents fall short of community requirements. Like the founders of the kibbutzim in Israel, the Puritans saw child development as a community issue first and a family issue second. This priority was expressed in the view that loyalty, affection, and submission to a husband or father should always be kept in careful subordination to corresponding sentiments toward God.[19]

Similarly, although the Puritans had no intention of encouraging self-expression or individuality in their children, their child-centeredness set severe limits on the exercise of parental authority. They were opposed to corporal punishment except in extreme situations since they viewed punishment as purificatory rather than educational. Children were to be trained with due attention to their individual peculiarities rather than by a general formula. Marriages were to be contracted with the voluntary agreement of the principals, since a coerced match might prevent the couple from carrying out their obligation to love each other. Nor should a child be forced into an occupation, for this might violate his or her particular "calling" and prevent the true service of God.[20]

This preoccupation with the *internal* development of the child shows that the Puritans already had the future orientation that has always dominated our culture. One sees them frequently struggling with this contradiction between (1) a theology that purports to know the only true course to be followed and hence allows no questioning or opposition and (2) the adaptation to the ambiguous physical and social environment that required faculties and skills more accessible to the young than to the old. The injunction to observe the child's interests before attempting to train him or her and the reluctance to force a marriage or a career against the child's will express some parental self-doubt, which was to increase in the ensuing centuries.

Community intervention was more important in undermining parental authority than the growth of a child-centered attitude. The Puritans, to be sure, saw themselves as bolstering rather than undermining parental authority, and their behavior largely substantiates this view: This was no revolutionary attempt to set up the state or the local community *in loco parentis.* Yet at the same time the Puritan community was more than an extension of parental authority on to a higher plane, like the village elders or clan heads, who continue and enlarge rather than oppose parental authority. The Puritan divines saw themselves as representing the authority of God and saw this authority as *competitive* with parental authority in the last analysis. The Puritans did everything possible to de-emphasize this conflict, but it appeared often in their discussions of familial affection. The child was told again and again, apparently with great effect, that love of parents, if too strong, constituted idolatry—that it must always be subordinated to love of God. What is important is the establishment of the community's independent claim on the child's future.

The significance of this claim is illuminated by Philippe Ariès' brilliant analysis of the changing role of the child from the Renaissance to the present day. Ariès points out that the concept of childhood as a separate period of life with special characteristics is relatively modern. A few centuries ago a child was simply a small adult, wearing the same clothes, engaged in the same activities, acting on the same assumptions as adults. He or she was in no way set apart or shielded from adult society as children are today, with pursuits and interests specific to their age. This change corresponds to the growth of a community investment in the child's future. We segregate children from adult life because we wish to do something special with them, to effect some kind of social change or to adapt to one. Such segregation insulates the child from the social patterns of the present and makes him more receptive to some envisioned future. Ariès says that medieval civilization lacked a concept of transition between childhood and adulthood, a transition now represented by formal education. Ariès calls it, quite appropriately, a quarantine. We might also liken it to the current fantasies about deepfreezing one's body until the cures for its diseases are invented. "Family and school together removed the child from adult society," making her amenable to new influences that might change the nature of her later adult behavior.[21]

The bases of a child-centered society and a democratic family system are: (1) a preoccupation with the future, (2) a desire to manipulate the child-rearing process to further community goals, and (3) a consequent confrontation between the community and the parent for the child's allegiance. The child emerges as the receptacle for future hopes and hence bears a higher status than her elders, whose authority is weakened by its doubtful relevance to this future. When this condition is achieved, the rate of social change is accelerated—or, more precisely, the gravitational forces that retard change are weakened—and the process becomes self-perpetuating.

The Great Immigration The third blow to family authoritarianism was the sudden influx, in the late nineteenth century, of many new immigrants from different cultures. It is almost as if fate had conspired to maintain a constant democratizing pressure, for immigration increased precisely as the frontier receded, and the degree of cultural shock experienced by the immigrants also increased as the shock effect of frontier life diminished.

American literature is rich in descriptions of the chasm between first- and second-generation immigrants: the child who is more acculturated than the parents and can act as an interpreter, the child who is a repository of parental hopes for social advancement but also an object of parental resentment for rebelling against Old World culture and parental authority. There are two points seldom made about this drama, however. The first is that without the development of the "quarantined" childhood that Ariès discusses, the acculturation of the child could not and would not have occurred. Immigration itself would not have created a chasm of such magnitude had the child instantly participated in the adult life of the transplanted community; it was the exposure of the child to the insulated life of the age-segregated school and play group.

The second point is that this experience of the immigrant is not a foreigner's experience but an American experience. There has never been a time when a child was not better adapted than his or her parents to live in American society, when he or she was not the bearer of aspirations for a better future. What the immigrant imagined to be a problem peculiar to being foreign was really an ironic initiation into American life.

There is additional irony in the fact that the newcomers brought with them a far more authoritarian family system than that prevailing here, and concentrated themselves in precisely those settled areas that might be expected to be most vulnerable to authoritarianism. Yet the net result of this infusion was further democratization. For although new pockets of familial authoritarianism did develop in unassimilated ghettos, those individuals who were able to enter the mainstream of American culture had to reject their parents all the more strongly. Social mobility always produces an experiential chasm even without an immigrant background. But since the immigrants typically began in poverty, assimilation and social mobility tended to occur simultaneously. Thus the price of entry into the American middle class was the pulverization of those conditions that nourish the authoritarian family. Paradoxically, the very existence of these pockets of familial authoritarianism served to heighten and dramatize the initiation process.

Technological Change Just as the tide of immigration was suddenly and permanently dammed, the fourth and most powerful force for democratization reached its peak. This force was technological change. Unlike the earlier ones, it has no natural limits. By World War I it had accelerated to the point that a disruptive invention could be counted on at least every 20 years, and it was driving wedges between family members fast enough to outmode parental assumptions before the child-rearing process was completed. Like the earlier colonists, frontiersmen, and non-English-speaking immigrants, *all* Americans of the present century must face the irrelevance of their knowledge and skills for the world into which their children will mature. It is not merely that parents cannot help their children with math and science problems, or that the children accept easily inventions that their parents still find a little mysterious or disconcerting. It is that parents cannot define the parameters of the future for their children—cannot even establish the terms of possible change or a range of alternative outcomes.

If this view is correct, we can predict that another hundred years or so will find the democratic family ensconced everywhere on the globe, barring nuclear disaster or some major deceleration in the rate of technological change and diffusion. Such a prediction, however, is bolstered by a fifth and somewhat less impersonal factor to which we may now turn.

THE STATE AND THE FAMILY

I have argued that familial democratization in America resulted from a series of environmental forces that widened the experiential chasm between parent and child. I suggested that any community intervention between parent and child would tend to produce familial democracy regardless of its intent. This argument becomes more significant when we survey the less industrialized segments of the world today, their aspirations and the models of change available to them. By this I mean that it would now be difficult to find a third world country that would be satisfied with the kind of gradual, spontaneous industrialization experienced by England and the United States during the nineteenth century. What most of them desire is a rapid and forced crash program that will close the enormous gaps that presently exist. For this the models are the Soviet Union and China—models that include a sharp centralization of power necessary to induce sudden and often painful changes.

At this point, however, the paradox begins. For in order to effect rapid changes, any such centralized regime must mount a vigorous attack on the family lest the traditions of present generations be preserved. In other words, it must artificially create an experiential chasm between parents and children in order to insulate the children and indoctrinate them with new ideas. The desire might be to increase submission to the state, but if one wishes to mold children in order to achieve some future goal, one must begin to view them as superior because they are closer to this future goal. One must also study their needs with care in order to achieve this difficult preparation for the future. One must teach them not to respect their tradition-bound elders, who are tied to the past and know only what is irrelevant. In other words, one must become child-centered and democratic in one's familial policies.

Thus far I have emphasized the causes more than the consequences of the democratic family system. We know that family and state tend to conform to each other in their authority patterns, and each seems to have the capacity to affect the other. As David and Vera Mace point out, "If the state and the family differ fundamentally in the principles and ideals that motivate them, one will ultimately destroy the influence and power of the other." [22] Changes in the state are somewhat more visible, but we have now seen how changes in the family can occur independent of political changes, and once this has taken place, it is easy to see how political authoritarianism could be undermined. It is in the family, after all, that attitudes of submissiveness and independence are learned. For the very small child, parents represent the entire universe, and one cannot build an automatic political submissiveness on a foundation of childhood independence. This is the paradox: One cannot teach the child to reject parental authority and be able to count on political authoritarianism, but one cannot permit submission to parental authority if one wishes to bring about profound social change.

The consequences of family democratization take a long time to make themselves felt. But even if policy makers decided that the benefits of rapid social change did not justify these dangerous consequences, it would be difficult to reverse the process once begun. What political intervention in the family initiates, technological change will carry forward. Technological advancement is a primary goal of those nations that are attempting to manipulate family relationships, and once the machinery of technological growth is set in motion, it will drive its own wedges into the family. Whichever force is most responsible, we seem to be witnessing the emergence of increasingly strong pressures toward democratization in the Soviet Union, and although they have been successfully parried thus far, they still appear to be growing.

Nazi Germany, the Soviet Union, and China have all shown great ambivalence in their approach to the family. The primary Nazi emphasis, as Lewis Coser observes, was on *strengthening* the authoritarian family, but the requirements of totalitarian control and the desire to monopolize individual loyalties forced a degree of competitive intervention. "Nazi policies for family and youth attempted to strengthen the paternalistic family and at the same time attacked and weakened it." [23] How much the familial democratization observed in postwar Germany can be attributed to this intervention is uncertain since there have been other powerful forces for change.

For the Soviet Union and China the balance is tipped the other way. Both revolutionary regimes began with a frontal attack on the traditional family, only to draw back as they became aware of the consequences. "The Russian policy-makers now realize that the authoritarian family acts to inculcate the authoritarian norms of the total society. They apparently feel that this task was not sufficiently well performed by the extrafamilial institutions for socialization." [24] But for the first 15 or 20 years after the revolution the assault on the traditional bourgeois patriarchal family was intense. We find Soviet leaders in the early period clearly supporting youth in opposition to a "reactionary" older generation. Actual public denunciation of parents by children was probably rare, but parents "tended to suppress their disagreement with the political opinions of their children, and to make the best of the situation. The evidence further suggests that Soviet parents, like most others, are eager for their children to make a success of life," which necessitated sustaining their loyalty to the regime. [25] In other words, once the wedge is driven, it makes very little difference how one tries to manipulate it. *Once uncertainty is created in the parent how best to prepare the child for the future—once the parent can in any way imagine his or her own viewpoint to be a possible liability to the child in the world approaching—the authoritarian family is obsolete,* regardless of whatever countermeasures may be taken. Indeed, it is likely that attempts to undo the process, such as the highly conservative Soviet family policies of the 1930s and 1940s, only serve to aggravate it. "The state, by its very interference in the life of its citizens, must necessarily undermine a parental authority which it attempts to restore." Official exhortations to respect parents "even if they are old-fashioned" can hardly serve to restore parental confidence that their way is the only way.[26]

China appears to have undergone a similar cycle. The old patriarchal family was, of course, in retreat long before the Communists came to power, but it was they who mounted the total attack that seems finally to have routed it. Yet only a decade after the defeat of the Kuomintang army, second thoughts about the attack on parental power began to appear. The slogan "all for the children" was surrounded with qualifications, and the positive side of filial piety received some attention. As Goode observes, these second thoughts "do not herald a return to the traditional family. They represent no more than official recognition that the propaganda campaign against the power of the elders may lead to misunderstanding on the part of the young, who may at times abandon their filial responsibilities to the state." [27] It will be several decades, however, before we can assess the impact of all this on Chinese society, which has always been more cohesive than our own.

The case of the kibbutz is also of interest in this connection, for initially there was no issue of protecting the power base of the state, and hence the attack on the traditional family was wholehearted and unhesitating. Like the Puritans, the kibbutz founders sought to establish an ideal community in the wilderness, uncontaminated by the viciousness of existing institutions. But unlike the earlier group, they viewed the authoritarian family as the foundation not of the new community but of existing corruption and attempted to eradicate it altogether. As we would expect, the second generation, being more comfortable in and better adapted to the new life than their parents, felt somewhat superior to them and regarded them as rather old-fashioned and bourgeois. Many rejected Judaism and evolved a highly negative stereotype of Jewishness. Others became apolitical and anti-ideological, bored with

Marxism and perfunctory in their commitment to their parents' Marxist ideals.[28]

An orientation toward the future tends to generate certain common attributes regardless of differences in ideology and intent. It seems clear that the entire globe is being swiftly drawn into such an orientation from a wide variety of positions and perspectives, and if my reasoning is correct, it follows with some inevitability that the democratic family, in some form or another, may become universal—along with all the troublesome issues familiar to us—by the time another century has passed.

Chapter 8

THE FAMILY IN ANCIENT GREECE

Power relations between men and women have always been a popular topic, but never in recorded history has there been so much serious analysis and questioning of those relationships as today—nor such sustained efforts to modify them. The history of all known civilizations, including our own, is patriarchal.

This makes it hard to conceive of alternatives or even to understand the workings of the system we have; it would be like trying to analyze our own culture if we had never seen or heard of another. We can't see without contrast, and those things in our environment that are most familiar, most unchanging, and most unchallenged are always the last to be understood.

Yet matriarchal fantasies have never been altogether absent from the human imagination for a very simple reason: Although men have dominated women throughout history, every man has a mother, hence every man has had the experience of being dominated by a woman. Furthermore, one can't help wondering, since this is virtually the *only* outlet for feminine dominance, if it doesn't get a little overcharged at times. And if it does, wouldn't that create in little boys a little anxiety, a little male chauvinism, a little need to control and dominate women and protect themselves from feminine emotion and power? If so, one could understand how the cycle could perpetuate itself forever, why patriarchy has been so long-lived.

These thoughts arose from looking at the culture of classical Greece, a culture that has given so much to our own in the way of literature, myths, and ideas. It was a culture profoundly patriarchal but not securely so—a society like our own, in which conventional standards were breaking down. The sexism of the fifth-century Greek male was strident and anxious, revealing more obviously a pattern that, in a more serene era, would perhaps be too subtle for our eyes to see.

There is a paradox regarding the role of women in fifth-century Athens. On the one hand, the status of women seemed to achieve a nadir. They were legal nonentities, excluded from political and intellectual life, uneducated, virtually imprisoned in the home, and appeared to be regarded with disdain by the principal male spokesmen whose comments have survived. On the other hand, as Arnold Gomme points out: "There is, in fact, no literature, no art of any country, in which women are more prominent, more important, more carefully studied and with more interest, than in the tragedy, sculpture, and painting of fifth-century Athens." Gomme rejects the traditional view of the Greek woman as a nonentity on these grounds and shows how one might arrive at a similar assessment of our own culture by the appropriate selection of sources.[1]

It is absurd to use statements like "a woman's place is in the home" as a reflection of reality, and the legal position of women often doesn't reflect their social position. It is also likely that the lower classes never participated as fully in the oppression of women as did the aristocracy, for the cultivation of bizarre and inconvenient social patterns is a luxury that the lower classes often cannot afford. The poor Athenian woman could not remain secluded in the home if peddling vegetables in the marketplace was her only source of livelihood.

But when all of these qualifications have been made, a core of male oppression and sex antagonism still remains. Women were legally powerless—a man could sell his daughter or even his sister into concubinage. Women of the upper classes could not go out unattended, and their social life outside the home was largely restricted to religious festivals and funerals. Among the well-to-do, men and women usually ate apart and often slept apart, and a wife who dined with her husband's guests was assumed to be a prostitute.[2]

Rejection and derogation of women mean rejection and derogation of domesticity—of home and family life and the rearing of young children. The Athenian male adult fled the home, but this meant that the Athenian male child grew up in a female-dominated environment. As an adult, he may have learned that women were of no account, but in the most important years of his psychological development he knew that the reverse was true. Men were at that time trivial to him; all of the most important things in his life were decided, as far as he could see, by women.

Nor was his view simply due to his ignorance of the outside world. We know from studies of the modern American family that participation and power go hand in hand. A working mother, for example, has more power in economic decision making than a nonworking mother but *less* power in decisions regarding household activities; the husband not only participates more in domestic activities but exerts more control over them.[3] Conversely, the more the male imprisons the female in the home and takes himself elsewhere, the more overwhelmingly powerful is the female within the home.

The social position of women and the psychological influence of women are thus quite separate matters. The Greek male's contempt for women was tightly bound to an intense fear of them and to an underlying suspicion of male inferiority. Why else would such extreme measures be necessary? Modern-day customs—such as the rule that a woman should not be older than her husband, of higher social status, more educated, paid the same as a male for the same work, or in a position of authority—show that males feel they are incapable of competing with females on an equal basis: The cards must first be stacked, the male given a handicap. Otherwise, as Plutarch felt, the male would simply be swallowed up and lose his identity altogether.[4]

There is strong evidence that women were powerful in the home. Greek literature shows that wives controlled the management of household finances; that while the husband earned the money the wife dispensed it. The home was also a factory, being divided into men's and women's quarters. The wife's control over her own domain, including the children, most of the slaves, and the economic heart of the household, was largely unchallenged and made the male vulnerable indeed. Isomachus, in attributing the outdoor life of the male and the indoor life of the female to a god-given division of labor, likens the wife's role to that of the queen bee, who supervises not only interior but also outside workers.[5] This is not to say that this division of labor completely eliminated marital power struggles—there are many allusions to sexual competition in comedy. But one cannot be a family patriarch at a distance. The role is an active one, involving the acceptance of interpersonal responsibility. The alcoholic who returns home only at midnight to beat his wife and children is not the most important figure in the daily life of the home. Women have great freedom of action in Greek drama and are usually more enterprising than the men; the tragic heroines are striking in their vigor, intelligence, vindictiveness, and uncontrollability.[6] But while one may agree that these women had contemporary models, we shouldn't assume that such modeling extended beyond the narrow range of the household. All that a playwright requires for drama is a vivid memory for his own childhood and family—and this is especially true of Greek drama, which is most intensely concerned with family conflict.

Attempts to simplify Greek attitudes toward women are thus thoroughly misguided. In Herodotus' description of the Battle of Salamis we find the Athenians so resenting the fact that a woman, Artemisia, commanded a ship against them that they offered a large reward for her capture alive. Yet, of the same battle, he reports a legend that the phantom of a woman appeared in the midst of the fighting and asked contemptuously, "in a voice which could be heard by every man in the fleet . . . if they proposed to go astern all day . . ."[7] The belief that an Athenian woman's place is in the home does not in the least prevent them from imagining her as an Amazon.

This same contradiction appears on Olympus. Despite its patriarchal superstructure, the goddesses are more intimately involved in the lives of mortals than are the gods. In particular, the enduring wrath of Hera is far more often the mainspring of mythological action than are the brief tantrums of Zeus, and has more far-reaching consequences. Like the Greek husband, Zeus wanders and philanders, but as the Greek wife was almost forced to be, Hera is faithful. Hera works out her jealous feelings primarily through the vindictive pursuit of her stepchildren, and there are several instances in Greek mythology (e.g., Medea, Procne) in which a mother kills her own children to spite her husband for his infidelity. Is it not possible that this phenomenon, too, reflects (in style if not in intensity) the situation of the Greek home? Is it not usual to expect the frustrated mother to work out some of her feelings on her children? It seems likely that some such tendency is responsible for the menacing aspect of women in so much of Greek myth.

Much has been written about homosexuality among the Greeks. All sources, from comedy to philosophy to litigation to history, indicate with compelling clarity that physical homosexuality was widespread and generally accepted, particularly among the upper classes, who attached more importance to homosexual affairs than to heterosexual ones. Now although psychological studies of male homosexuals are infected with a clinical bias that makes them somewhat suspect, there does seem to be a trend in the families of at least some male homosexuals for fathers to be absent or irrelevant and the mother-son relationship to be "of the close-binding, intimate type, where often it seemed that the mother might select the son as a kind of surrogate husband," leading to a subsequent fear of women.[8] This description fits the Greek case rather well.

Greek fear of women, however, was more particularized than this. It was mature, maternal women who were most feared and regarded as most dangerous. In the tragedies, young women and virginal goddesses are helpful and benign, while the mature ones tend to be jealous, vindictive, and destructive. In Greek religion we find two goddesses, Athena and Artemis, being transformed, over the centuries, from mother-goddesses to youthful virgins. And in the daily life of Athens we find a tendency for males to marry barely pubescent girls and to encourage their women to shave off their pubic hair.[9]

Bettelheim mentions the frequency with which disturbed boys are concerned about the "hairy vagina" and we may also recall that during the persecutions that periodically convulsed Europe between the thirteenth and seventeenth centuries, witches were shaved to uncover the mark of the Devil. The meaning of this preoccupation seems clear.[10]

Freud, for example, discusses the Medusa's head by pointing to its appearance on the shield of Athene: "Thus she becomes a woman who is unapproachable and repels all sexual desires—since she displays the terrifying genitals of the Mother." [11] But it is somewhat misleading to talk of Athene as someone who frightens and repels, inasmuch as she emerges as the most personal, most helpful, and least punitive of all the major Olympian females. In fact, the only repellent aspect of Athene *is* the shield, suggesting that from the Greek viewpoint kindness could be anticipated from a woman only so long as she remained a virgin. Perhaps the inhibitory value of the shield lies in the fact that it is a reminder that the alternative to a helpful Athene is a vindictive Hera.

A more compelling interpretation is suggested by Karen Horney's paper, "The Dread of Woman," in which the fear of female genitalia is derived from a fear of maternal envelopment. She describes "typical" dreams of male homosexuals: falling into a pit, sailing a boat in a narrow channel and being sucked into a whirlpool, being in a cellar full of "uncanny, blood-stained plants and animals"; and she comments on the widespread myth of the pool maiden (there are several in Greek mythology) who lures the male to his death.[12]

Trobriand Island women also shave their pubic hair. The Trobrianders believe in a mythical island inhabited only by women who don't shave and whose pubic hair grows long enough to form a kind of grass apron. They are very fierce and sexually insatiable. "When they cannot have intercourse, they use the man's nose, his ears, his fingers, his toes—the man dies." Boys born on the island are treated in the same way, become tired and sick, and die before growing up.[13] For the Trobrianders, also, then, pubic hair is associated with being overpowered by a mature and lustful female.

Both the practice of pubic depilation and the preference for immature females might derive from a phobic attitude toward the maternal genitalia. Freud and Ferenczi believe that the head of the Medusa is a representation of this fear, which, I would suggest, springs from the frustrated mother's hostility and seductiveness toward her male child.[14]

It seems likely that the mother's body becomes menacing to the child only as a function of what she does. A cross-cultural study by Stephens for example, found a positive correlation between variables suggesting sexual arousal of the child by the mother and a number of sexual anxieties and taboos (e.g., menstrual taboos, sexual prohibitions, desexualization of breasts, kin avoidance); and a study by Baruch provides an excellent illustration of this relation in a boy unable to cope with his mother's sexual needs.[15] Wherever one finds a mother unfulfilled in her sexual life, one may expect also to find a mother whose aspect may be menacing to her child. And wherever one finds a mother who, by virtue of being a woman, is deprived in some way of self-expression or forced to endure narcissistic wounds of various kinds, one may expect also to find a mother whose aspect is menacing to her sons.

MARITAL STRAINS AND MATERNAL SCAPEGOATING

If sexual deprivation and humiliation by males both lead to anxiety-provoking maternal behavior toward sons, we would expect Greek males to be doubly fearful since these seem to have been combined in the Greek household.

However much she may have looked forward to it in fantasy, marriage for a Greek maiden was somewhat traumatic. She moved abruptly from the life of childhood and the security of her family into the seclusion of a stranger's house. Her husband was chosen by her father and was probably never seen by her before the marriage, since deception in marriage contracts seems to have been common. Marriage also involved a religious change, the relinquishing of the household gods of her youth: "She must abandon her religion, practice other rites, and pronounce other prayers.

She must give up the god of her infancy, and put herself under the protection of a god whom she knows not." These sudden changes took place, furthermore, when she was still very young. In most Mediterranean countries the age of marriage was seldom later than 16. Blümner notes:

> It was not uncommon, since Greek girls married very early, for them to play with their dolls up to the time of their marriage, and just before their wedding to take these discarded favorites, with their whole wardrobes, to some temple of the maiden Artemis and there dedicate them as a pious offering.[16]

The bride, then, is an ignorant and immature teen-ager, totally dependent on a somewhat indifferent stranger for all her needs—a stranger who regards marriage at best as a necessary evil, and certainly a tiresome interruption of a pleasant and well-established pattern of daily living in which social and sexual needs are already being satisfied through concubines and young boys. Semonides of Amorgos concludes a long tirade in which women are compared to sows, vixen, bitches, donkeys, weasels, and monkeys by saying: "No one day goes by from end to end enjoyable, when you have spent it with your wife." [17] The husband has normally had little say in choosing his bride, marriage being defined as having a purely procreative function.

It may be objected that these dour jokes about exchanging freedom for slavery or equating marriage with death may be found in our own society as well as in many others. They receive greater force, however, when we see the structural realities associated with them. Many Greek cities, for example, punished celibacy as a crime, and at one time Sparta denied the rights of citizenship to the man who did not marry. While Athens had no such law, custom forbade bachelorhood, and it was viewed as impious. Athens did have a law, moreover, which made it a duty of the city's magistrate to prevent any family from becoming extinct. Only a man who had an elder brother with children could avoid the general rule. Yet despite all this pressure, marriage was frequently avoided.[18]

The age at which the male married was probably around 30,

more than a dozen years later than that of his bride. In the case of some, it was apparently a great deal more; when Socrates, for example, was over 70, his wife Xanthippe was still at childbearing age. This age difference was viewed as desirable since the beauty of the female was considered of briefer life than the strength of the male. Since for some Greek males beauty and maturity could not coexist, this period of sexual desirability was brief indeed.[19]

On her side, the bride was equally unprepared for a mature heterosexual relationship. Her relationship with her father had probably been rather tenuous, partly because of his emotional distance from familial life but also because of his overriding concern with preserving his daughter's chastity by means of strict control and seclusion. The pervasive segregation of, and antagonism between, the sexes meant that she understood of men only that they had the best of things. In the Greek wedding ceremony it was the mother and not the father who performed the ritual analogue of giving the bride away.[20]

Even though an unmarried girl led a "retired and . . . joyless existence," and even though marriage may have brought "somewhat greater freedom," it was nevertheless a disappointment:

> When we are young, in our father's house, I think we live the sweetest life of all; for ignorance ever brings us up delightfully. But when we have reached a mature age and know more, we are driven out of doors and sold, away from the gods of our fathers and our parents, some to foreigners, some to barbarians, some to strange houses, others to such as deserve reproach. And in such a lot, after a single night has united us, we have to acquiesce and think that it is well.[21]

However restricted her childhood years, maternal protection and affection were hers, as well as the companionship of siblings and playmates. The marital relationship provided little compensation for the loss of these advantages. Socrates could ask, "Are there any men to whom you entrust more matters of importance, or with whom you have less conversation, than with your wife?" and know the answer.

This shallowness of the marital bond is not new with the classical period. Finley points out that in Homer there is no marital relationship, even that between Odysseus and Penelope, that contains the emotional intensity found in the attachment between father and son or between male friends.[22] But in most societies or subcultures in which the marital bond is weak, the partners are deeply invested in other relationships, which are strong and enduring and supp rted by a stable and permanent environment.[23] When this external stability breaks down, the marital bond becomes more important, and if marital roles are still structured along the older principle, substantial misery can result. This seems to have happened in fifth-century Athens, particularly for the wife; the husband still had many external ties. Whereas in Victorian England one could talk of a *wife's* "marital duties," in Athens it was more likely to be the male who would view marital sexuality in this light—not, of course, for prudish reasons. Plutarch captures something of the spirit of the Greek male's attitude toward marriage in his discussion of a law of Solon: "that a man should consort with his wife not less than three times a month—not for pleasure surely, but as cities renew their agreements from time to time . . ."[24] When marital love occurred, even between newlyweds, it excited special comment.

The marital relationship thus came to resemble that of an older brother and younger sister, when the brother has been entrusted with his sister's care against his will, and she is longing for her mother and resents his coldness, irritability, and contempt. But in the case of brother and sister, the mother will eventually return, and the sister can even complain of her brother's ill treatment. The wife is alone among strangers and will remain so. As a child, she could perhaps vent her feelings in doll play. As a wife she can only vent them on her children.

This is particularly likely to affect the male child. If the wife resents her husband's superiority, she can punish arrogance (or even masculinity) in her son. Such vengeance was especially appropriate in Greece, inasmuch as the son was the sole means of perpetuating the father's lineage and property. Furthermore, lack of a son meant not only lack of an heir but also the disappearance of the family religion and rites and condemnation of the father to eternal unhappiness beyond the grave. Since the direct expression of hostility toward the husband was inhibited by the wife's dependence, youth, and social inferiority, destructive unconscious impulses toward male children must have been strong. Both the impulses and the need to repress them would be increased, furthermore, by the greater value assigned to male children. A woman who failed to produce an heir for her husband was viewed as not having performed her most elemental function, and women could be divorced for barrenness.

The male child was thus of vital importance to the wife, her principal source of prestige and validation. Yet how much she must secretly have resented the callous and disparaging male attitude toward female children, who were an economic liability, a social burden, and of no redeeming religious significance to the household, of which they were, in any case, only a temporary member. The mother-daughter bond seems nevertheless to have been the closest, most affectionate, and least conflicted of all the familial relationships, as is true in most sex-segregated societies. One sees it in the Demeter-Kore myth, which is unique in having parental affection as its primary motivational theme. Yet it was a perfectly acceptable practice in Athens for a healthy female infant to be left out to die, even if the family were rich, if the father willed it. When the dramatists based Clytemnestra's hatred of Agamemnon on his having casually murdered his daughter Iphigenia to further his military adventures, they were tapping a contemporary emotion. To be a woman was to be "nothing," and if women consciously and automatically shared this social assumption, this did not prevent them from resenting it. The male child aroused both feelings, and the casualness with which female children were denied found its negative counterpart in the mother's ambivalent overinvolvement with the son. His life, in other words, was given preference at a measurable cost. Sex antagonism is a two-edged sword, and if men could feel secure only in a heterosexual relationship in which they were unambiguously superior, the same was true of the woman. The male child was hers, under her control and subject to her whims, and it was here that her feelings could be given full expression. He was at one and the same time a scapegoat for and an antidote to the inferior position of the mother.

In myth the use of the son as a scapegoat for the father is both well-known and baldly expressed. Medea kills her sons in jealous rage against Jason, while Procne, for identical reasons, kills her son and serves him up to his father in a stew. In Ovid's version she expresses the desire to burn, blind, and castrate her husband and then remarks pitilessly, upon seeing her son go by, "How like your father you are!" [25]

But the positive side of the ambivalence was just as difficult for the son to handle. Imprisoned and isolated by her indifferent and largely absented husband, some of the mother's sexual longing was turned on her son. Along with, and in direct contradiction to, her need to belittle and discourage his masculine striving, she attempted to build him up into an idealized replacement of her husband, fantasying that "her little man" would grow up to be the perfect hero and take care of his mother all of her days. Such fantasies would also gratify her own masculine strivings—though *she* might be confined and restricted, her son, an extension of herself, was free and mobile, and she could live her life through him. This may be an additional reason why Greek men married at such an advanced age, and also why the mother of the groom played such an important part in the marriage ceremony.

This maternal ambition for the son is reflected in myths such as those of Perseus and Achilles. In both cases the mother has been slighted or injured in some way by a male, and the exploits of the son serve directly or indirectly to compensate for this. An analogous relationship is that between Hera and Jason, the goddess using the hero to revenge herself on Pelias.

The ambivalence of the Greek mother toward her son was, in other words, a deeply narcissistic ambivalence in which the mother does not respond to the child as a separate person but as both an expression of and a cure for her narcissistic wounds. Her need for self-expansion and vindication requires her both to exalt and to belittle her son, to feed on and to destroy him.

GREEK NARCISSISM

Theories of psychopathology permit us to anticipate two consequences of the ambivalent attitude of the Greek mother. The first
is a generally narcissistic personality structure in the child. Since
she alternately accepts him as an idealized hero and rejects his
masculine pretensions, one would expect him to develop an abnormal concern about how others view him and to have an extremely
unstable self-concept. He will feel that if he is not a great hero, he
is nothing, and pride and prestige become more important than
love. This is perhaps the basis of the Greek idealization of and
preoccupation with the body, and we may also assume that the
homosexuality of the Greeks rests on a firm narcissistic foundation:
An unknown poet says, "Seeing a kindred shape I swooned away."
It is, after all, his physical maleness on which his mother's ambivalence is focused, and it is his childish pride in it that she is unable to tolerate with the relaxed indulgence of an unenvious
mother—although she continually stimulates and encourages it.
Consequently, his physical maleness becomes of enormous importance to him. The male body dominates his art and his sexual life.

It also expressed itself through athletics. Homosexual love in
Greece centered very much on the gymnasium, and many love affairs began with the admiration of bodily grace. The Greek word
gymnos, in fact, means "naked," for naked athletes were a Greek
innovation, dating apparently from not long before the Pelopon-
nesian War, and looked upon askance by non-Greeks. But women,
except in Sparta, were excluded from this world of male bodily
display. They were forbidden to watch athletic performances and
were themselves rather fully covered. The nude forms that one
sees in Greek art are, until rather late, almost entirely male forms.

But Greek male vanity was not only physical. It expressed itself
in the preoccupation with honor and glory, in boastfulness, and
even perhaps in the willingness of Athenians to spend the better
part of their daily lives in myriad and tedious official positions. It
appears early: in Achilles' desire to trade a long uneventful life for
a brief one filled with honor and glory and in Agamemnon's willingness to trade several months of his life for an honorable death

on the battlefields of Troy. Perhaps the most dramatic demonstration of narcissism is Achilles' readiness to sacrifice his comrades to his own glory. When Patroclus goes out to do battle, Achilles cautions him not to diminish his honor by winning the entire war without him. And he concludes his instructions by praying to the gods that not one of the Trojans *or the Greeks* would survive the war save Patroclus and himself.

What was merely an exaggeration of a trait one would expect to find in any aristocratic warrior culture did not, however, diminish as the Greeks became more civilized; instead, it was generalized to embrace all of life. "Nothing defines the quality of Greek culture more neatly than the way in which the idea of competition was extended from physical prowess to the realm of the intellect, to feats of poetry and dramatic composition." [26] Indeed, as Huizinga remarks, "The Greeks used to stage contests in anything that offered the bare possibility of a fight"—beauty (male, of course), singing, riddle solving, drinking, staying awake.[27] Nothing seemed to have meaning to the Greek unless it included the defeat of another. So absorbed were the Greeks in the quest for the unwilling admiration of their peers, so universal were vanity, boastfulness, ambition, competitiveness, and invidiousness, that there was no attempt to hide the feelings of envy and vindictiveness that the success of another aroused. To achieve revenge and arouse envy were the twin delicacies of everyday life.

Aristotle observes that men pursue honor in order to assure themselves of their own worth. This need derives from a mother-son relationship in which the most grandiose self-definitions are at once incited and punctured. Alvin Gouldner shows how the incessant Greek striving after honor and glory is closely linked to a deep pessimism and notes that the self is seen "as a precarious entity which is difficult but vital to maintain—an entity that might perish with only one discrepant, unfitting act," such as one of the many seizures of madness with which Greek mythology is dotted. Feelings of weakness, dependence, passive surrender, desires to be protected—all must be hidden from consciousness, forming, as Gouldner notes, the hidden "underside" of the Greek self-image, achieving expression in the weak, dependent, anxious, fearful, and submissive tone so often taken by Greek choruses.[28] These feelings are also expressed, as we shall see, in the fact that the women-hating heroes of Greek myth can rarely achieve any of their goals without extensive feminine assistance. The rejection of and dependence on women mirror the mother's own ambivalence.

This phenomenon is familiar to the psychoanalyst: " 'Narcissists' suffer regularly from repetitive, violent oscillations of self-esteem." Such men tend to be preoccupied with, and overvalue, the penis, while regarding the female organs as dirty, injured, and repellent. Furthermore: "The tiniest disappointment, the slightest physical indisposition, the most trifling experience of failure can throw the patient into extreme despair . . . The grandiose body-phallus fantasy . . . turns *suddenly* into one of total castration . . ." [29]

A society that derogates women produces envious mothers who produce narcissistic males who derogate women. The anxiety that success aroused in Greek males had its origins in the nursery. For was not *hubris* fundamentally masculine pride and phallic self-satisfaction, even exhibitionism?

GREEK MADNESS

A second consequence one might anticipate from the ambivalence of the Greek mother is psychosis. This expectation derives from the theory of Gregory Bateson and his associates that schizophrenia originates in what they call the "double bind." A "double bind" is said to occur when a parent deals with ambivalent feelings by explicitly or covertly directing the child to respond to two contradictory ideas and punishing him for failure to do either.[30] The factors operating in the Greek family agree with those discussed by Bateson, and the ambivalent maternal injunctions might be expressed as follows:

1. You must be a strong and adult male, treat me as a woman, and by your conspicuous male achievements express my own aspirations.

2. You must not aspire to maleness nor flaunt your masculinity before me nor remind me that I am a woman.

3. You must not desert me nor find any contradiction in my demands.

Our expectation receives a shadowy confirmation from Greek fantasy. No other mythology with which I am familiar contains so many explicitly designated instances of madness. All of these, of course, involve a superhuman agent, but certain characteristics are easily identified.

The most striking fact is that of all the clear instances of madness deliberately produced in one being by another, none is caused by a truly masculine or paternal agent. Most are inflicted by goddesses, the remainder by the androgynous Dionysus, himself a previous victim at the hands of Hera. In all but a handful of cases madness is induced in persons of the opposite sex.

Narcissistic disorders tend to be emotionally contagious, particularly between parents and children. Hera's injured narcissism leads her to persecute her stepson, Dionysus, whose injured narcissism in turn leads him to persecute the women of Argos, who express their madness in the destruction of their children. This cycle has its milder counterpart in the dynamics of the Greek family. The jealous, neglected mother injures the narcissism of the young boy. He, upon reaching adulthood, selects, because of doubts about his adequacy with mature women, an immature, inadequate wife, whom he treats with contempt and neglect, thus ensuring a malignant disturbance in the mothering of his own sons, and so on. His precarious self-respect compels him to disparage women and to demand "a feminine type which is infantile, non-maternal and hysterical, and by so doing . . . expose each new generation to the influence of such women." [31]

MATERNAL BOGIES

While fathers tend to be idealized in Greek fantasy, the exact reverse is true of the mother. Blümner points out that "naughty children were brought to obedience or quiet by threats of bogies, but, curiously enough, these Greek bogies were all female creatures." Similarly, there were witches but no sorcerers in Greek folklore, and the statue of Fear was a woman.[32]

These female bogies—Lamia, Gorgo, Empusa, Mormo, and others—are fundamentally nothing more than that; they are often named plurally and have little attached myth. When they are assigned characteristics, however, their connection with fear of the mother's sexuality becomes apparent. That they should prey on children is intrinsic, but what is important is the sense of deprivation that often attaches itself to them. They have lost their own children, they are devouring and cannibalistic, and, above all, they are sexually ravenous and insatiable.[33] Whatever the origin of these bogies, it seems apparent that at some point they were derived from the male child's fear of the emotional needs of the mother—needs often directed toward himself and in relation to which he felt helpless, inadequate, and frightened. This is one reason why intense feelings that are difficult to control tend to be viewed as having a feminine origin.

Thus we find that the first Greek love-tragedy—Sophocles' lost *Phaedra*—consists of a chaste and prudish boy being pursued by his passionate stepmother, who responds to his refusals with vindictive and lethal rage.[34] Aristophanes treats the same constellation farcically in the *Ecclesiazusae,* in which a law is passed requiring any man who wishes to copulate with a young girl first to satisfy some old hag; as a result, a young man is almost torn to pieces by two old harlots.

Mature and conspicuous female sexuality was in itself sufficient to call bogies to mind. Courtesans were frequently called names like Lamia and Charybdis, Sphinx, or Phryne ("toad")—names that expressed depth of avarice as well as of sexuality. Indeed, even married women were frequently called *lamiae* if they showed any spirit.[35] It was only young girls who escaped these epithets. The feminine ideal in art was correspondingly youthful—even boyish,[36] and benevolence among goddesses was highly correlated with virginity. As Kitto pointed out, the two oldest cities in Greece worshiped mother-goddesses: One of these goddesses, Athene, was "dematrified" and became not only virginal and boyish but also the most helpful female deity in the Greek pantheon. The other, Hera, retained her maternal form and became the most vindictive and persecutory.[37] Finley describes her, with magnificent understatement, as the "complete female . . . whom the Greeks feared a little and did not like at all." [38] It is in fact fair to say that Greek males, as a group, were terrified of any female who was a whole woman.

One origin of this cycle was probably the breakdown of the extended family system and an increase in mobility—both of these changes throwing an emotional burden on the family, which was unusually poorly equipped to handle it. Sex segregation is a manageable system only under conditions of strong kinship ties and residential stability. When ties of blood weakened, there was no strenthening of the marital bond to fill the gap. (See Chapter 5.)

However the cycle began, Greek myths, as refurbished in the classical age, express its forms in every conceivable elaboration. Not only are most of the major myths clothed with themes of mother-son ambivalence, but the male gods and heroes exhibit every conceivable kind of psychological defense against the maternal threat. One of the most interesting is the myth of Orestes, which, although derived from varied and complex origins, became clothed with ideas and symbols expressive of the familial tensions of the classical period.

ORESTES

The earliest versions of the Orestes myth seem to concern little more than a battle over succession to the Argive throne, with women playing a secondary role. Orestes is not the infant son and matricide of later versions but simply the exiled pretender who comes unaided to claim his throne.

But this simple tale of war and politics was later transformed into one in which the matricidal revenge was the central theme. That it was the woman-hating Athenians who filled the story with women and made it a tale of family conflict is not very surprising. A people reared in such a culture would obviously be more impressed by the story of a woman plotting against her husband than by anything else. It would tap their fear of women and lead them to occupy themselves with the process of filial revenge. But given this fundamental concern, why was Electra, Orestes' sister, introduced?

In Euripides' *Orestes*, when Orestes cries out that the Erinyes, his mother's Furies, are pursuing him, Electra puts her arms around him to comfort him, but Orestes is little soothed by this protection and accuses her of being an Erinys herself. It is particularly interesting that Orestes identifies Electra with his mother's Erinyes at the moment when she offers encircling comfort and protection. It is also significant that the attack of madness itself occurs when Orestes is telling Electra not to be like Clytemnestra.[39] The very thought is enough to unhinge him, to start him talking to his dead mother and accusing Electra of being an Erinys—for the Greek male's defensive structure was highly dependent on maintaining some sort of benign (i.e., sexless, virginal, boyish, youthful) feminine image to contrast with the more prevalent and malign maternal one.

The Orestes myth, in its fifth-century form, became a story of sex antagonism and mother-son conflict. This conflict is "solved" by the killing of Clytemnestra. Yet the story continues; the solution is ineffective, the feelings remain. When he is asked if the matricide did not slake his thirst for blood, Orestes replies: "I can never have my fill of killing whores," a sentiment frequently expressed by sex-killers.[40]

There are three plays that deal in a major way with Orestes' life after the matricide. In Euripides' *Iphigenia in Tauris* he is saved from death and enabled to accomplish his mission by his sister Iphigenia. In *Orestes*, he is protected and nursed by his sister Electra, and it is her bold stratagem that rescues him from death. In *The Eumenides* of Aeschylus it is Athene who saves him from the Erinyes by casting her deciding vote in the trial and by pacifying them when they threaten revenge. Apollo, his sponsor, instigator, and much-touted protector, is in fact utterly unable to rescue his protege.

In other words, the mother-rejecting solution blindly ignores the intense, frustrated craving for maternal love and protection. How to placate the maternal rage and bring back maternal love is the theme of Orestes' psychosis, while how to find nurturant substitutes is the theme of his everyday life.

Unfortunately, there is no simple solution to ambivalence. A craving so intense leads to fears of being utterly swallowed and cannot, therefore, be permitted free expression. Far from selecting motherly figures to satisfy his dependent longings, Orestes chooses three notorious virgins: Electra, Iphigenia (priestess of Artemis), and Athene herself. Since virgins are often seen by men as less feminine, more neuter, they are less threatening to masculine narcissism than are sexually mature women. A "real woman" required a more secure masculinity than Greeks of the classical period felt able to muster.

But there is still another twist to the Orestean nightmare. Helpful virgins may be found, but can they protect him against the fears that this very nurturance arouses? Iphigenia threatens his life, and Electra seems to turn into Clytemnestra. And does not Athene herself wear the snake-festooned Medusa head on her shield? And what of the Erinyes themselves, the "Gorgon shapes" with snaky hair? Are they not also virgins? The Orestean dilemma is never really resolved, any more than the Athenians resolved it in real life.

The Greeks, nevertheless, were proud of Orestes. Indeed, if dramatic preoccupation be an index, he was their greatest hero. The nature of his achievement is made clear in his speech to the Argives in *Orestes*, when he argues: "I helped you no less than my father when I slew my mother; for if the murder of men by women is to be sanctioned, then the sooner you die, the better for you; otherwise you must needs become the slaves of women." [41] Perhaps the reason that the Greeks held him in such affection and esteem was that the solution he adopted—total rejection of the mother and devotion to the father—was most particularly their own.

Our society has produced the most voluminous literature on the mother-son relationship since ancient Greece. The Greek family system was in one way similar to our own, in depriving women of contact with and participation in the total culture and in creating a domestic pattern peculiarly confining and unfulfilling. They thus both encourage a vicarious involvement of the mother in the life of the son as well as a deep resentment in the mother toward the son and what he represents.

Male fear and oppression of women, in other words, is addictive. The more women are prevented from either being whole persons or finding adequate substitutes, the more their frustration and ambivalence will direct itself toward their sons, the only helpless males in their environment. Such feelings may coexist with deep maternal love and kindness, but they will be picked up by the son as frightening and mysterious overtones, often leading to the familiar male fear of emotional intensity. The mother's warmth and kindness will arouse affection in her son, but her frustration, hidden anger, and manipulation will arouse more sexism—particularly a fear of being overwhelmed by a woman, hence a need to dominate and control women and to flee from their emotionality. All of which, of course, leads to still more oppression of women and a continuation of the cycle.

What the cycle teaches us is that men have to face up to women as full human beings at some point, either as children or as adults. And if an adult male can't meet a woman face to face without the protection of his superior status, his power, his emotional frigidity, his detachment, his need to control and manipulate through "logic," and all the other trappings of sexism, he certainly can't expect his son to do it.

Yet for countless generations men have passed the buck for this emotional task to their sons, and this has been an extremely costly piece of cowardice. The flight from emotional honesty has played a large part in the creation of the push-button misery we live in: the ugly and oppressive cities, the polluted environment, the inhuman bureaucracies, the cruel wars, the ravaged countryside, and the pervasive feelings of alienation. Men are forced to manipulate the natural and human environment partly because they have so much difficulty in discharging their own feelings, especially the softer, more vulnerable ones. Often they are utterly out of touch with what the feelings are. Those who are free from this emotional impactedness can weep or wail when they feel bad, and this usually leads to relief. Since most American men believe they should be unemotional, they have no easy way to achieve such relief and must manipulate the environment (especially women) to get it to make them feel better. The ugliness of the world we live in is testimony to the futility of this method. And as we shall see in the next chapter, the suppression of emotion is not unrelated to the prevalence of war itself.

Chapter 9

TRAITS OF WARLIKE CULTURES

The last chapter traced the relationship in Greek culture between maternal ambivalence toward sons and male vanity and competitiveness. A cross-cultural study confirmed this relationship.[1]

The Greeks were a quarrelsome and warlike people, and the cross-cultural data suggested that some of what I had described might be generally characteristic of warrior societies. I became curious to discover what other traits might be typical of warlike cultures.

In the Greek study the relationship between maternal ambivalence and male narcissism was circular: Each served to maintain and reinforce the other. The same is probably true of any traits found to characterize warlike cultures: The traits keep people warlike, and making war reinforces the traits. I decided to base my study on two cross-cultural scales that Dori Appel Slater and I had developed for our cross-cultural study of narcissism and maternal ambivalence. Both scales appear in Textor's *Cross-Cultural Summary*, a compendium of cross-cultural interrelationships.[2]

The first scale I shall call "Militarism" for simplicity's sake. A society was rated "high" on this scale when the ethnographer reported that war was regarded as glorious; or that it was the principal source of prestige in the society; or that men actively sought death in battle as a means to earthly or otherworldly glory; or that military virtues (valor, recklessness, fighting skill) were the most important ones in the society. A "low" rating was given when the ethnographer reported indifference to military virtues, abhorrence of war, or approval of saving one's skin in a battle. This scale, then, is not just a measure of a society's readiness to engage in war but reflects a psychological dependence on fighting as a·means of ego building.[3]

A good example of a society with a "high" rating is the following description by G. B. Grinnell:

> The Cheyenne men were all warriors. War was regarded as the noblest of pursuits, the only one for a man to follow; and from earliest youth boys were encouraged to excel in it. They were taught that no pleasure equaled the joy of battle; that success in war brought in its train the respect and admiration of men, women, and children in the tribe, and that the most worthy thing that any man could do was to be brave. It was pointed out that death in battle was not an evil, and that such a death, besides being glorious, protected one from all the miseries which threaten later life and are inevitable to old age.[4]

Grinnell also points out that this orientation led them to take great risks and lose many men, made them eager for revenge when injured, and hungry for public applause.

The second scale, which I shall call "Sadism," is related to the first. Societies are rated "high" on this scale when ethnographers reported that prisoners were taken in battles or raids for the express purpose of torturing them; or when elaborate tortures were described; or when prisoners were sacrificed or slaughtered under conditions approximating torture (e.g., extreme pain, gradual dismemberment, being eaten alive, etc.). "Low" ratings were given when prisoners were taken as slaves, or given freedom, or when battles were concluded without either mass killing or the taking of prisoners.[5]

The Araucanians of Chile are a good example of a society rated "high" on this scale. Prisoners captured in war were often flayed alive or tied to a tree and taunted for hours while their captors hacked pieces of flesh from them until their bones were stripped.

Sometimes the prisoner's heart was torn out of him before he died and eaten collectively. One ethnographer described them making a flute from a live prisoner's shinbone and forcing him to play on it.[6]

These two scales both go considerably beyond a mere tendency to engage in war; both involve an enthusiasm that far outstrips the necessity for self-defense under conditions of general conflict. Yet they are naturally correlated quite highly with other measures that simply reflect the tendency of the society to engage in war. (See Appendix A.) The society that fights all the time but only to defend itself is a figment of propaganda. When peaceful societies fight, they either lose or become militaristic.

In a simple "fishnet" operation I first listed all the variables correlated with Militarism and Sadism in Textor's *Cross-Cultural Summary* (see Appendix A), which includes such things as geography, climate, language, economics, work patterns, technology, social structure, political systems, marriage and kinship systems, crime, child-rearing practices, group activities, religious beliefs, medical practices, recreational pursuits, personality characteristics, and so on.

When this was done, I found that the strong correlations were overwhelmingly concentrated in the areas of sexual and child-rearing practices. For Militarism, only 6 out of the 15 correlations fell in any other area, and for Sadism, only 3 out of 12.

Furthermore, when we look at the sexual and child-rearing variables that dominate the correlations, they convey a strong sense of emotional and sexual repression: the inhibition of pleasure seeking and bodily gratification and the imposition of social restraints. Specifically, we find correlations with low sexual satisfaction in infancy, with high "castration anxiety," with punishment of extramarital coitus, with lack of demonstrativeness toward infants, with delay in meeting the child's needs, with anxiety in the child about behaving responsibly and about achieving or failing to achieve, with conflict in the child over achievement and obedience behavior, with pressure on the child to be self-reliant, and with low overall indulgence of the child. Other correlations, such as the custom of avoidance behavior between a man and his son's wife or the custom of having a growing child sleep exclusively with the mother, seem to be part of a constellation of oedipal traits—customs reflecting a cultural emphasis on a highly charged mother-son relationship, channeling sexual energy into a tabooed area in which it becomes blocked.[7] The impact of such customs on the adult male was discussed in the last chapter.

Militarism seems to be more strongly related to specifically sexual issues. Sadism, on the other hand, is more strongly related to lack of nurturance. Militaristic societies seem more preoccupied with making children responsible and successful, sadistic ones with making them obedient. The overall picture for Militaristic societies reminds one of the classic "high achiever" syndrome in our own society: the strong mother who loves and is adored by her son but who makes extremely heavy demands on him for successful adult behavior. The pattern for Sadistic societies suggests pure deprivation: The child is neglected, unsupported, expected to take care of himself or herself, behave properly, and not make any trouble.

Since this is a preliminary exploration, however, it seems wiser simply to say that the data suggest some kind of relationship between militaristic and sadistic practices on the one hand and the suppression of pleasure seeking in both children and adults on the other.

Once again, it's important to recognize the circularity of relationships like these. Militaristic and Sadistic societies tend to withhold gratification from their participants, and children from whom gratification is systematically withheld tend to grow up with militaristic and sadistic tendencies. Those who would argue that the relationship is only one way—that militarism "causes" suppression of pleasure but not the other way around—find themselves in an awkward situation. For if we ask *why* militaristic societies frown on pleasure seeking, the answer comes quickly that they want to create a tough, fighting populace. In other words, militaristic societies suppress pleasure seeking because they *know* that such suppression engenders militarism. Those who argue against the psychological interpretation of militarism are thus in the position of arguing that militaristic policy-makers everywhere are committed to the same erroneous psychological assumptions, which nevertheless seem to work. As a theory, this seems unduly cumbersome.

Theories of human belligerence tend roughly to fall into three categories. First there is the biological argument of a kind of innate human surliness, based on some sort of no-longer-functional instinct. Many statements by Freud, Lorenz, Ardrey, and others fall into this category. The flaw in this position is the extraordinary cross-cultural variability in human belligerence. If it were simply a biological given, a study like this one would yield no correlations at all, for there would be no peaceful societies.

The second argument holds that humans are by nature peaceful but are corrupted by their institutions—especially capitalistic ones—into belligerence. Vulgar Marxism falls into this category. This position has more to recommend it since it allows for differences between societies, but it pays little attention to how the corrupt institutions arose in the first place and finds very little support from our exploratory study in which things like social structure and technology bore little relation to militarism and even less to sadism.

The third argument holds that belligerence is learned as part of the child-rearing process, and this is the one that receives most support from the clustering of relationships in our exploratory study. But social variables relate to each other in very complex ways, and it would be foolish to dismiss any possible connections on the basis of such preliminary findings. All one can say on the basis of these findings is that there does seem to be some relationship between certain forms of socially approved belligerence and the tendency of a society to suppress pleasure seeking.

About seven years after this preliminary study was conducted, a more thorough analysis was carried out by William Eckhardt, using the full Textor sample.[8] Eckhardt used two additional scales in his analysis: a simple measure of bellicosity and one expressing the mere prevalence of warfare in the society. His results were similar but somewhat more extensive, partly as a result of having a larger sample.

Sexual variables showed the same strong pattern of relationship, particularly with bellicosity and militarism, less with sadism and prevalence of war. The differences were most marked in the case of the oedipal variables—those that imply a weak marital bond and a strong mother-son bond. In this study, however, socioeconomic scales emerged far more powerfully. Generally speaking, the more complex, developed, urban, and hierarchical the society was, the more warlike. Social classes and slavery were particularly important.

Eckhardt's study suggests that war involves the interplay of belligerent personal traits—engendered by harsh child-rearing practices and repressive and oedipal sexual attitudes—and social conditions brought about by technological development and class oppression. He sees these findings, based on "primitive" societies, as essentially duplicating studies of militarism in modern industrial states, which show that "militarism in the modern world is associated with . . . capitalism and religiosity . . . frustrating discipline and sexual repression . . . conformity and egoism." Furthermore, preliminary studies suggest that "most of these same variables are associated with militarism in some Communist and some developing nations as well as in the Western world."

My own interest in these questions was part of a larger concern with the triangular relation between sexual repression, egoism, and cultural development. Everything seems to point to a positive relation between all three, recalling again Freud's skepticism about whether civilization can really show a net profit in human terms.

What are the benefits and what are the costs, for example, of social institutions that place some kind of limitation on pleasure seeking? Are they really at the root of civilization? Are they also at the root of egoism, war, and violence? In this chapter we have concentrated on the debit side of the ledger, but if cultural development is equally tied to repression—if, as Freud argued, the evils of civilization are inseparable from its assets—a serious choice confronts us. The next chapter attempts to come to grips with this question.

Chapter 10

CIVILIZATION, NARCISSISM, AND SEXUAL REPRESSION

Many of the most important theories in the social sciences are neither accepted, rejected, nor tested but remain as academic curiosities in a kind of historical limbo, whence they are removed from time to time for the edification of students, who are permitted to handle them but not take them home. Freud's attempt to understand the relationship between sexual repression and culture seems to be one of these unfortunates, apparently doomed, despite revivals by Herbert Marcuse and Norman O. Brown, to an inglorious semi-retirement in the vaudeville of the Western Civilization course, along with Plato's parable of the cave and Hume's billiard-ball dilemma.

Anthropologists detest it because it violates the credo of cultural relativism that has dominated their field for so many years. To argue that sexual repression facilitates cultural development would be to relinquish anthropology to the same intellectual aborigines who controlled it in the nineteenth century: Missionaries, ethnocentric travelers, and colonial administrators. This was the view of Murdock, who dismissed the repression theory as the position of "moralists," [1] although his own research showed a strong relationship between restrictive premarital sexual norms and several indices of cultural complexity.

Prior to Murdock's study, which was not designed as a test of

Freud's theory and makes no mention of him whatever, I know of only one direct test of the relationship between sexual repression and cultural complexity: The pioneer cross-cultural study done in 1934 by J. D. Unwin. Unwin found a strong positive relationship, and although the study has many flaws, its historical depth carries it far beyond the kind of work being done today.

My own goal here is simply to add more information on the question and to elaborate the theory somewhat. I see no point in trying to hide a conspicuous correlation; as yet we are a long way from seeing what it means. And if few people today want to see a return to sexual repressiveness, a growing number are becoming disillusioned with civilization as well.

CIVILIZATION AND SEXUALITY

Freud's basic contention was that cultural development was only made possible by "borrowing" libidinal energy to counteract what he felt to be the inherent aggressiveness of the species. His argument can be roughly broken down into four parts:

1. Human beings are inherently aggressive:

"Men clearly do not find it easy to do without satisfaction of this tendency to aggression that is in them; when deprived of satisfaction of it they are ill at ease." [2]

". . . aggression is an original, self-subsisting instinctual disposition in man, and . . . constitutes the greatest impediment to civilization." [3]

2. Human communities must "borrow" energy from sexuality both to offset this aggressiveness and to prevent society from dissolving into a collection of sexual pairs:

In consequence of [the] primary mutual hostility of human beings, civilized society is perpetually threatened with disintegration. . . . Hence the restriction upon sexual life . . . [4]

. . . the conflict between civilization and sexuality is caused by the circumstance that sexual love is a relationship between two people, in which a third can only be superfluous or disturbing, whereas civilization is founded on relations between larger groups of persons. . . .

. . . we might well imagine that a civilized community could consist of pairs of individuals such as this, libidinally satisfied in each other, and linked to all the others by work and common interests. If this were so, culture would not need to levy energy from sexuality. But . . . in actuality culture . . . endeavours to bind the members of the community to one another by libidinal ties as well. . . . Restrictions upon sexual life are unavoidable if this object is to be attained.[5]

3. Thus humans achieve the benefits of civilization at the cost of direct and immediate gratification:

If civilization requires such sacrifices . . . we can better understand why it should be so hard for men to feel happy in it. In actual fact primitive man was better off in this respect, for he knew nothing of any restrictions on his instincts. As a set-off against this, his prospects of enjoying his happiness for any length of time were very slight. Civilized man has exchanged some part of his chances of happiness for a measure of security.[6]

4. Yet it isn't clear that the exchange was profitable, or that the maneuver was even successful:

"With all its striving, this endeavour of culture's has so far not achieved very much . . ."[7]

". . . one is bound to conclude that the whole thing is not worth the effort and that in the end it can only produce a state of things which no individual will be able to bear."[8]

"Men have brought their powers of subduing the forces of nature to such a pitch that by using them they could now very easily exterminate one another to the last man."[9]

In view of these last considerations, one might well raise the question as to whether "borrowing from sexuality," if indeed it occurs, has all the effects Freud attributes to it, or some quite opposite. For Freud the only negative consequences of this borrowing were the occasional foreclosures made by sexuality on harmless guilt-ridden neurotics. We are more familiar today with the sexual pathology of murderers, rapists, racists, and fascists and may well wonder whether restrictions on sexuality increase or decrease the "natural" aggressiveness of humans. Any anthropologist can point to a dozen nonliterate societies that combine relaxed sexual norms with a pacifism far exceeding what "civilized" nations exhibit.

The last chapter suggested the possibility that the imposition of restrictions on sexuality may not only fail to neutralize but actually serve to *intensify* the aggressiveness of humans—that the price of civilization is not merely the corruption of erotic life but also (and therefore) an intensification of human malevolence. It also raised the possibility that not all sexual restrictions have the same impact—that the frustration of purely sexual needs may encourage militarism, while frustrating a child's need for nurturance may foster sadism. In this chapter I would like to ask two questions:

1. Are sexual restrictions related to cultural complexity ("civilization")?

2. How do sexual restrictions affect relationships between people? Do they unite or divide?

Obviously these questions are easier to ask than to answer. In the first place, the questions imply causality, and I have no data that can answer a causal question. All I can do is point to a relationship and leave it to the reader to solve the chicken-and-egg problem. Obviously, I've made my own inferences, for reasons spelled out in the last chapter.

Second, the questions are very broad, and—as is usual in social research—the data are much more narrow. The easiest problem is the one of finding indices of sexual restrictiveness. We already encountered several in the last chapter, in which we made use not only of various kinds of taboos against sexual intercourse but also of restrictions on diffuse bodily pleasure, mostly in connection with child rearing. This seems particularly appropriate in view of Freud's statement that the community must repress sexuality in childhood in order for adult prohibitions to be maintained.[10]

Cultural complexity is more difficult to measure, although several efforts have been made.[11] Freud's theories suggest that sexual restrictions could have two different effects on culture: First, they would make possible the formation of larger and larger social units, from which we would infer that the larger and more complex the social unit, the greater the "levy" on sexuality. Second, Freud seemed to see sexual restrictions as generating an accumulation of energy that could be directed into culturally useful channels:

> Sublimation of instinct is an especially conspicuous feature of cultural development; it is what makes it possible for higher psychical activities, scientific, artistic or ideological, to play such an important part in divilized life. . . . It is impossible to overlook the extent to which civilization is built up upon a renunciation of instinct, how much it presupposes precisely the nonsatisfaction (by suppression, repression or some other means?) of powerful instincts.[12]

For this exploration, then, I used measures reflecting both *social* complexity and *technological* complexity. The latter is admittedly a poor representative of "scientific, artistic, or ideological" activities, but one must begin somewhere.

NARCISSISM

While Freud argued that inhibiting erotic gratification serves to bind people together in larger groups, Grace Stuart, proceeding from the same psychoanalytic premises, maintains that it produces "narcissistic" individuals—"touchy, possessive, acquisitive, jealous, aggressive"—and that the "banished god" (Eros) returns in the form of aggression.[13] Indeed, she argues eloquently that such inhibition unleashes feelings that can only culminate in war. She sees narcissism as originating in the failure of the mother to provide the purely physical comforts and satisfactions for the infant that a spontaneous love for it would necessitate:

"We love out of our leisure from self-concern, and we are always self-concerned unless we know that someone other than ourself is prepared to maintain the significance of our being."[14]

Thus. while Freud sees sexual restrictions as uniting people, Stuart sees them as divisive. In any case, we are now in a position to rephrase our original questions in slightly more specific terms:

1. Are social restrictions on sexual behavior correlated with either (a) social complexity or (b) technological development?

2. Are social restrictions on diffuse bodily gratification in infancy

correlated with either (a) social complexity or (b) technological development?

3. Are restrictions on sexual behavior correlated positively or negatively with "narcissism"?

4. Are restrictions on infant gratification correlated positively or negatively with "narcissism"?

Before discussing the specific measures used in our exploration I would like to say a few words about social cost or inconvenience. Sociologists and anthropologists often seem to me unduly impressed with the effectiveness of various social customs in fulfilling some function or other. I must confess to an antithetical response: Faced with the most compelling functional analysis, I am usually struck with the wastefulness and inaccuracy of such customs in performing the functions attributed to them. Every social mechanism, while performing important functions for a society, also produces heavy social costs, and the heavier these costs are, the more pressure is generated for finding some substitute mechanism. This is what social change is all about. A police state, for example, performs the function of maintaining order but is sometimes felt to be too costly a mechanism for doing so; its gratuitous oppressions and rigidities begin to seem too expensive, and people look around for a more economical form of order.

Furthermore, the mechanism may trigger lasting consequences, consequences that eliminate the necessity for its existence. Under these conditions the drag or friction created by its social costs will cause it to atrophy. Yet, on the other hand, its social costs may be so burdensome that they smother any such evolution. Indeed, if the social costs are closely tied to the function itself, a vicious circle may ensue: The mechanism will hypertrophy because it never quite manages to meet both the original need and the new needs generated by its own costs.

Let's take as a hypothetical example the postpartum sex taboo, which might conceivably play an important role in relation to cultural development. John Whiting has offered evidence that the long postpartum sex taboo—a common form of sexual restriction in nonliterate societies—originated in dietary concerns having nothing to do with cultural change. Culturally speaking, in other words, the origins of this sexual restriction may well have been "accidental."

We have a wealth of data on the correlates of the postpartum sex taboo, most of it making a rather compelling case that it's a socially noxious institution, producing fear and hostility between the sexes and requiring a cumbersome array of other social mechanisms (other sexual taboos, harsh initiation rites) to counteract its effects. It also bears a strong relationship with narcissism.[15]

The impact of the postpartum sex taboo rests on the prior existence of the incest taboo, for it shifts erotic stimulation and interest from the marital relationship, in which they can be satisfied, to the mother-child relationship, in which they cannot.[16] The libidinal "surplus" thus created could conceivably lead to increases in social or technological complexity. But consider in comparison the equally common institution of prohibiting premarital sexual intercourse, a custom that blocks erotic expression in the adolescent population but doesn't affect marital relations or the erotic experiences of infants. The two mechanisms may be equally efficient in accumulating blocked libido, but the premarital restrictions seem less expensive, and we might therefore expect them to persist at levels of greater cultural complexity.

I'm suggesting a kind of accidental theory of cultural change. A taboo emerges for extraneous reasons, is maintained either because it fosters an addictive cycle (i.e., creates tensions for which it is itself the only "cure"), or because it leads to further cultural development and is reinforced by virtue of becoming essential to the continuance of a new and valued pattern. Once change has occurred, however, the mechanism becomes increasingly vulnerable since the greater level of complexity it has created may in turn yield an energy surplus that permits the luxury of selection between alternative mechanisms. We don't know if any society ever "switched over" from the postpartum sex taboo to premarital sex restrictions in response to anything other than European influence, although a study by Alice Ryerson suggests that this happened in at least some Western societies themselves. We can also observe an analogous process taking place in the Western world today, as premarital and extramarital prohibitions give way to more subtle mechanisms for erotic blockage and accumulation, particularly the displacement of libido on to nonhuman objects through mass media.[17]

THE STUDY

My sample [18] consisted of 100 societies previously selected for a cross-cultural study of narcissism. I used five kinds of *sexual restriction:*

1. The duration of the postpartum sex taboo (i.e., is sexual intercourse prohibited for only a month or two after birth, or until the child is weaned, at two years old or more?).
2. Restrictions on premarital sex.
3. Prohibition of extramarital sex.
4. Curbing of sexual gratification in childhood.
5. Restrictions on diffuse physical gratification in infancy.

I used three kinds of *cultural complexity:*

1. The size of the local community.
2. The number of levels of political jurisdiction in the society.
3. The amount of technological development.

My measure of *narcissism* was based on a composite index of ratings of sensitivity to insult, invidiousness, military glory seeking, belligerence, sadism, boasting, and exhibitionistic dancing. (See Appendix B.)

All of the correlations between the five measures of sexual repression and the three measures of cultural complexity are in the expected direction and most of them were statistically significant. (See Table 2, Appendix B.) On the whole it seems clear that sexual restrictiveness is positively correlated with cultural complexity.

The relationship between narcissism and the sexual repression measures is also strong and in the expected direction. And to round out the picture, narcissism correlates positively with the three measures of cultural complexity, although the relationships are weaker and most likely an artifact of the stronger correlations both show with sexual repression. (See Table 2.) In general, then, narcissism and cultural complexity both vary with sexual repression: As one increases, so do the others.

CULTURE THROUGH FRUSTRATION

The results above provide preliminary support for our crude model of the relation between sexual restrictions and cultural complexity, and while such findings say nothing about causality, they at least raise the possibility for consideration. Since sexual restrictions are related to narcissism as well as to cultural complexity, the view that institutionalized narcissism is the price paid for cultural development seems worthy of further exploration.

One might object, of course, that all of these relationships are self-evident: In *Civilization and Its Discontents,* Freud remarked that he had never felt so strongly that what he was saying was "common knowledge".[19] That civilization seems to rob people of some kind of spontaneity, some totalness of sensation—substituting instead a vague tension and restlessness—is also a common observation. And Shakespeare long ago sensed the connection between sexual frustration and narcissism and portrayed it vividly in *Richard III,* a point noted by both Freud and Grace Stuart.[20] Yet what seems obvious to some is bitterly rejected by others and not taken seriously by most. I would therefore like to share some speculations and observations of my own on this hypothetical process.

Interference with immediate gratification generates a rich variety of substitute goals (wealth, power, fame), forming the raw material of many complex social institutions. Human energies are more consistently tapped by this procedure since substitute gratifications never entirely appease the individual, who strives incessantly for more.[21] While this is rather hard on the individual, it obviously has an enormous social advantage since the individual's energies will be fixed on a goal at all times rather than intermittently. Hunger, thirst, and erotic desire are readily extinguished. Once satisfied, a man untrammeled by "higher" motives becomes dormant—his energies are not available for cultural purposes. To an imaginary social architect he presents the same problem as does solar energy to physical engineers: great potential energy that is difficult to tap because it isn't constantly available. Colonial employers imbued with the Protestant ethic, for example, employing workers who are not, complain that their work force evaporates whenever they are paid and only return when their money is gone. (We call this an inability to delay gratification; it is also an ability to obtain it.) A desire for power or prestige, on the other hand, cannot easily be appeased and thus ensures that a constant supply of energy from the individual will be poured into the economy.

This diversion of pleasure seeking into chronic striving after unattainable goals may be a blessing for technology, but it clearly creates problems for social organization. The very energy that makes it possible (through technological improvements) for larger and more complex social units to exist is a threat to their integration. Furthermore, with each technological gain the need for such taxation of human energy is diminished, allowing more "expensive" libidinal restrictions to be dropped.

Unwin argued that premarital restrictions were most important in differentiating very simple from intermediately complex societies, but that the emergence of "advanced" civilizations was related to the imposition of extramarital restrictions as well. His historical analysis attempts to show how several of the "great" civilizations reached their peak as a result of such restrictions and then declined following their decay. If Unwin is correct, an interesting line of thought is opened up, for extramarital restrictions are the most profoundly patriarchal of all those included here since the restrictions, like sexual restrictions everywhere, are applied primarily to *women* and thus tend to place married women in the position of being considered as property. The transition from relative sexual equality (always referred to as "matriarchy" by patriarchal males) to the system of male domination that exists in most of the world today is often located in the so-called "neolithic revolution." Mary Jane Sherfey, for example, argues that the invention of agriculture necessitated a "ruthless subjugation of female sexuality," and our data seem to bear her out.[22]

A serious deficiency in these data is that the narcissism index is not sensitive to the more subtle forms taken by narcissism in complex societies such as our own. The narcissism scales were originally designed with nonliterate societies in mind, and our confidence in their validity is correspondingly diluted when they're applied to modern industrial societies. Perhaps our narcissism index should be retitled "Subtype A: primitive epic narcissism," and other ways will be found for measuring the processes that enable modern industrial societies to maintain so much war with so little of the warrior ethos.

"Narcissism" isn't a very precise term. One problem with it is that it makes no distinction between forms of self-absorption that are immediate, impulsive, and bodily and those that are cerebral, long-range, and highly controlled. We could imagine at least four identifiable positions on this continuum, moving from the more physical to the more cerebral, away from the body toward more delayed forms of gratification. The first position would emphasize physical vanity—adornment, cosmetics, and so on—preoccupation with one's physical appearance. It is clearly the least toxic of all forms. The second form would involve short-run ambition: *machismo*, the warrior ethos, conspicuous consumption, and so on. The narcissism index used in this study mostly deals with this second level.

The third form would involve long-run ambition: the accumulation of wealth, complex planning to gain and hold power, lifelong goals to achieve professional eminence, artistic fame, or whatever. The fourth form would represent other-worldly ambition: efforts to be the most virtuous, most loving, most enlightened of all beings.

Obviously there are precedents for this continuum: Sophisticated religious doctrine has always tended to see personal vanity as venial and spiritual pride as the ultimate sin, something available only to the most highly developed individuals—a fallen angel like Milton's Lucifer.

This leaves us with two alternative models for the role of narcissism in cultural development. If we stick closely to our data, that role is best viewed as essentially negative. Assuming—quite arbitrarily—that sexual restrictions are causally central to all this, one would attribute both primitive narcissism and the emergence of intermediate (neolithic?) levels of cultural complexity to the growth of these restrictions without seeing narcissism and complexity as having any relation at all to each other. Statistically, this would be the sound conclusion since it is quite clear that narcissism and complexity have no relationship if sexual restrictions are held constant. In this model, then, sexual restrictions channel energy into "constructive" cultural activities, leading to the development of agriculture, larger social units, use of metals, ability to make war on a larger scale, and so on. Narcissism, which also increases, is simply to be viewed as the negative side of this process: the "cost" of sexual restrictions. As civilization proceeds, this cost becomes so high that further "progress" is blocked: The energy made available by blocking gratification and maintaining a higher level of frustrated restlessness is drained off in warfare and unproductive competition (e.g., the invidious destruction of wealth, as in potlatches, boastful posturing, and so on). Our data support this model (there are even hints of the appropriate curvilinear relationships).

In the second model, narcissism plays a positive role. Here we compound our arbitrary assumption that sexual restrictions have some causal significance by attributing a similar significance to the narcissism itself. Restrictions create complexity and narcissism, but narcissism also creates complexity. Narcissism becomes not merely a social cost but also a driving cultural force in its own right.

Even to entertain such a possibility may seem to some readers heretical since there are no data whatever to support it, and the data presented tend to argue against it. Until more data are in, however, I'm not quite ready to discard the possibility that narcissism might play some significant role in cultural complexity. Technology, for example, is referred to as "extensions of man" and is usually discussed in terms of human mastery over nature, with a great deal of self-congratulatory exultation over this power. Is it conceivable that all this phallic pride over technological achievements could exist without narcissistic impulses having provided fuel for these achievements in the first place? Certainly war and economic competition—two highly "narcissistic" activities—have always been viewed as important for technological growth.

At a much more primitive level, Gouldner and Peterson seem to be dealing with the same relationship in their discussion of pottery, which they use as a measure of technological development.

(This seems far-fetched enough so that Gouldner and Peterson take some pains to justify it.) They argue that pottery made humans more *aware of themselves* and their instrumental powers. I would suggest that the direction could as well be reversed—that a heightened self-preoccupation led to attempts by humans to impose their own formal ideas on nature and natural products.[23]

A case could even be made for narcissism as facilitating *social* complexity. Narcissism dilutes all social bonds, and although in most respects this might be seen as interfering with the formation of larger social units (as we shall see in the next chapter) there is a paradoxical process leading to the precise opposite. The erosion of intimate group bonds, the reduced cohesiveness of the community, opens the way to the imposition of authoritarian rule by a chief or a warrior class. Narcissistic aspirations can lead to true military ambition—one tribe can conquer another and enslave it instead of merely scuffling from time to time. Class and caste divisions, autocratic rulers, chronic warfare and militarism—all are generally associated with an intermediate level of cultural complexity. They seem to depend on the development of agriculture or animal husbandry, with fixed settlements. Hunter-gatherers, on the other hand, tend to live in small, property-less, roving bands. They tend to be modest, informal, democratic, peaceable, and classless. Disagreements are handled by fission.

This is not to say that narcissism is a boon, or that the change toward large social units held together by the arbitrary rule of warrior-kings or class oppression is not a "social cost." On the contrary, one could make the case that the whole neolithic revolution was a wrong turning—that we are still paying for the fact that the entire edifice of social complexity as we know it was built around a narcissistic core, flawed from the very beginning. Or, more optimistically, one could just view it as a necessary experiment in suffering and chaos. Perhaps there is no direct way to build intense, intimate, small groups into large ones without first interfering with that intimacy. Nevertheless, to suggest that narcissism plays some role in generating cultural complexity is not to deny it its role as a "social cost." One could even take the position that the defects Freud found in civilization are due less to the loss of erotic fullness than to the fact that the development of civilization has been indissolubly tainted with narcissism from the very first, a view echoed in the Judaeo-Christian myth of the fall of Adam, especially as portrayed by Milton in *Paradise Lost*, at the dawn of the industrial age.

At the moment there is no way to choose among these various historical models, and I would now like to lay them aside and speculate a bit on the role played by the sexual restrictions themselves. There are, as we have seen, many different kinds of sexual restrictions, each with its own side effects, and the number of possible combinations is almost infinite. Evolution occurs not so much because new elements appear but because old ones are recombined in new ways. Hence the same restriction might appear at many different times and places, with effects that vary according to how it's combined with *other* restrictions. Premarital sexual restrictions have been imposed and lifted several times in English history, for example, but each time in conjunction with different child-rearing practices and marriage patterns. The disappearance of the long postpartum sex taboo in Europe coincided with the imposition of a great variety of new restrictive child-rearing practices; while the Puritan attack on sports, which bore intermittent fruit between 1650 and 1850, corresponded with the abandonment of swaddling, an even more elementary restriction on motor discharge.[24]

While each combination can be assumed to have unique by-products, both beneficent and malign, I would suggest that underlying all of this variety is a purely quantitative factor: How *much* overall manipulation of the impulse has been achieved. While individual restrictions may wax and wane, giving an impression of alternating periods of severity and permissiveness, the overall trend in the West seems to have been to continually lengthen and complicate the circuitry of gratification.

It may be, for example, that all restrictions begin with simple prohibitions, which later lead to more subtle and sophisticated channeling. The prohibitions may spring from extrinsic causes. The postpartum sex taboo, for example, seems to have arisen from considerations of nutrition or population control.[25] It would be ridiculous to assume that primitive peoples got together and decided that prohibiting intercourse between husband and wife for two years after childbirth would concentrate sexual energy in the mother-child relationship. The heavy "oedipal" impact of the taboo was essentially accidental.

The impact was crude. Ambition was evoked, fear of women, and a compulsive need for male bonding, but no ability to sustain a complex ambitious undertaking. The problem with the postpartum sex taboo seems to be that it weakens the marital bond *too* much, which seems to be associated with poor impulse control and an inability to delay gratification.[26] The impetuous braggart warriors and vain exhibitionists of our most narcissistic cultures, while perhaps well equipped to conquer or exploit a preindustrial society seem ill adapted to the more sustained complexities of empire building.

Other forms of sexual restriction (premarital and extramarital, for example), far from weakening the marital bond, serve to intensify it since they block alternative sexual outlets. The self-concern that sexual suppression engenders is thereby alloyed with stronger controls and with a measure of foresight. The use of shame to control behavior gives way to guilt, which eliminates a great deal of cumbersome repressive machinery for the society, but places a heavier damper on the instinctual life of the individual.

The generalized negative attitude toward sexuality (usually called "Puritanism," although by no means restricted to that sect) that began to spread over Europe in the seventeenth and eighteenth centuries also seems to have had an extrinsic origin, this time in the virulent syphilis epidemic that raged in the sixteenth century. Ryerson and others have observed a radical change in attitudes toward sexuality beginning in English writings around 1600, and increasing steadily until the twentieth century.[27] Since this parallels Western technological growth rather closely, Freud's theory of libidinal "borrowing" seems appropriate. At the same time, the more optimistic view that a level once achieved no longer requires so much energy to maintain it—that the erotic "debt" can be repaid, in other words—would be supported by the reversal of this trend in the twentieth century.

The stress placed on internalization of controls by the Protestant movement not only "bit deeper" into the individual's instinctual life than did ecclesiastical prohibitions and penances but also changed the quality of the self-concern that emerged: Vanity was given a moral flavor. This contrasts sharply with the societies in my sample, in which the narcissism index is significantly correlated with the amount of personal crime.[28]

The narcissism of the Protestant ethic is thus considerably disguised since it is always geared to gaining approval from parent-like deities. Through this device one can assign moral worth even to such baldly narcissistic phenomena as Bunyan's hero, who rejects his worldly family in favor of his eternal self-interest, or to Franklin's exhortation to *appear* modest so that one's ultimate glory will be increased. Max Weber notes that ethical reform was of little interest to the Puritan divines, that the isolated individual seeking personal, if ultimate, glory was the focus of attention, and that "individualism" still characterizes "peoples with a Puritan past." He cites the frequent warnings against placing trust in friends and the intense opposition to worldly authorities.[29]

Another relevant point in Weber's analysis is his emphasis on sexual repression. He makes the interesting statement that "mediaeval Catholic laymen lived ethically, so to speak, from hand to mouth" since guilt was discharged through expiation, and asceticism was limited to a group of religious specialists. He seems to be raising the problem I mentioned earlier: how to harness human energies so that they are constantly rather than intermittently activated. He says of the Reformation that "the drain of asceticism from everyday worldly life had been stopped by a dam" and refers to confession as a "periodic discharge" eliminated by Calvinism.[30]

The analysis of historical change is made difficult by (1) the enormous unevenness of social change (for every evidence of a transition someone can point to places where it has not occurred) and (2) the uncertain length of the interval between action and reaction (if such a complex process can be viewed in such simple terms). The second difficulty is particularly acute when one assumes, as I do, that the focal point of change is the child-rearing process, thus necessitating an interval of at least a generation. Unwin argues that a full *three* generations must pass before changes in sexual norms influence cultural development.[31] None-theless, certain broad changes can be observed.

Taylor speaks, for example, of a particularly repressive phase in European history as beginning in the middle of the eighteenth century.[32] This view is confirmed by Alice Ryerson's study of med-ical attitudes toward child-rearing practices. Ryerson notes that from 1550 to 1750 medical advice on child rearing in the West (particularly England) was typical of contemporary nonliterate tribes with regard to parental approaches to all five of Whiting and Child's infant behavior categories (oral, anal, sexual, aggression, dependency). From 1750 to 1900, however, there was a sharp increase in the severity with which all these behaviors were treated, with the single exception of aggression. In Whiting and Child's study the modern American middle class was rated as among the two or three *least* indulgent societies for oral, anal, and sexual behavior, and in the bottom 20 percent for dependency. Specifically, the 1750–1900 period saw a drastic increase in medi-cal advice that suggested (1) early weaning; (2) early toilet training; (3) having the child sleep in a room apart from parents and siblings; (4) ignoring the baby's crying; (5) evading the child's sex-ual questions; (6) forbidding and punishing sex play and masturba-tion; (7) avoiding physical demonstrativeness on the grounds that kissing and handling the child would "overstimulate" it and lead to sexual precocity.[33]

This increase in repressiveness seems to correspond roughly with increases in achievement imagery in English and American literature during the same period. It also parallels the industrial revolution, and the tendency for puritanical norms to evolve in na-tions undergoing rapid industrialization is a familiar phenome-non.[34]

The twentieth century presents a more complex picture. For while sexual norms for adults have relaxed considerably, this has involved very few concessions to childhood sensuality in terms of the Ryerson variables just discussed. What is perhaps more signifi-cant is that our culture combines a minimum of physical gratifica-tion in childhood with a maximum of symbolic sexual stimulation (largely through the mass media). David and Vera Mace describe the difficulty experienced trying to protect Soviet visitors from such artificial stimulation, so pervasive in the United States and so absent in Russia, while McLuhan's *Mechanical Bride* illuminates beautifully the segmented and mechanical nature of contemporary sexual stimulation in media.[35]

We seem to have stumbled on the cleverest form of sexual restriction yet practiced: fragmenting the impulse and attaching sexual interest to purely symbolic images or material objects, through which gratification is impossible. Despite contemporary efforts to free Americans from their sexual trammels—the "sexual revolution," the human potential movement, and so on—erotic life in America is uniquely disturbed and self-conscious, matching our extraordinary, culturally approved egoism and the unprecedented complexity of our social and technological existence.

Chapter 11

SHORT CIRCUITS IN SOCIAL LIFE

If we view sexual energy, or libido, as being able to expand and contract, then we can throw some light on a familiar process—the withdrawal of energy from larger groups to smaller and more exclusive ones. These contracting tendencies of libido drive it toward closer and more intimate relationships along simpler and more direct paths of gratification. At other times, however, sexual energy seems to diffuse, with forces driving it toward more and more remote people, along more and more circuitous paths of gratification, and toward involvement in larger and larger groups.

But if this diffusion of energy involves not only an increase in the number of people attached to an individual but also an increase in the extent to which gratification is delayed and incomplete, why does it occur at all? Why does a person make these ever more complicated detours? Apparently because an individual who participates in a community has competitive advantages when it comes to natural selection and variety of options, and the community benefits from the higher degree of organization and integration. Libido diffusion is the social cement that binds living entities together.

The incest taboo is one institution that works to encourage libido diffusion. It enforces marriage outside of the nuclear family, preventing it from becoming an autonomous unit. It also serves to

114

block withdrawal of energy from larger groups whose maintenance is essential to tolerable human existence in most parts of the world. Involvement in an incestuous relationship, which would more fully and immediately gratify emotional needs, would weaken an individual's bonds to the larger community. The more people an individual can love at once, the larger the number of individuals who can cooperate in a joint endeavor. Furthermore, as libido becomes further diffused and gratification becomes less complete, the individual experiences a constant tension and restless energy that can be harnessed to serve socially useful ends. So long as an individual loves more than one person, he or she will feel this continuing tension and so always remain available for collectivization.

THE LIMITS OF LIBIDO DIFFUSION

However, because ultimate diffusion would lead to ultimate extinction, libidinal contraction must be permitted to go far enough to ensure sexual union and procreation, yet not far enough to threaten the existence of communities. The incest taboo marks the point at which further contraction is prohibited, and it has to be a very powerful barrier since the forces propelling the individual across this line are just as powerful.

Although incest constitutes the nearest danger to larger communities, there are other and more extreme forms of libidinal contraction. If energy can be withdrawn from larger communities and centered in the nuclear family, it can also be withdrawn from the family and centered in any single dyadic relationship. Finally, it can be withdrawn from all relationships and centered in the ego—what we call "narcissism." All three are simply positions on a continuum of libidinal contraction.

The normal response of other people to signs of libidinal contraction in an individual with whom they participate in some group is what I call "social anxiety." They may also show anger, moral indignation, ridicule, or scorn, but the anxiety is clearly the primary response. It is a common and familiar sensation to all of us, experienced whenever someone physically or psychically deserts a group in which we are emotionally involved. The latent danger with which it is concerned is the collapse of the group. The anxiety does not spring, however, from any rational consideration of the advantages of societal existence but is emotional and automatic and appears concurrently with awareness of group membership.

Social anxiety generally evokes behavior designed to reform the deviant member who has withdrawn his or her libido from a more inclusive to a less inclusive entity. In all surviving societies we also find anticipatory institutions that serve to hinder such withdrawal.

Three principal forms of libidinal contraction exist. Each of these forms has an anticipatory institution designed to prevent it.

1. The most immediate form—withdrawal of energy from larger groups to the confines of the family—we will call familial withdrawal. Its anticipatory institution is the incest taboo.

2. Withdrawal of energy from groups to a single, intimate dyad we will call dyadic withdrawal. Its anticipatory institution is marriage.

3. The most extreme form—withdrawal of energy from all people to the self—we will call narcissistic withdrawal. Its anticipatory institution is socialization.

These institutions are for the most part so successful in counteracting withdrawal that we are usually unaware of the conflict taking place; it is only at certain rough spots in the social fabric that it becomes visible. The examples that follow pit individuals experiencing libidinal withdrawal against others who are not. This is not to say that there is no inner struggle in all this, or that we are talking of different types of people. Everyone at some time in his or her life experiences and defends libidinal withdrawal, and everyone fights against it.

In the same way I have ignored the issue of guilt. Guilt is not aroused by withdrawal itself but only by violation of the norms associated with the anticipatory institutions. For to the extent that withdrawal has occurred, the person is emotionally unavailable to the group. He or she feels no commitment to it and cannot therefore perceive having violated that commitment.

NARCISSISTIC WITHDRAWAL

Narcissistic withdrawal takes many forms, the most familiar of which are psychosis and physical illness. In these instances, the internal emotional process is often given some kind of concrete physical or behavioral manifestation.

Resocialization of a withdrawn person is based on the same control mechanism as the initial socialization process: the kindling and fanning of dependency needs. By placing him in the sick role and catering to his needs, the "deviant" is seduced into once again directing his energy onto social objects. For the more severe "crimes," the sick person is incarcerated, partly to facilitate dependency but partly also to offset the possible contagious effect of his libidinal withdrawal.

The logical extreme of both of these types of narcissistic withdrawal—in fact of all libido withdrawal for the human organism—is death. Death naturally arouses more social anxiety than illness, however, because it is total, permanent, and irreparable. Furthermore, the dead man does not even decently take himself off but leaves a putrefying corpse as a reminder that he has "laid his burden down," and that others may do the same if they wish. For this corpse is impervious to social pressures and sanctions; no matter how others plead, nurture, threaten, and cajole, it is obstinately, defiantly asocial. Death is thus a desertion without the saving grace of absence. Nor is there any threat of punishment involved, for the corpse is clearly immune.

All of this serves to make funeral rituals an urgent necessity. First of all, the social fabric must be repaired, the ranks closed, and the virtue and unity of the group dramatized in such a way as to bolster the waverers, who might be seduced into following in the footsteps of the departed. Second, the corpse must be incarcerated in the ground or isolated to remove the "bad influence" from sight and awareness. Third, the "independence" of the corpse must be symbolically denied in some way through ritual interaction between mourners and mourned. The corpse is thus almost always bathed, cosmetically treated in some way, and decorated or dressed—in some societies even held in the arms, rocked, and kissed—as if, by treating it like an infant, to make one last effort at resocialization through gratification of the now-extinct dependency needs. Furthermore, by performing these various operations on the corpse, and particularly by disposing of it, the group recaptures the initiative. Instead of being abandoned by him, they have now expelled him and often do not consider him officially dead before doing so. This desire to deny the independence of the deceased is also revealed by the almost universal denial of the possibility that death could be a voluntary act of withdrawal, which, as every general practitioner knows, it often is. In primitive societies this denial takes the form of a belief that all death is caused by sorcery. In our own society it takes the form of an insistence on a specific physical cause of death on death certificates, even in those cases in which no lesion can be found to serve as the scapegoat. Finally, the social immunity of the deceased may be denied by the myth that existence does not cease with death but continues in another world, so that he has not in fact "escaped" and may even be punished.

In some instances the individual takes the initiative in causing his or her own death. Although suicides are sometimes attributed to sorcery in primitive societies, the more usual response is to accept such blatant evidence and condemn the deceased. For disapproval always varies in accordance with the degree of personal responsibility for the crime, and as malingering is the most disapproved form of illness, so suicide is the most disapproved mode of dying. This disapproval, it must be emphasized, is a response to the suicide's shockingly individualistic conclusion that his life is his own affair. Without the theory of energy withdrawal the social attitude toward suicide becomes incomprehensible.

THE WITHDRAWAL IN "STRENGTH"

The forms of narcissistic withdrawal considered so far have been those associated with a weak and beleaguered ego, but more robust forms of narcissistic withdrawal exist in reality and play an even more important role in fantasy.

Of greatest interest is the individual actively engaged in communities but with no emotional commitment to them. Insofar as others are aware of his total self-interest he will be viewed as an ambitious and unscrupulous manipulator, but there is no lever by which such an individual can be persuaded to serve social ends. He is the complete "economic man," motivated solely by rational self-interest. He will conform when it is dangerous not to but will never hesitate to violate any social norm or betray any individual or group if it will further his ends. The great villains of literature and mythology, for example, are courageous, ambitious, and proud but also heartless, calculating, and unscrupulous. They achieve their goals without "going through channels." The epitome of this type is Milton's Satan, who is flagrantly individualistic and hostile to any social organization he cannot dominate. His self-sufficiency and sturdy ego defenses enable him to withstand extreme tortures:

> The mind is its own place, and in itself
> Can make a Heaven of Hell, a Hell of Heaven,
> What matter where, if I be still the same?

The fact that "pride" is the cardinal sin in most religious systems is enough to make it clear that the strong ego is seen as a great menace to social existence.

Great villains are often ambivalently regarded. They are villains to society, but as representations of the ego they are heroes to the individual. Their deaths are doubly satisfying, for while social control is thus re-established and evil punished, the villain achieves a secret victory, having established his narcissistic withdrawal on a permanent and invulnerable basis.

These narcissists arouse the most social anxiety because they appear to have overcome the dependency and guilt that are used as levers to resocialize the more fragile narcissist. The most important anticipatory institutions that meet this threat are the child-rearing process and the tendency of the family and peer group to punish narcissistic behavior with deprivation of love before the ego is strong enough to tolerate it. These mechanisms are so effective that we have been forced to cull our major examples from fiction, where their existence serves further to ensure their absence from real life.

Before leaving the subject of narcissistic withdrawal, we should note one fact that seems at first to contradict much of what has been said. While we might expect narcissistic individuals to be innovators, it is rather strange to think of them as charismatic leaders, which they often are. How can they be feared as evil villains and followed as saviors at the same time?

First, it seems to be true that strongly narcissistic individuals have a certain seductive fascination for most people, particularly those with intense dependency needs. Great leaders are often sought among those who do not have a strong need to depend on others, that is, people who are willing to sacrifice security to vanity.

Narcissistic withdrawal is often tolerated in people who are expected to be of great benefit to society; leaders, prophets, shamans, inventors, artists, scientists, innovators of all kinds. This expectation relieves social anxiety and social control mechanisms are waived—there is no harm if the prophet temporarily leaves the group and goes into the desert because he will return in time, replete with marvelous visions. Similarly, if the leader is selfish, unfeeling, unscrupulous, and vain, this is acceptable because he will take upon himself the group's burdens and lead them to the Promised Land. This is the basis for the intensive use of narcissistic rewards in the form of deference, flattery, and exhibitionistic display to motivate leaders in all cultures and all ages. Shakespeare shows an understanding of the nature of this exchange in *Henry V,* when the king reflects dolefully on the heavy burden of responsibility laid upon him by his subjects:

> what infinite heart's-ease
> Must kings neglect, that private men enjoy!
> And what have kings, that privates have not too,
> Save ceremony?

Yet the next day Henry reveals that he is not an unwilling victim to the contract by wishing he had fewer soldiers with whom to share his glory.

The basis of this tolerance is perhaps some vague awareness that great enterprises require an abundance of libidinal energy, which must be withdrawn from the usual social objects. The stronger narcissists have this energy available for creative innovation, and to the extent that the social value of this innovation is perceived, the rest of the group will respond with proportionate acceptance.

In the case of the charismatic leader the relationship is simpler and more primitive. The person who has stored up energy will attract the energy of others to him, after the physical principle that the greater the mass the greater the attraction. A person of this kind can be a focus for group loyalty.

We can summarize these observations by saying that a group will not punish narcissistic withdrawal if such withdrawal seems to increase the energy diffusion of other group members. We shall see that the same principle applies to other forms of withdrawal.

Freud saw this principle as operating on the biological level. Starting with the familiar observation that the association of cells is a means of prolonging life (one cell helps to preserve the life of another, and the community survives all individuals), he sees the cells as "cathecting" one another and "sacrificing themselves" for the whole. Then he notes that germ cells are an exception to this rule, behaving "in a completely 'narcissistic' fashion . . . The germ cells require their libido for themselves, *as a reserve against their later momentous constructive activity.*" [1]

DYADIC WITHDRAWAL

Our discussion of narcissistic withdrawal would suggest that the social danger it raises is almost entirely hypothetical. When combined with a weak ego, it is impotent as a social force, while when it appears in conjunction with ego strength, mechanisms have evolved that tend to channel it into socially constructive paths. What diminishes the threat of both forms, then, is the fact that all human beings have needs that can best be satisfied through other human beings. When the ego is weak, the individual is compelled to depend on others. When it is strong, he will seek out others because they will maximize his gratification, although he will expend very little love on them and will try to use and exploit them ruthlessly.

But what if most of the physical and psychological needs of a person could be satisfied without immediate recourse to the larger collective? Suppose that the energy of the person were concentrated on only one other person who gratified all of these needs, and that a reciprocal concentration were made by that other person. A lower level of ego strength would then be needed to effectively withdraw from larger groups, and the anticipatory institutions described in the previous section would no longer be adequate.

This is the case with dyadic withdrawal. An intimate dyadic relationship always threatens to short-circuit the energy network of the community and drain off its source of sustenance. The needs binding the person to the group are now satisfied in the dyadic relationship, and the energy diffused through the members of the community is drawn back and invested in the dyad.

There are several reasons why the dyad lends itself so well to this kind of short-circuiting. Both persons are indispensable to the maintenance of the bond. More energy is thus concentrated in the dyad than in any other group. All other groups consist of multiple relationships that influence one another, while the dyad consists of only one relationship, influenced by none. In triads and larger groups the energy of the individual is divided and distributed, and there are many points of "leverage" at which he or she may be influenced or controlled.

THE DYAD AND THE COMMUNITY

If we assume a finite quantity of libido in every person, then it follows that the greater the emotional involvement in the dyad, the greater will be the withdrawal from others. This agrees with the popular concept of the oblivious lovers who are "all wrapped up in each other" and somewhat careless of their social obligations. All of the great lovers of history and literature were guilty of disloyalties of one kind or another. Disregard for the norms governing family and peer-group ties in the story of Romeo and Juliet becomes, in the affair of Antony and Cleopatra, a disregard for societal responsibilities that embrace most of the civilized world. In the latter, a war of global significance is treated as a courtly tournament by the lovers, and their armies are manipulated as if the outcome were related only to the complexities of their relationship. In Shakespeare's drama this is epitomized in a remark by Cleopatra, who expresses her satisfaction with a day of military victory by saying to Antony, "Comest thou smiling from the world's great snare uncaught?"

The inverse relationship between dyadic attachment and social attachment suggests that the more totalitarian the community (in terms of making demands on the individual to involve every area of his or her life in group activity), the stronger will be the prohibition against dyadic intimacy. A similar relation holds for suicide and other forms of narcissistic withdrawal.

Strong opposition to dyadic intimacy is often found in youth groups that are formed on the basis of common interests, such as music, camping, travel, or mountain climbing. Solidarity in such groups often runs high, and when it does, avoidance of pairing is usually a firmly upheld norm. Extreme prohibitions are also characteristic of utopian, communistic communities, religious and otherwise, such as the Oneida experiment. In some instances the intimacy prohibition is enforced at the same time that sexual promiscuity is encouraged, revealing that the basis of the proscription is not fear of sexuality but fear of libidinal withdrawal, fear that the functions that the community performs for the individual could be performed for each other by the members of the dyad. An insightful literary portrayal of this antagonism may be found in Orwell's *1984*, in which a highly centralized state evinces overwhelming hostility to dyadic intimacy as a potential refuge from its all-pervasive influence.

In some nonliterate societies the prevention of privacy is managed through such devices as barracks-type living arrangements, but there are many other methods of blocking dyadic intimacy: child marriages, restriction of the pool of eligible spouses, isolation of adolescents from prospective mates, and peer-group control.

The principal issue in this conflict between dyadic intimacy and collective life is whether the relationship shall be an end in itself (as in "romantic love") or a means to a socially desired end. The intimate, exclusive dyadic relationship is essentially "playful" and nonutilitarian, and this is the source of the antagonism of "totalitarian" collectives toward it. Some kind of organized societal intrusion, like the institution of marriage, is required to convert it into a socially useful relationship, and insofar as this intrusion is successful, the playful aspect of the relationship will tend to disappear. We may thus directly equate energy diffusion with the de-eroticizing of the sexual life of the individual, the transformation of hedonistic activity into utilitarian activity. Freud says flatly that "direct sexual tendencies are unfavorable to the formation of groups," remarking that the sexual act is the one condition "in which a third person is at the best superfluous." "Two people coming together for the purpose of sexual satisfaction, insofar as they seek for solitude, are making a demonstration against . . . the group feeling. The more they are in love, the more completely they suffice for each other . . ." [2]

THE PREMARITAL DYAD

Let us look now at examples of dyadic withdrawal in our society. It occurs most often in adolescence, when experiments in enduring sexual intimacy first begin. The dyad soon meets various kinds of resistance and control from parents, other authorities, and the peer group. "Going steady" is generally opposed by adults, but peer groups handle it with more inconsistency. In some groups zealous opposition is the rule, while in others there is an equally enthusiastic group endorsement of pairing off, but only when transformed by group regulations so it no longer constitutes withdrawal. Criteria of sexual desirability are established by group norms to eliminate the importance of personal characteristics. The partners are expected to spend most of their time in group activities and to have a relationship of short duration (often measured in weeks). Such institutionalization of "going together" is clearly a far more effective instrument against withdrawal than adult opposition.

Before the days of Women's Liberation the norm for such groups was sex antagonism and exploitation. The boy achieved prestige within the male group by maximizing physical contact and minimizing expenditure of money on a date. The girl achieved prestige within her group by maximizing expenditure and minimizing sexual contact. The date then became a contest between adversaries. Each had much to win or lose in the way of prestige, depending on how effectively they could control their tender and sexual feelings. It is easy to see how dyadic intimacy was minimized in this situation. If each partner, even in the midst of sexual caresses, is "keeping score" in terms of the peer-group norms, little emotional involvement can take place. The boy, for example, knew that his friends would later ask him if he "made out," and his sexual behavior was determined more by this than by any qualities inherent in his partner. It is significant that the beginning of dyadic withdrawal and intimacy was always signaled by the boy's sudden reluctance to talk about the relationship, a reluctance that always aroused social anxiety and ridicule.

The control mechanisms of the adult community during this early period are less subtle. Like the peer group, adults depend heavily on ridicule, and lay similar stress on promiscuity and an exploitative attitude toward the opposite sex. In the adult's exhortation to the adolescent, however, to "play the field," "keep 'em guessing," or "don't get tied down at your age," it is not hard to detect the expression of their own suppressed promiscuous urges—so that the advice serves a psychological as well as a social purpose.

Adult opposition is not limited to these casual pleas, however, but sometimes takes the form of censure by church and school authorities. Prohibitions by these authorities are an expression of the breakdown, under changing social conditions, of older and more subtle methods of control. Marriage and peer-group regulation block withdrawal by intruding on the dyad—ritualizing and regulating it, drawing its members back into their other relationships. For the most part these forms of control are so effective that it is only in large, "loose" pluralistic societies such as ours that dyadic withdrawal occurs with enough frequency and intensity to permit easy observation of the forces opposing it. In many primitive societies dyadic relationships are so highly institutionalized and diluted by group bonds that withdrawal has little opportunity to emerge. Our own society has seen an extension of heterosexual dyadic intimacy into a younger and younger age group in an era in which teen-age marriage is felt to be socially undesirable. In the colonial period, when an unmarried woman of 20 was considered an "old maid," the threat of dyadic withdrawal in adolescence was dissipated by marriage, but this is less feasible today, when the educational process is so prolonged and so valued.

About twenty years ago a Roman Catholic paper expressed unqualified disapproval of couples "going together" and a parochial school actually banned it. Arguments stressed, as usual, the dangers of sexual "transgression," but since sexual intercourse may also occur within the context of a promiscuous dating pattern, something more than sexuality was clearly involved. The parochial school ban revealed intense social anxiety over possible dyadic withdrawal and consequent loss of interest in church, state, school, community, and God. Thus the priests argued that going steady "creates distractions to make concentrated study impossible" while a school superintendent claimed that it "robs the youngster of one of the finer experiences of growing up: the friendship and companionship of as wide a circle of acquaintances of both sexes as possible." [3] But it is not only the "younger" who is being "robbed" but also the community and the peer group, and the quotes reveal the anxiety of people when they are reminded that the entire social structure, upon which they are so dependent, rests on borrowed libidinal energy.

THE MARRIAGE CEREMONY AS AN INTRUSION RITUAL

The real focal point between dyadic intimacy and social allegiance is, of course, the marital relationship. Every marriage poses the threat of social withdrawal by creating the possibility of a self-sufficient and exclusive subunit, emotionally detached from the larger group.

In a society such as ours, with small nuclear families, monogamy, mobility, and relatively weak kinship ties, the threat of dyadic withdrawal is a very real one. The marriage ritual then becomes a series of mechanisms for pulling the couple apart somewhat, so that it complements rather than replaces the various group ties of each member. The discussion that follows is primarily concerned with the social rituals surrounding the traditional Protestant middle-class marriage in our society, but the pattern differs only in detail from those found elsewhere.

As the marriage approaches, there is usually a rapid acceleration of the involvement of the families of the couple in their relationship. Increasing stress is placed on an awareness of the ritual, legal, and economic significance of the relationship and the responsibilities that must be assumed.

But invasion of the free and exclusive intimacy of the couple is not limited to such overt influence. The entire ceremony constitutes a rehearsal for the kind of social relationship that is expected of them later. First of all, the ceremony is so involved that it requires many social decisions by the couple. Much of their interaction during this period will thus concern issues external to their relationship, and there will be a great deal of preoccupation with loyalties and obligations outside of the dyad itself. Guests must be invited, attendants chosen, and gifts for the attendants selected. The ceremony has the effect of concentrating the attention of both individuals on every *other* affectional tie either one has ever contracted.

Similarly, the ceremony serves to emphasize the *dependence* of the two partners on other groups. In addition to the gifts given to the couple, it is made clear to them that much of the responsibility for their wedding rests with their families, who bear a far greater burden in this regard than they themselves. They are, in essence, "given" a wedding.

Their feelings of harassment and anxiety over the coming event, coupled with the realization that their role is relatively minor, instills a feeling that the dyadic relationship is not their "personal affair." They become more aware that after marriage, too, life will involve extradyadic personal obligations, responsibilities, and social dependence. It is usually during this period that the impulse toward dyadic withdrawal reasserts itself and one or the other will half seriously suggest elopement. But it is usually felt that things have "gone too far"—parents and friends would be disappointed and hurt, eyebrows would be raised—there is no turning back.

The role of the clergyman who is to unite the pair is of the utmost importance during this period. It is he who usually verbalizes the intrusion most explicitly, and he speaks from a position of considerable prestige. For he is the central person in the proceedings and represents, emotionally, the paternal figure who can fulfill or deny their wishes. He will speak the magic words that will join them, and the accumulated experience of hundreds of movies, novels, soap operas, and comic strips tells us and them that until the last word is spoken, the marriage is in danger of being thwarted.

In many denominations it is explicitly stated that marriage is a contract involving three parties—husband, wife, and God—and that He is always present so long as the marriage lasts. This is a vivid symbol of the institutionalization of the dyad and a clear equation of God with society. Not only is the dyadic relationship no longer a "personal affair," it no longer is a dyad. The privacy of the relationship is seen as permanently invaded. This supernatural symbol of societal intrusion is given more concrete form in Orwell's *1984*, in which the couple cannot escape from Big Brother, who is "always watching." One wonders what effect this fantasy of an omnipresent parental figure has on the sexual relationship of couples who take it seriously.

The actual process of intrusion, however, is more mundane. As the time for the wedding draws near, the forces drawing the couple apart become more intense. It is often believed to be "bad luck" for the groom to see the bride in her wedding dress before the ceremony, and, in general, contact between the couple on the day of the wedding is considered bad form. They enter the church from opposite ends, as leaders of separate hosts of followers. Prior to the wedding day there are showers or a bridal supper for the bride and a bachelor's dinner for the groom, in which peer-group ties are very strongly underlined. This tends to create the impression that in some way the couple *owe* their relationship to these groups, who are preparing them ceremonially for their marriage. This impression of societal initiative is augmented by the fact that the bride's father "gives the bride away." The retention of this ancient custom serves explicitly to deny the possibility that the couple might unite quite on their own. In other words, the marriage ritual is designed to make it appear as if somehow the idea of the dyadic union sprang from the community and not from the couple itself. The ceremony, its corollary rituals, and the roles that pertain to it all tend to create an image of two individuals propelled toward each other by a united phalanx of partisans.

THE HONEYMOON

To everything that has been said thus far the honeymoon would seem to be an exception. The wedding ritual seems designed to emphasize that, indeed, marriage is *not* a honeymoon. Yet this wedding is actually followed immediately by a socially approved dyadic withdrawal, involving the very kind of exclusive, private intimacy that is at all other times forbidden. The couple is permitted, even expected, to "get away from it all" and remove themselves entirely from collective life. Some secrecy is usually preserved about their destination, with only a few chosen persons in on the secret. Seldom in the life of the average individual are the threads binding him or her to society so few and so slackened.

At the honeymoon resort they are entirely without obligations and responsibilities. No one knows them or expects anything from them. They are more or less taboo, and others leave them to themselves. The emotional privacy so difficult to obtain at all other times is for the moment almost universally granted. But this period is characteristically brief, save for the very wealthy; the couple returns to the community, establishes a household, resumes old ties, assumes new responsibilities, "puts away childish things," and "the honeymoon is over."

But how are we to account for the exception? The most reasonable interpretation would seem to be the same as was applied to the narcissistic leader: The married couple is allowed to hoard their libido between themselves "as a reserve against their later momentous constructive activity." By this I refer not only to the begetting and raising of children but to the more general process of creating a home and becoming a family. For marriage is after all a compromise institution—one that attempts to generate a substructure that will be solid enough to perform its social functions without becoming so solid that it begins to seek autonomy. The wedding ceremony tends to guard against the latter, while the honeymoon helps to ensure the former. Some marriages, after all, do not begin with a withdrawn dyad but with one that has scarcely experienced any privacy, intimacy, or freedom.

The reaction to honeymoons expresses itself primarily in going-away pranks of various kinds, whereby the most serious honeymoon taboos may be broken in a joking context. A great deal of hostility is expressed directly toward the departing couple in the form of such gestures as throwing rice and confetti. Some of the customary jokes have the covert purpose of hindering the couple's departure. These include tampering with the couple's automobile, hiding their luggage, etc. Furthermore, signs, streamers, or tin cans fastened to the car, stones put in the hubcaps, and confetti serve to make the couple conspicuous and thus minimize or negate the sense of privacy that has been granted to them. The importance of this maneuver appears when we recall that lack of self-awareness is commonly seen as an essential attribute of intimate lovers.

These practical jokes show the social anxiety aroused. In more totalitarian communities in which the honeymoon does not exist, the mere possibility of an emotional withdrawal on the part of the newlyweds may call forth more extreme antiwithdrawal mechanisms such as the charivari or shivaree, which serve as a reminder that the couple has not and cannot evade the community in which it is rooted.

POSTMARITAL INTRUSION

The birth of the first child tends to weaken the exclusive intimacy of the couple, first, by providing an important alternative (and narcissistic) object of attachment for each member and, second, by creating responsibilities and obligations that are partly social in nature, and that strengthen the bond between the dyad and the community. This helps to explain the intense and often hostile reaction toward young couples who announce their decision not to have any children.

The phenomenon is also striking in recreational activities, which fall largely into two categories: those that involve a reshuffling of partners and those that separate the sexes. Occasionally we find both, as in the case of the traditional Victorian dinner party during which husband and wife were always seated apart and after which the sexes retired to separate rooms. In our society, separation by sexes is more prevalent in the working class, while the reshuffling of partners prevails in the middle class. It would not be too much an exaggeration to say that all types of mixed-group recreational activities in the middle class are rooted in larval forms of adulterous flirtation. Married couples who stay too much together in such situations are disapproved.

The extent of such flirtation varies a good deal. The more traditional groups limit themselves to mixing bridge and dancing partners and frown on spontaneous expressions of sexual interest. More commonly one finds groups in which open flirtation in a joking context is expected but must be carried on in the presence of the group. Finally, there are those communities that are organized on a completely adulterous basis, wherein spouse trading is widely practiced. Here the group norms merely prohibit permanent attachments.

While this latter form is something of a special case, it may in general be said that adulterous flirtation in social groups is a cohesive force that prevents the marital bond from disintegrating the community.

EXTRAMARITAL INTRUSION

If the marital dyad is institutionalized, the extramarital dyad usually is not. In our society as a whole, extramarital sexuality is prohibited, although often approved by subgroups within it. Since it is forbidden, one would expect the extramarital dyad to be the most free from societal intrusion and control—to provide the most favorable context for dyadic withdrawal.

To a certain extent this is true. It is not accidental that most of the great love affairs of history and fiction are extramarital. In most societies, past and present, there has been very little choice in marriage, and intimacy has often been restricted to the more voluntary extramarital relationship. But it is easy to exaggerate the freedom of such relationships. In general, it may be said that the higher the incidence of affairs in a given society, the greater will be the society's intrusion on them, especially with regard to sexual choice. In many societies in which extramarital sexuality is universal, choice is restricted to a few relatives.[4] The stronger the prohibition, the more individual choice is limited by situational factors; while the weaker the prohibition, the more choice will be limited by group norms.

To begin with, there are the general norms that decide sexual attractiveness and that apply to all relationships, not only the extramarital. Sexual appeal has been based on painting the body and face, wearing bizarre clothing, putting rings in the nose, in the ears, around the neck, on the wrists, fingers, ankles, or arms; disfiguring (by scarring, stretching, or pitting) parts of the body—to mention only the cosmetic conventions. To foreigners these embellishments often seem strikingly ugly and sexless, and in a complex society such as our own it is not unusual to hear complaints to this effect even from natives.

Left to themselves, human beings would mate entirely in response to instinctual demands and psychological attraction. The establishment of socially defined aesthetic norms brings sexual choice under social control—one can maximize one's sexual attractiveness by conforming to social codes of taste. The fact that such a code may create an effect that is asexual or even repulsive (by foreign standards) is an index of the need and ability of collectives to control eroticism—to socialize sexuality.

An excellent example of this process may be found in our own society. Comments have often been made on the enormous emphasis placed on deodorants, perfumes, and colognes in the

United States. Body odors are of paramount importance in the sexual life of animals and have always played a large, but apparently decreasing role in human sexuality. Sexual appeal was once determined primarily by the intensity of odors emanating from sexual secretions. But these have now become taboo. Erotic value is instead attached to absence of natural odors and has been displaced on to odors that are advertised and packaged and may be purchased in a store. This means that sexual appeal can be restricted to certain people and made conditional upon certain acts. It also means that the criteria of attractiveness may be integrated with the other values of society: If beauty can be bought, it becomes a part of the society's monetary reward system. "Rich" becomes "beautiful."

What applies to choice also applies to the conduct of the affair. When extramarital relationships are tolerated or encouraged by the community, they are usually governed by a variety of conventions that tend to forestall dyadic withdrawal. These conventions may be grouped roughly into three categories:

Impermanency It is often considered poor form in such groups to retain the same lover for long periods. The person who changes partners rapidly gains the most prestige, while the one who is slow in shifting affections suffers ridicule from the group. In such a situation the end of the relationship becomes almost a more important issue than its beginning. Each partner is constantly on the alert for signs of flagging interest in the other, lest he or she be caught in the embarrassing predicament of not being the first to find a new partner. The effect of this pattern is to keep the dyadic ties weak and shallow and prevent the kind of emotional commitment that is a precondition for dyadic withdrawal.

Romantic Stylization Communities that approve extramarital sexuality often develop elaborate and detailed customs for initiating, maintaining, and terminating love affairs. This has generally been the rule in aristocratic groups. When it occurs, intimacy becomes difficult due to the formal, gamelike manner in which the affair is conducted.

Romantic stylization is simply one further example of the socialization of sexuality through appeal to vanity. Just as there are fashions in sexual desirability, so also are there fashions in sexual etiquette, and these rules, while they last, will be just as indispensable and just as asexual as a ring in the nose or paint on the face. The important issue is that behavior, like perception, be socially conditioned, not left to the instinctual tendencies of the dyadic partners.

Time-Space Constriction Whether an extramarital relationship is short-lived or lasting, stylized or free, it is often the rule that it must be conducted only at specified times and places. Such constriction of the relationship may, of course, arise purely from the fact that it is forbidden. But often it is a socially prescribed limitation. The affair is approved so long as it is "kept in its place."

One example of this is the demand that affairs be conducted on a clandestine basis even when everyone knows of their existence. The explanation usually offered for this practice is the alleged attraction of "forbidden fruit," but this does not account for the motivation of the community to collaborate in the pretence. I would suggest that the demand for clandestine behavior is a way of limiting the scope and depth of the relationship. Time-space restriction ensures that each of the partners is drawn away from the dyad and into the community during the greater part of his or her everyday life. The intimacy of the relationship is decreased by the fact that each partner knows the other only in a very limited and narrow context. If a degree of intimacy does arise in such a relationship its first expression is a demand for more freedom and "sunlight," but when the couple comes into the open the reaction of other group members is typically one of shock and contempt. Extension of the dyadic relationship into other areas of everyday life is considered "out of place."

DYADIC WITHDRAWAL AND DEATH

In the preceding discussion it might seem as if we had pursued dyadic withdrawal into its last remaining stronghold only to watch this stronghold collapse. Where intimacy is frequent, it appears to be ephemeral, and where it is lasting, it seems to be rare. Societal intrusion seems effectively to forestall whatever tendencies toward dyadic withdrawal may appear.

It is perhaps for this reason that dyadic withdrawal is such a popular theme in the myths, legends, and dramas of Western civilization. Yet even in fantasy such withdrawals are always short-lived, ending usually in dissolution or death. Apparently a lifelong dyadic withdrawal is unimaginable, for to my knowledge there is no instance of such a phenomenon in the fantasy productions of any culture.

But in death a kind of permanent dyadic withdrawal *is* achieved, and this is the appeal that stories of tragic lovers hold. In real life and in comedies dyadic withdrawal usually ends in societal absorption unless the couple separates. This does not mean that the relationship is any less satisfying—the couple may indeed "live happily ever after" as in the fairy tale. But the dyad loses some of its exclusiveness and self-sufficiency and ceases to be a social threat. Some of the libido previously withdrawn into the dyad flows back into larger groups, and some of the needs funneled into the dyad begin to seek fulfillment in a wider setting.

The great tragic lovers of fiction, however, are always set in opposition to social forces and are always destroyed by them. But their relationship is not. They die or are buried together, the dyadic bond untainted by social intrusion. The immortality of this bond and of their withdrawal is often symbolized by plants or trees growing out of their graves and entwining.

We have encountered this theme before in our discussion of the death of the narcissistic villain-hero: The crime of narcissistic withdrawal receives public punishment, that is, death, and private reward, that is, escape from socialization. So also with the crime of dyadic withdrawal in fiction. It is initially achieved, satisfying the desire of the spectator, and subsequently punished, relieving his social anxiety. But in spite of the punishment, society is really cheated since the withdrawal is never really reversed, and both the couple and the withdrawal remain immortally intact. A moral victory is won for the forces of withdrawal, one in which the spectators can privately participate with secret applause, like Irishmen applauding an Irish villain in an English play.

Thus, the great tragic lovers of fiction actively desire and seek death. But this longing for death is a longing for an end to life in a social context. It is a desire to return to a more primitive, more simple, and more fully satisfying form of libidinal involvement and a turning away from what is felt as an over-diffusion of libido.

THE POSTPARTUM DYAD

Let us now complete the circle and return to the living, for while in fantasy life ends in a dyadic withdrawal, in reality it begins in one. The dyad in question is that of the mother and newborn infant. For it is extremely rare for a woman to undergo pregnancy without a certain amount of narcissistic withdrawal or to tend an infant without entering into a dyadic relationship with it that involves considerable withdrawal from other people. The fact that one member is experiencing libidinal withdrawal (the mother), while the other merely has not yet undergone libidinal diffusion (the child) differentiates it from all other forms of dyadic withdrawal.

Both the earlier narcissistic and the later dyadic withdrawal are tolerated by the community for reasons that the reader will by this time have anticipated. Temporary withdrawal is permitted because it is perceived as creative and as leading to greater long-run diffusion on the part of all concerned.

Narcissistic withdrawal during pregnancy can be explained in terms of the mother's increased dependency needs. She must be allowed to hoard libido in order to later extend it to include another person: the child whom she sees as an extension of herself.[5] So the mother retravels the lowest levels of libidinal withdrawal in order to seduce the child—through emotional involvement, narcissistic rewards, and nurturant gratification—into normal diffusion.

But whenever withdrawal takes place, there is a social danger. Here the danger is that the mother will remain fixed in her narcissistic withdrawal, as in the case of postpartum depression, or be unable to relinquish her early symbiotic relationship with the child.[6]

There are a number of social mechanisms that serve to offset these withdrawals. Rituals taking place when the child is born, for example, resemble the marriage ceremony in their tendency to stake a social claim in the new relationship. In our society it is the hospitalization rite that creates the illusion that the mother would be unable to bear a child without community assistance—the physicians merely replacing the old women who gather around in so many primitive societies. Instead of producing a child herself, it is "given" to her, first by the obstetrician, later by nurses; and her own role in the situation is often obliterated by anaesthesia. It is typically several days before she can call it her own, and by this time she will be highly conscious of the extent to which the birth of her child has been a group effort.

At a more informal level, there are showers and other gift-giving arrangements to provide reminders of group ties, to let everyone participate in the event in some way, and to create group obligations that must be repaid.

Normally, this flurry of social activity around childbirth serves to inhibit dyadic withdrawal to a considerable extent. A strong marital dyad also drastically limits the likelihood of withdrawal, but where this does not occur, dyadic withdrawal in the form of a continued mother-child symbiosis arouses unanimous social disapproval.

FAMILIAL WITHDRAWAL

A major social limitation of the withdrawn dyad is that, however self-sufficient it may appear to be, it cannot reproduce itself. This limitation is remedied when we move to the third potential product of withdrawal, the autonomous nuclear family. Here for the first time we encounter a true collective, a miniature society that is potentially immortal.

Familial withdrawal occurs whenever a nuclear family becomes emotionally or libidinally sufficient unto itself, and partial expressions of this state are often seen. But it is quite obvious that such a condition can neither go very far nor persist very long without the occurrence of incest.

Since the danger of total familial withdrawal is as hypothetical as

in the case of the other forms, and since it is the least extreme of
the three, why is the incest taboo stronger than the taboos surrounding more severe forms of libidinal withdrawal?

The answer is that the incest taboo does not militate specifically
against familial withdrawal but is a general "outpushing" force, and
can be seen as having its most direct influence against incestuous
dyadic withdrawal. The three types of withdrawal necessarily par-
take of each other and are not entirely separate and unique. Dyadic withdrawal is far more likely to occur if the attachment is narcissistic (based on resemblances between the partners), and
incestuous relationships are in part tabooed because they are
closer to absolute narcissism than any other relationship can be.

Let us bear in mind that while there are only three types of heterosexual incest, there are almost as many types of family organization that could be based on *some* form of incest as there are
types that reject *all* forms. This is usually ignored in discussions of
the functions of the incest taboo, it being assumed that a lifting of
the great ban would be followed by unbridled promiscuity and
chaos. Yet when we look at the variety of family patterns, both in
"primitive" and civilized societies, we must believe that some
limiting and structuring would take place. This is true of the few
instances of a full-fledged and enduring incestuous family pattern
that we have: The Ptolemaic and Hawaiian royal families were
both based on brother-sister incest alone.[7]

Even if we assumed some kind of primeval normlessness, with
the family structure based on physical power alone, we would not
expect random mating but a pattern reflecting the power structure. The prevailing form of incest would thus be father-daughter
incest, with the other forms strongly inhibited by force. This is
Freud's "primal horde."

It would be more difficult to envision a stable family structure
built on mother-son incest simply because the potential for dyadic
withdrawal would be so high. Intimate communication is very easily established between incestuous partners due to the biological
and cultural similarities between them, not to mention the great
range of shared experiences. But this essentially narcissistic ele-
ment is particularly strong in the relationship between mother and

son since each has at one time viewed the other as a part of or extension of the self. It is in part for this reason that mother-son incest is of all forms the most severely prohibited.[8]

We should not leave the topic of familial withdrawal without considering the tolerated "exceptions" that we have found in the other forms of withdrawal. George Murdock points out that institutionalized violations of the incest taboo are restricted to royal or aristocratic families, the conscious purpose being to keep such families separate and impermeable.[9] The position of these families is identical to that of the narcissistic leader, in whom libidinal withdrawal is encouraged so that he or she may bear the burdens of responsibility more easily.

Although this exception appears rarely in actual royal families, it is very much the rule in mythological ones. Not only are all major deities the world over narcissistic, but in all polytheistic systems the divine families are incorrigibly incestuous. One of the few traits held in common by Greek and Judaic gods is that they are motivated almost exclusively by vanity, and are aroused to anger only by narcissistic injuries. In order to create a powerful and attractive nucleus that will focus libidinal diffusion for the earthly community, the libido of the gods must be concentrated and intense, according to the principle that libido attracts libido. For upon these deities rests the solidarity of the community.

But it is not only as leaders and libidinal foci that the gods must hoard their energy; it is also as creators. The demiurges and ancestors of the gods are most particularly likely to be incestuous; theirs is, after all, the most "momentous constructive activity" imaginable.

A LITERARY ILLUSTRATION

The best examples of social and psychological processes always come from literature. Although inadmissible as evidence, they provide superior illustrations, by forcefully condensing many trends into a compact and dramatic instance.

Thus the best example of libidinal withdrawal is a story by Thomas Mann entitled "The Blood of the Walsungs," which deals with an incestuous relationship between a twin brother and sister, identical in feature, personality, and attitude.[10] Familial withdrawal is expressed in the contrast drawn between the family and outsiders; dyadic withdrawal in the twins' gaze "melting together in an understanding from which everybody else was shut out"; narcissistic withdrawal in Mann's comparing them to "self-centered invalids," in the brother's constant contemplation of his own image in the mirror, and in the final outburst of identification that immediately precedes their climactic copulation, an outburst in which the brother mutters (with rather careless oversight), "Everything about you is just like me."

The "erotic," nonutilitarian quality of the relationship is emphasized repeatedly by Mann. He speaks of their absorbing themselves in "trifles," of days passing "vacantly," of their having "doffed aside the evil-smelling world and loved each other alone, for the priceless sake of their own rare uselessness." The lower senses, particularly of smell, are insistently stressed:. "They loved each other with all the sweetness of the senses, each for the other's spoilt and costly well-being and delicious fragrance."

Finally, the absence of other social ties is conveyed both explicitly and symbolically. The most telling expression is their journey to the theatre in a carriage, in which their social isolation is dramatized by the nearness of the city: "Round them roared and shrieked and thundered the machinery of urban life. Quite safe and shut away they sat among the wadded brown silk cushions, hand in hand."

This relationship epitomizes libidinal withdrawal, or contraction, in its introversion, its rejection of partial and scattered attachments, its conservatism. One can argue about its satisfactoriness, but it is clear that it does not leave a sufficient residue of tension on which to build a group structure. Only when a man falls in love with a stranger while some of his energy is still harnessed to an incestuous relationship will he be inclined to attach himself to a larger agglomeration that embraces them both. In so doing, he sacrifices total gratification and gains whatever benefits accrue from social existence. One might also maintain that he gains life, for it is only in death that utter peace is found.

"Life is impoverished, it loses in interest, when
the highest stake in living, life itself, may not be
risked."

—Freud

Chapter 12

EMOTIONAL PRIORITIES

Psychoanalysts speak of illness, aging, and death as a process of
withdrawing "libido" from the world, especially from other people.
At times they seem to mean that some sort of *interest* is being
withdrawn, at other times a kind of *energy*.[1] Freud gives the
clearest clue when he argues: "The future may teach us how to exercise a direct influence, by means of particular chemical sub-
stances, upon the amounts of energy and their distribution in the
apparatus of the mind."[2] He seems to be talking about the distribution of some sort of energy in the brain itself.

G. Rattray Taylor, in a summary of the remaining differences
between computers and the human brain, notes that the brain cell
"does not treat (the inputs it receives) as being equivalent . . .
some signals are given greater importance than others." But "the
methods by which it judges relevance remain completely mysterious."[3]

> The exact way in which feeling becomes attached to data is
> crucial . . . it can become attached to elements in the situation
> and even to words . . . In a practical physiological way, we
> know absolutely nothing about how this takes place. We can
> suspect it is connected with the changing chemical patterns in
> the brain. . ."[4]

141

Some mechanism must exist to give some pieces of data more importance than others, and it would seem logical that this should be connected in some way with stimulation of the pleasure centers of the brain.[5] When we talk about libido flowing here and there— out on to social objects, back on to the ego or a part of the body— we are referring to the energizing of brain cells. We are saying that some messages or connections are being given priority over others, and that these priorities are in turn determined by the strength of their connection with the pleasure centers of the brain. When we say that libido "flows" on to an object, or that a person "cathects" another person, we are saying that some chemical adjustment has taken place whereby information relating to that person is given higher priority, and that this adjustment has occurred because of the expectation of greater stimulation of the pleasure centers. When we speak of "transference" in the psychoanalytic sense, we are referring to the fact that when connections are established between new stimuli (teachers or therapists) and highly charged old stimuli (parents), some of the "emotional charge" from the old will attach itself to the new. Furthermore, the brain constantly searches for such connections since the early stimulus or person carries such an emotional charge. This search takes the course of least resistance, following the pathways already determined by the characteristics of the original stimulus (or person) and seeking resemblances to the new one.

Ambivalence toward the original person or relationship, usually a parent, might inhibit the permanent transfer of the "emotional charge." We would expect, for example, that stimuli coming from the mother (or whoever provided the early nurturing) are given the highest priority for many years since most erotic gratification comes from this source. This will be particularly true in a society like ours, less in societies in which feeding, holding, caressing, etc., are shared by many persons, or in which the amount of erotic stimulation is minimal. Psychoanalysts use the term "maternal fixation" to refer to the persistence of this priority far beyond the age when it is appropriate.

Paradoxically, however, such persistence seems to occur when it involves painful experiences as well as when the child receives much gratification. The more unhappy a relationship, the more the individual seems to be unable to move beyond it. The truly idyllic childhood often seems to be the easiest left behind, while the miserable child may grow up to a nostalgic and regressed adulthood.

It seems that painful experiences with a high-priority person act to inhibit the transfer of this "emotional charge" to a current relationship, while the relative absence of such experiences permits it to move more freely to new connections. Perhaps the expectation of pain from the new experience prevents the transfer, forcing the person back into the same old patterns, endlessly repeated. It is not so much a compulsion to repeat as a compulsive inability for the brain to cathect a new pathway.

The most striking example of this phenomenon is found in mourning. As Freud implies in "Mourning and Melancholia," it is when there is strong hostility toward the lost person that mourning becomes difficult and slow.[6]

Freud also observes that a mourner may hallucinate about a lost love. This hallucination takes the same form no matter whether it is another person or a part of one's own body that is lost. What perseveres is the structure of priorities in the brain, and it doesn't matter what they refer to in reality. The "phantom limb" experiences of amputees are precisely the same as the hallucinations of the bereaved. Indeed, the use of the term "phantom" in the above phrase serves to remind us that the very idea of ghosts, which is practically universal, is an expression of this phenomenon. Most societies hold the belief that the spirits of the dead hover around the living for a time and are dispersed only at the conclusion of funeral rites or a prescribed mourning period, or upon finally being told or magically compelled to depart. These ancestral shades are simply the "phantom limbs" of the society, persisting until they have been decathected by their loved ones, that is, until the mourning process has fulfilled its course as described by Freud:

"Each single one of the memories and hopes which bound the libido to the object is brought up and hyper-cathected, and the detachment of the libido from it accomplished."[7]

In other words, the priority system must be restructured by

consciously reassessing its structure piece by piece in this ritualistic fashion.

INTROVERSION

Another variable affecting the way "emotional charges" are shifted is the overall speed or rate at which they are transferred. Freud called it "adhesiveness of libido," and viewed it as one of the "fundamental characteristics of the mental apparatus." Those with high "adhesiveness of libido", he says, "cannot make up their minds to detach libidinal cathexes from one object and displace them to another." There is increased "psychic inertia," so that "all the mental processes, relations and distributions of energy are immutable, fixed and rigid. One finds the same state of affairs in very old people." In those with low "adhesiveness," on the other hand, libidinal cathexes are "evanescent" and never to be counted upon.[8]

From this description "adhesiveness of libido" seems to be identical with Jung's term "introversion." [9] The terms "shallow-broad" for extrovert and "deep-narrow" for introvert seem to describe aptly the different nature of the priority systems of the two.

This suggests a continuum that we might call "steepness of the emotional priority system"—the extent to which a person tends to put all of his or her emotional eggs in one basket. "Steep" people tend to invest in few people deeply; "level" people tend to treat all people as having equal potential for providing gratification. Steepness is associated with introversion, "adhesiveness of libido," age, and the inability to adapt to alterations in the gratificatory economy of the environment. "Levelness" is associated with extraversion, nonadhesiveness, youth, adaptability, fickleness, and impulsivity. Levelness occurs when all social stimuli are equally important to the child (many adults and siblings provide nurturance), steepness when the child is more exclusively nurtured by one person. Lack of *any* gratification leads to extremely shallow and impermanent relationships, while intense ambivalence in the maternal relationship leads to a relational life built entirely on transference. Romantic love, for example, is rooted in the persistence of such intense oedipal fantasies and is an extreme form of "steepness."

We are now in a position to understand more fully what "delay of gratification" is all about. For note that we have linked a "level" priority system with impulsivity, with the inability to postpone satisfaction. To find the reason for this we must turn back to the child's relationship to the mother.

Clearly, the ability to delay gratification is linked to the idea that people and objects are *differentially* gratifying. One would not be willing to wait if all people and things were viewed as equally rewarding. The underlying principle of postponement is one of relinquishing an immediate but lesser gratification for a more distant but greater one. Delay of gratification cannot be separated from the concept of an emotional hierarchy.

But the establishment of such a hierarchy, as well as its steepness, comes from the nature of the child's experience with the mother. Insofar as a single person (a) provides intense gratification and (b) provides far more gratification than any other person, a steep hierarchy will develop. The child will be willing to forgo immediate gratifications because of confidence in the availability of a more complete one—the love, protection, and caresses of the mothering one.

The steepest type of priority hierarchy, occurring most strongly in Western societies, is the so-called oedipus complex. Increased focus on the sexual organs, together with increased understanding of marriage as a possessive and exclusive contract, achieved by the adequate performance of adult roles, generates in the male child the fantasy that by relinquishing childish pleasures he can obtain total possession of the mother, and hence a gratification superior to any heretofore imagined. The situation is a little different with female children since these changes are typically associated with a partial transfer of emotional cathexis from the mother to the father.

Normally, this fantasy is associated with growing attachments to others, increasingly distant from the original love object (though usually cathected because of some resemblance), so that by the time adulthood is reached, much of the energy bound up in the fantasy is available to attach itself to new and unrelated relationships.

But occasionally, as Freud has described so tellingly, the fantasy remains in its original form, unconscious and clinging to its first love.[10] A man with a priority system organized around such an oedipal fantasy may build his entire life and career on it. Underneath his ceaseless striving, his harsh self-imposed deprivations, and his unflinching determination, lies the romantic and totally unconscious assumption that one day, in this world or the next, he will, by his having achieved fame, glory, power, wealth, or whatever, win access to exclusive possession of his mother. As the years go by, this woman becomes withered and old and ultimately dies, but as Freud emphasizes so repeatedly, nothing changes or ages in the unconscious, and as a fantasy she remains beautiful, ageless, and eternal. Indeed, our hero may "delay gratification" with the same permanence and pursue his fantasy right into the grave. The fascination of poets with the beauties of bygone ages and with unavailable and lethal women in general testifies to the intensity and pervasiveness of this fantasy.

This agelessness of the fantasy mother, who remains young and beautiful while her real counterpart fades and dies, represents the unchanging mental system: Connections involving "mother" still have extremely high priority, even though they involve imagined gratifications that are no longer sought in actual interactions with the mother or in any real relationship at all. Gratification becomes a kind of ultimate fantasy prize, to be awarded when the tasks that the person has for this reason been able to get involved in are finally performed.

PAIN AND LIBIDO

It is universally known . . . that a person suffering organic pain and discomfort relinquishes his interest in the things of the outside world, insofar as they do not concern his suffering. Closer observation teaches us that at the same time he withdraws his libidinal interest from his love-objects: so long as he suffers, he ceases to love. The banality of this fact is no reason why we should be deterred from translating it into terms of the libido-theory. We should then say: the sick man withdraws his libidinal cathexes back upon his own ego, and sends them forth again when he recovers. 'Concentrated is his soul,' says W. Busch, of the poet suffering from toothache, 'in his jaw tooth's aching hole.' " [11]

The normal priority system has somehow been superseded by another principle during suffering. Regardless of the flatness or steepness of the priority system, pain or other bodily discomfort is a signal for a concentration of interest in the affected area. We are thus dealing here with the extent to which energy is diffused over many connections or contracted into a few.

Our assumption that energy is concentrated in the affected organ may be doubted, for all that we can actually observe is a *loss* of libidinal interest in other objects and people. How can we say that there is an accumulation anywhere else? We can see that a sick or wounded person is enormously preoccupied with him- or herself, but have we any grounds for calling this libidinal, even in the sense in which we have used this term? What is the anticipated gratification in the poet with the toothache? Is it simply the cessation of the pain or discomfort?

We can best understand the libidinal nature of this process from making a few simple observations. If a person bumps a leg on a chair, the automatic and immediate response will be to rub the injured part. If I cut my hand, I will rapidly put it to my mouth and suck the wound unless I have been rigidly trained from early childhood not to. In a purely physiological sense this is not necessarily functional, and doctors often forbid such instinctive reactions, particularly with children, lest they aggravate the injury. It may even increase the pain, as when a person rubs a fracture; or create a new one, as when a tongue is rubbed raw on a broken tooth. What, then, is the basis of this response? Why does an animal lick its wounds?

It seems clear that what is involved is a kind of primitive caress. The organism attempts to give pleasure to its injured part. In these gestures we observe the same fusion of sensuous eroticism on the one hand and solicitous nurturance on the other, which we normally associate with the care of an infant. Certain peculiarities of language also express this relation, such as the verb "to nurse," which means at once to give a child the breast and to care for the ill. We talk of "nursing a cold," and almost all folk remedies involve either ingestions of some substance through the mouth or titillating the skin in some way. We speak of "dressing a wound," and the French make the connection even more dramatic with the verb *panser*, which means not only to "dress a wound" but is also used in relation to the grooming of horses. How is it that this complex of rubbing, brushing, washing, petting, and pampering comes to be applied to illness and injury in the same way as to babies and pets?

Let us consider another phenomenon. We observe that although animals and humans may seek to "retire from the field to lick their wounds," humans, at least, are usually unable to achieve such withdrawal. The moment a person falls ill, there is a tendency for others to cluster around and take care of him. This is mitigated in our own society somewhat by our magical fears of contagion but is institutionalized in the practice of hospitalization. In some nonliterate societies in which there is less belief in contagion, a severely ill person may draw 30 or 40 people into a small dwelling. The process of treating the sick person, furthermore, again recalls the care of the infant. He is relieved from all normal responsibilities and permitted the total passivity and dependency of the infant. He is "nursed back to health" by being put to bed, fed, and generally cared for as if he were helpless.

With the onset of illness, one may become "narcissistic," withdrawing libidinal interest from those around him. (See Chapter 11.) They, on the other hand, seem to be unusually interested in him—we may even say that they have "hypercathected" him. Most important of all, when the illness is over, when he has been "nursed back to health," we discover that his "narcissistic" behavior has vanished, that he has "recathected" those around him and diffused his libido into the world again.

We suspect that the community attempts, through nurturant

behavior, to seduce the person into energizing those mental connections that involve the seeking of pleasure from other people. I am suggesting, in other words, as I did in the previous chapter, that people spontaneously respond to narcissistic withdrawal on the part of one of their number with behavior designed to terminate it.

Furthermore, the animal that licks its wound is applying to a part of its body the same principle as the group applies to its injured member. In both cases a contraction of libido occurs, and an effort is made by those systems from which it has been withdrawn to bring about its rediffusion throughout the system. The human organism is, after all, merely one link in a long chain of organic structures, and we may assume that there are important biological principles that operate through all of these. It seems reasonable to imagine that libido serves to bind structures of all kinds and hence can be said to exist quite independently of specific organisms.

We have consistently compared treatment of ill or injured parts with the treatment of infants, and we might now observe one additional parallel, namely, that the infant is also outside of the system and in the process of being drawn into it. Life begins with erotic stimulation—the child is, as it were, seduced into the world through pleasurable stimulation. As we know from the studies of Spitz this seduction is vital for human existence: The child must be eroticized in order to live, just as the wound must be eroticized in order to heal.[12]

With many mammals this relationship is even more dramatic. The mother animal will wash her offspring by licking them all over, and if this stimulation is for any reason omitted, they will usually fail to begin breathing. The sexual basis of this process is sharply underlined in a study by Birch [13] of female rats who were prevented from licking their genitals by placing large collars around their necks until just prior to parturition. When they had their litters they neither licked their own genitals nor their offspring, and the latter died. This would seem to be rather strong evidence of the importance of sexuality in the economy of social interaction—one might even say it is the medium of exchange, just as Talcott Parsons has suggested that pleasure is the money of the

organism. (See Chapter 15.) The newborn will not live until it receives erotic stimulation from the mother, and the mother will not
perform this social function until she has associated the newborn
with erotic self-stimulation.

I am reminded here of Grace Stuart's analysis of narcissism as
resulting from a lack of erotic stimulation. Of particular interest is
her notion that the selfish, self-indulgent behavior of the narcissist
is in reality an awkward attempt at therapy—that is, through nurturing and gratifying his own ego, he tries to cure the disease by
removing its cause.[14] Presumably this would be successful insofar
as the cause is immediate, and unsuccessful insofar as the condition is a more chronic one arising from earlier deprivations. People
often advise one who shows signs of becoming ill to "take care of
himself" or to "pamper the flesh a little."

One may even wonder if the orgasm that occurs when a man is
hanged or undergoes a similar agony does not involve a similar
process. The trauma is so violent that the usual libidinal forces are
activated with a comparable intensity. The brain engages in a
rapid and desperate search operation to determine what connections should be energized to prevent dissolution, but in vain, and
the accumulated energy is orgasmically expended in a final and
useless adjustive response.

But, as I said in the last chapter, it is not only the individual
who makes such attempts to ward off death through collective
seduction. One frequently finds the community behaving the same
way. A death almost always activates collective behavior of some
kind or another—a drawing together, a social integration—as well
as some sort of loving behavior toward the corpse.

We thus find an analogous process occurring at several different
organic levels. It would seem crudely correct to say that (1) organisms show a tendency to de-energize their attachments to other
organisms when under stress, and that (2) these other organisms
show a tendency to hyperenergize their connections to the organisms that withdraw.

To understand how libido organizes social structures, let us return to Parsons' analogue of pleasure as the currency of the body,
"a way of imposing order on still lower level processes." [15] Just as

money organizes activity by creating a common motivation for that activity, so the pleasure principle organizes structures through similar consolidation of motivation. (See Chapter 15.) Each organic structure borrows libido from those of which it's composed.

The prevention of total tension discharge is the "goal" of this transfer. So long as libido is diffused over several objects such complete discharge is impossible, and life will go on.

According to psychoanalytic theory, for example, the early incestuous attachments of a person are never entirely abandoned. While in a healthy person the bulk of this involvement is transferred to new loves, fragments always remain, generating residual tensions whose discharge is relegated to the realm of dreams and fantasy. The incest taboo, of course, enforces this transfer, pushing the libido outward—diffusing it, in other words. In the absence of such a taboo there might be total libidinal quiescence. That is, if all of the sexual energy of an individual were tied up in one object, then it could be utterly discharged through that object, and the "goal" of the death instinct would be achieved. The incest taboo and a host of other social norms effectively see to it that this never occurs, for so long as an individual has libidinal attachments to more than one person, he or she will be unable to achieve a total absence of libidinal tension. Such tension can be diverted into a variety of new attachments, which serve to link together and bind large numbers of people in libidinal networks, further ensuring the permanence of this same tension. Any tendency toward short-circuiting this network arouses anxiety in all those who participate in it, as we saw in the last chapter.

TENSION REDUCTION AND DEATH

For Freud, death was the ultimate end of tension, the quiescence toward which all living matter moved. He saw life as a state of tension thrust on us by some overwhelming catastrophe of stimulation that not only began all the turmoil but continually drives us farther and farther from our goal, like a panic-stricken child lost in the forest. The increasingly roundabout paths to gratification prolong tension and thereby life itself. Death is hence a kind of ultimate orgasm, an escape from stimuli and motion. The person who consciously seeks death is expressing a longing for closure, an end to the uncertainty of human experience in which every ending is but another beginning, and every simplicity hides another complexity.

Yet while such feelings arise in all of us (for even sleep is a form of libidinal withdrawal, needed to shut off input and discharge the tensions of the day), it is by no means clear why or when stimulation becomes uncomfortable to the point at which a tension-reduction theory of this sort seems to make sense.

Freud confronts this problem rather briefly in his paper on narcissism:

> Of course curiosity will here suggest the question why such a damming-up of libido in the ego should be experienced as "painful." There I shall content myself with the answer that "pain" is in general the expression of increased tension, and thus a *quantity* of the material event is, here as elsewhere, transformed into the *quality* of "pain" in the mind . . .[16]

Since very mild stimulation can be experienced as pain, however, while very intense sexual stimulation is not, this hardly seems a solution to the problem. We could suggest a threshold effect; that is, that a certain level of accumulated tension must be reached before discharge can take place, and hence stimulation will be sought in the service of ultimate tension reduction. One could also argue that a stimulus is sought in order to unlock a *structure* that is tension-generating. In other words, we must think not in terms of a single impulse being discharged in a single moment, but rather of a complex system of interrelated impulses that is incapable of simultaneous total discharge so long as a person lives. It is always unclear whether a given stimulus will increase the overall tension level or decrease it (as a kind of unlocking mechanism).

It may be that the desire for pleasurable stimulation is initially linked to reduction of more basic tensions (e.g., hunger) and retains this association throughout life. But the licking of newborn mammals by the mother is independent of the feeding process, and is not followed by stimulus avoidance but by an awakening interest in living. Hence it is a stimulus that seems to be both independent and pleasurable in its effect. The drive toward pleasurable stimulation may in the short run either raise or lower the tension level of a person, combating the drive toward tension reduction or being harnessed in its service; but in the long run the two stand in basic opposition, the drive toward pleasurable stimulation holding our search for quiescence in temporary abeyance.[17]

THE PROBLEM OF BOUNDARY MAINTENANCE

The maintenance of psychic boundaries separating the self from the rest of the world is an energy-consuming, tension-generating task. Boundary maintenance is, in fact, one of the major sources of tension, as we can observe in the fact that the subjective experience of boundary dissolution—if not resisted—is always accompanied by an intense feeling of tension release. The description of *nirvana*-like states always includes the notion of complete destruction of the artificial boundaries that make one feel separate from the unity of life.

This relationship between boundary maintenance and tension guarantees a certain delicacy in the handling of stimulation. An overloading of stimuli may lead to boundary destruction in an effort to discharge the accumulation, and indeed, peaks of stimulation and tension are often experienced subjectively as ego shattering. It's possible that certain somatic failures, such as heart attacks, are examples of this process.

On the other hand, the bodily structures themselves are highly dependent on erotic stimulation for their maintenance. Ferenczi and Alexander have both described vividly the way in which body functions are first exercized for the erotic pleasure they provide and are only later organized into a complex interdependent system in which the erotic goal of each individual organ is relinquished in favor of a utilitarian one that benefits the whole structure. At this point, according to Ferenczi, the system develops a specialized organ, the genital, to discharge libidinal tension and thus free the other organs for these utilitarian functions.

An end to stimulation, then, particularly of an erotic kind, would be equally devastating to the equilibrium of the system. In fact, both overstimulation and understimulation produce loss of consciousness, and disruption of the constancy of stimulus input may produce permanent boundary loss. One cannot escape a peculiar metaphorical image of eroticism as a kind of Ariel-like, catalytic messenger in the service of biological development, appearing at every point at which growth and evolution are problematic. Although purely poetic, we may carry the metaphor to the point of wondering whether, as organisms and communities age, utilitarianism wins the day altogether so that no organic function is any longer an end in itself, the spritely messenger having taken himself off to where he was more strongly needed.

Chapter 13

DUALITIES

It is a common error to view a whole as developing historically from its parts. A complex structure arises not from its current elements but from a simpler structure. The human organism was not created by a union of cells but through an evolution from a simpler structure of cells. Similarly, the 13 American colonies did not create a new structure but already represented a whole: a common language, common customs, common problems, and a prior political edifice. The "union" they created was simply an improvement and elaboration of their existing structure.

Such improvements are in essence a rearrangement of the internal contradictions that every system contains. For the internal contradictions of a system are not merely historical accidents to be swept away by utopian logic but are essential to the maintenance of the system itself. Every system needs change and stability, deviation and conformity, creation and destruction, cooperation and competition, individualism, and collectivism.[1]

Compromise is, of course, the temporary outcome of most contradictions, but it does little to remove the tension of the conflict. One frequent outcome of compromise is overelaboration: Unusual complexity in rules and procedures, for example, is a handy index of conflict in bureaucratic settings.

There is no meaningful compromise (to use one of Gideon Sjoberg's examples) between adhering to scientific procedures and violating those procedures, although both are essential to the growth of science. It is no solution to satisfy each contradictory need halfway any more than it is a solution to divide a quart of blood between two injured men when each needs the whole quart to survive.

Sometimes, instead of compromise, separate institutions emerge to satisfy the contradictory needs. Because this often threatens the integrity of the whole, the belief systems often emphasize and idealize one of a contradictory pair over the other. (Satirists, for example, have always delighted in contrasting the one-sided Christian emphasis on love and peace with the unrivaled blood-thirstiness of its proponents.) One of the pair thus tends to become overt, the other covert, one formal and official, the other informal and unofficial. Black markets, drug traffic, organized vice, pornography, and political machines are examples of informal, covert institutions that emerge to balance such one-sided belief systems.[2]

This creates a strain, however, between the belief system and the concrete institutions, between the need to suppress the covert institutions and the need to maintain them. One can try either to modify the belief system to make it more realistic (this will cause radicals and fundamentalists to cry out against the compromising of ethical values) or to eradicate the unofficial institutions so that the reality conforms to the belief. Such eradication is often attempted during revolutions and reform movements (such as the Inquisition). The savagery often shown in trying to establish consistency may occasionally achieve lasting results but, sooner or later, in some form or another, the "repressed" side returns. Needs that run counter to official ideology can be limited and suppressed only for a short time.

Actually, these two ways of resolving strain are always taking place simultaneously.[3] But social change comes more by rearranging the structure in which contradictory behaviors occur than by changing the behavior itself. This fact often converts idealists into cynics, since they are motivated by the vain hope that one of the contradictory needs can be altogether dispensed with. They are disappointed when they find some expression of it creeping back into the system in a new form, even though the new contradictory institutions may be vastly superior to the old in some respect.

CONTRADICTION WITHIN THE INDIVIDUAL

Ambivalence may be considered the keystone of individual motivation, just as contradictory needs are central to social systems. We can never be totally committed to any action, or totally absorbed in a single feeling toward a person, an object, or a goal. There are always competing and contradictory feelings and wishes: hate mixed with our love, love mixed with our hate. As in the case of social systems, tension arises when our belief system ignores this ambivalence. Since action seems to require a certain minimum level of simplicity and constancy, some such ignoring seems necessary in order to make action possible. In communication, statements such as "I am well," "I am sick," "I love you," and "I hate you" are gross oversimplifications, but one does not give the inquiring passer-by a catalogue of physical blemishes and minor complaints, although no one is without them; nor does he recite to the doctor the numerous ways in which his body is functioning brilliantly; nor does he qualify his declaration to his lover with a description of the situations in which he is irritated, disdainful, enraged, frightened, or even indifferent toward her; nor, finally, does he point out to his enemy the fascination that the latter has for him, the frequency with which he thinks of and talks about him, or how excited and alive he becomes when he has an opportunity to fight with him.

We also demand constancy in our perceptions of others. We take for granted the enormous mental effort that goes into maintaining a stable concept of another person in the face of changes in context and mood. Schizophrenics and people on LSD may experience these changes as real physical alterations in size, shape, and texture, at times so great as to bring into question the identity of the person. We tend to see this as pathological, but we should remember that the "normal" approach of saying that all events from birth to death, from morning to night, are experienced by the same entity is merely a conceptual convenience, however fundamental. And even "normals" occasionally suggest that someone has become a "different person."

A man who is too aware of the contrary forces operating within him is considered "indecisive," and many people considered "decisive" are also considered "capricious" because one side of their ambivalence is expressed one day and the other side the next. In order to act, we must exaggerate the differences between each feeling and its opposite. This is the basis of majority rule. The two-party system, precisely *because* it is a poorer reflection of the complexity of popular sentiment than a multiparty system, seems to lend itself more easily to decisive action. In the individual, action is achieved in part through repression.

We can understand this process through a familiar analogy. After a national election in the United States, we say that the nation "went Democratic" or "went Republican." By this we may mean that only a dozen seats in Congress changed sides, or that a fraction of 1 percent of the population changed its vote from the previous election. We do not call attention to the fact that about 90 percent of the vote never changes but remains more or less evenly divided. We treat the matter as in some sense finished, although the range of opinion on issues and candidates in the country is exactly as it was before. All that changes is that some individuals who were previously in the role of candidates are now in the role of incumbents and, as such, will receive more support. In the case of the President of the United States, about 20 percent of the population switches support to him the moment he is elected.

These 20 percent are responding to nothing in the personality of the individual but only to a change in his *role*, a change from candidate to President. Because he has assumed this new role, their feelings toward him as a person change.

This change in opinion—this collapse in the ability to distinguish between personality and role—is analogous to what we call repression in the individual, that is, the inability to distinguish between deciding not to act on a feeling, desire, or idea and believing that the feeling, desire, or idea is not a part of oneself at all. Just as the newspapers will refer to a "Democratic congress," so all of us as individuals go about viewing and presenting ourselves as "extraverted," or "shy," or "frank," or "easygoing," or "orderly" and, to a lesser extent, accepting the similarly one-sided self-descriptions of others.

This is a convenient shorthand, but it causes one form of gross distortion. In terms of the distribution of opinion and sentiment in the nation, an election that went 52 to 48 percent for the Democrats would resemble one that went 52 to 48 percent for the Republicans more than it would resemble one that went 80 to 20 percent for the Democrats; yet the first two outcomes would be considered opposites, while the two Democratic victories would be considered identical. This is even more marked on the interpersonal level, where we seldom appreciate the similarity of two people who share a common ambivalence but have "elected" different sides of it to be uppermost. Since the closer the balance is to 50 percent, the more it threatens to reverse, people will tend to show more tension around evenly divided sentiments than any other; they are preoccupied and absorbed with them and seek out other people with the same preoccupation regardless of which side they have "elected."

Let us take, for example, as one ambivalent pair, the desire for independence and the desire for dependence, both of which are present in all of us. Many people have a more or less comfortably lopsided distribution (for instance, 70 to 30 percent) of these desires; they can view themselves as having some consistency and can act or make choices with little difficulty. Their "minority" need is expressed at specific times and in specific relationships without threatening the individual's overall, "majority" view of himself. People with such comfortable "majorities" seem "unconflicted," that is, able to behave contrary to their "majority" tendencies when the situation demands it.[4]

Now consider two people in whom these traits are distributed on a 52 to 48 percent basis. These two people are obviously very similar, but one is a little higher on the dependent side, the other a little higher on the independent side. They are continually threatened with a reversal of this predominance, and hence with being unable to act or to maintain a constant self-image. Both will be preoccupied with the problem of freedom. Those with a dependent "majority" are chronically concerned with suppressing rebelliousness and deviance everywhere, and invest a great deal of energy in maintaining a consistent image of loyalty and devotion to authority. Those that have an independent "majority" are obsessed with combating authority wherever they find it, and invest their energies in upholding an image of rebelliousness. Both stances are naturally brittle because the "minorities" are so large. Since the "majority's" power must be constantly exercised to survive, both types will often seek out the other in order to join in ideological dispute. This has the additional function of permitting the dissident "minority" to express itself vicariously. The authoritarian will be attracted to situations in which there is deviance to be suppressed, while the rebel will seek situations in which he can be tyrannized over and nobly resist it. While the two may seem opposite, they are basically like-minded and share an identical problem. We should not be surprised, therefore—although we usually are—when they occasionally "convert," going to what seems like the opposite extreme. We can be sure that the new position will be just as brittle and exaggerated as the old. Just as societies like Germany and the United States, with a history of difficulty in achieving internal unity, lay exaggerated stress on loyalty and patriotism.

COMPARTMENTALIZATION

What keeps most people, most of the time and on most dimensions of feeling, from either a brittle absolutism or from being paralyzed with indecision is the convenient fact that contradictory tendencies in the individual can be expressed in different places and at different times. A college student, for example, may reject his parents' values but send his laundry home or write for money. Different relationships, different groups, and different occasions will be used to express contrary tendencies. Indeed, all cultures contain built-in institutions for such separation: personal relationships that require and others that forbid the same behavior (hostility, sexuality); special areas and special times of license, and other areas and times of taboo. The phrase "there is a time and place for everything" is not merely a tight-lipped New England reproof; in its most literal sense it is a profound cross-cultural generalization. There is no conceivable kind of human behavior that is not socially acceptable somewhere at some time under some conditions. Many societies have a special time of the year or occasional orgy in which all the usual rules do not apply and "anything goes," even incest. The "Feast of Fools" (of which the Christmas office party, New Year's Eve, Mardi Gras, and April Fool's Day are in one way or another lineal descendants), which was popular for more than a thousand years in Europe, was this kind of a festival, and involved such usually forbidden behavior as public ridicule of the clergy, transvestitism, and public copulation in the church.[5]

Less dramatic but more important are the short-term temporal rhythms: working in the day and playing in the evening, "sinning" and confessing, parties and hangovers. We work or play, are active or passive, in different places and in different relationships. The nuclear family of husband, wife, and children is, in our society, an exception to this rule, for all feelings and desires tend to converge here no matter how contradictory they may be. For this reason most tragic dramas are set within the home and center around family relationships—ambivalent conflict, the heart of drama, always seems a little less necessary in other settings. But even here some compartmentalizing is possible, particularly for males. The manager who is dominant on the job but submissive to his wife, for example, is a familiar phenomenon, as is the browbeaten clerk who plays domestic tyrant. Studies of the adjustment problems of the elderly have made us aware of the shattering impact that compulsory retirement can have on these elaborate systems of compartmentalization and on the families who collude in maintaining them. Historically, women have been forced to manage with far less opportunity for compartmentalization, but this is now changing.

ROLE

Since all groups and all individuals have contradictory needs, it might seem to be a simple matter to mesh one with the other. Since both also have needs for unity, consistency, and homogeneity, however, the problem becomes highly complicated. Every group requires the performance of certain roles whose existence it cannot admit, so initiation into these roles must be subtle. At the same time, there are roles that no individual can admit he or she is able or willing to perform. Furthermore, there is likely to be a correlation between the function denied by the group and the behavior denied by the individual, so that generalized "shortages" may emerge.

The concept of "role" is useful primarily as a mental lever to free us from the erroneous notion that the unit of a social system is a person. It serves to remind us that there is no group anywhere, nor has there ever been one, that includes the whole person—every aspect of his or her instinctual, emotional, and cognitive being. In our own complex society everyone belongs to many different groups in a lifetime, each with a special claim on some aspect of his or her personality. Even in primitive societies, nuclear families, unilineal clans, local village groups, age groups, and sex groups create a very elaborate system of cross-cutting relationships.

Any group, then, is made up, on the one hand, of group functions to be performed and, on the other hand, of *pieces of people* performing them. It is not only that "one man in his time plays many parts" and in different groups, but also that he uses only the relevant segments of his personality in a given group, while much of the rest of himself he excludes altogether. Every group, to an extent, violates the integrity of the people in it, while at the same time it restores their integrity in other respects from the limitations imposed by other groups.

Some groups and roles permit a greater range of behavior than others—a man will have a wider range of behavior in his role as husband than in his role as bank president, for example—and we generally view these groups as permitting us to relax and "be ourselves." This attitude cannot be taken at face value, however, since it may mean only that some single aspect of ourselves that is suppressed in most other roles is finally permitted to emerge. The sense of release that this entails blinds us to the fact that other aspects are being repressed at the same time. Nor should we imagine that we are "ourselves" when alone, since a vast range of our behavior is thereby made impossible. We are the sum total of our feelings, ideas, and behavior—regardless of what sort of truncated self-label we typically parade before our now indulgently gullible, now tactfully skeptical audiences—and neither any single group nor the lack of any group can embrace this totality.

AGE AND SEX ROLES

Human beings vary far more in their role behavior and self-concepts than in their instinctual emotional makeup. Everyone experiences hunger, thirst, fatigue, sexual excitement, anger, dependency, affection, jealousy, and pride in some form or another. Any role that makes a person seem unique will thus tend to do violence to his or her emotional economy and will be experienced not as freedom but as constraint.

A person who performed a role perfectly would be regarded as a little inhuman—lacking the richness of normal human endowment—while a role that didn't damage personality structure would be a social paradise. It is not merely that a servant's need to be dominant is frustrated, or that a ruler's need to be submissive, private, or retiring is thwarted. It might even be argued that these needs do not exist since individuals are socialized from birth to accept these limitations. But the variety of roles that a person must learn produces a full range of needs: The ruler learns submission in relation to his parents, the servant dominance in his childhood peer group. Society inculcates attitudes of superiority and inferiority through class stratification in classes, but because this greatly increases the individual's contacts with peers instead of with class superiors and inferiors those attitudes never get developed to their extreme. Conceivably, a person who from birth experienced only domination or only submission from others might lack this response himself, but as yet no documented case of such a person has been found.

Even the most diffuse and vaguely defined roles would be crippling if they monopolized a person's behavior. Fortunately, in most instances, there are compensations that moderate this effect in the form of cross-cutting roles or latent contradictions built into the role itself. A good example can be found in traditional American sex roles. What was a woman to do with her common sense, for example, in a culture that regarded woman as "by nature" impractical and delicate? What did a man do with his aspirations for elegance in a culture in which it was obligatory for a "real man" to be clumsy? The answer is that a man of the pre-World War II generation could be as graceful, surefooted, and foppish as he liked on a football field so long as he fell over his feet and looked sheepish in the living room. And even in Victorian England women were assigned most of the practical care of the household despite their vaporousness; and they retained their monopoly over the management of illness and death despite their alleged squeamishness. The constrictions imposed on personality by sex-role definitions nevertheless create problems of one kind or another in every culture and, as Margaret Mead points out, are extremely wasteful of individual potential.[6]

Even more dramatic are the constraints imposed by age roles. Everyone is, of course, familiar with the injunction "act your age," but few are conscious of the great limitations that it places on behavior in all age groups. This is most striking in the case of the elderly, who must relinquish patterns of behavior that have been ingrained for decades and that may have formed the core of their self-concepts. A man of 80 may still think of himself privately as he did when he was 20, but if he were to behave along these familiar lines he would probably be hospitalized.

What is amazing is that these drastic changes do not cause more difficulty than they do. Most people effect the transition so well that children often cannot grasp the fact that old people were once young. The secret is, of course, in the gradualness of the change. As people grow older they drop certain behaviors bit by bit—in part modeling themselves on parents and other old people they knew when younger, in part being inducted into old age roles by those around them, who caution them to "slow down," "take better care" of themselves "at your age," and gently ridicule the persistence of too-youthful behavior and interests. One must learn to be decrepit, just as one must learn to talk, even if the physical capacity is already present.

Such drastic changes in behavior, however, are characteristic of all role induction. People often become disillusioned at how little effect a change in Presidents has on American foreign policy, for example, and how much more the remarks of different incumbents resemble each other than they resemble their own statements and beliefs out of office. The fun-loving Prince Hal becomes the coldly ambitious Henry V; the married man no longer seems so congenial to his unmarried friends. We even find such changes in small informal groups. When a member has sharply specialized in some bit of behavior useful to the group and subsequently departs, we are often surprised to see how quickly someone else slips into the gap.

MARITAL AND FAMILY ROLES

Ezra Vogel and Norman Bell describe a particularly instructive form of personality change through role induction in the family. They note that parents who have severe but covert tensions in their own relationship often lead one of their offspring into the role of "problem child," obliquely rewarding him for the very behavior they complain of. By maintaining emotional distance from each other, avoiding confrontation in areas of conflict, and scapegoating the child, the parents are able to preserve a fragile equilibrium. Sometimes each parent will pressure the child to behave in opposite ways, thus permitting "one spouse to express annoyance to the other indirectly without endangering the marital relationship." When a child's problem shows signs of responding to therapy the latent marital conflict often erupts violently, and threatens to lead to the breakup of the marriage or to personality disturbances in one of the spouses.[7]

As we would expect, the initial attraction of the parents in cases of this kind is based partly on "the fact that they shared many of the same conflicts and understood each other quite well. Not long after marriage, however, they seemed to have become polarized in their conflicts, so that one parent represented one side of the conflict and the other represented the other side." [8] Thus the induction of the child is really derived from the mutual polarization of the parents.

All of us are familiar with informal role specialization in marriage relationships. ("So-and-so is a different person when his wife [her husband] isn't around.") One spouse tells the jokes, the other fills in contexts; one is expressive, one judicious; one initiates new social contacts, the other provides excuses for withdrawal by being prone to illness or chronically busy. In some cases this distribution of traits is regulated by sex roles or occupational roles: Thus women often manage social arrangements and the expression of emotion in our society, while husbands are often expected to be the authorities in business matters. In some cases, however, the matter tends to be settled in terms of whose inclinations are most intense. If both husband and wife are eager and able storytellers, the most eager is likely to develop the skill to new heights, while the other permits it to atrophy. A new husband may abandon his bachelorhood culinary skills, or he may accentuate them and become the "fancy cook," his wife falling into the role of "plain cook." Gradually the traits and abilities are sorted out and assigned (usually, but not always, unconsciously), atrophying or hypertrophying as the case may be, and eventually achieving an almost stereotypic rigidity. ("He's the smart one of the family." "She's always right about *people*.") Widowhood and divorce often produce what appear to be startling personality changes as the conditions for suppressing or exaggerating some characteristic are suddenly removed. A retiring, dependent wife becomes competent and forceful upon losing a dominant husband, while the dour spouse of a vivacious woman reveals a humorous facet when separated from her. Unsuspected talents suddenly emerge or are revived, and many other relationships must be readjusted. Those who experience this process often describe it as a kind of self-discovery, albeit a very painful and disruptive one.

The process of polarization can be observed at any time in any relationship. Suppose, for example, a husband and wife are deciding whether to spend an evening out or at home. Both are ambivalent—a little bored and restless, but a little tired and comfortable as well—but perhaps the husband is a bit more inclined to stay home and the wife a bit more inclined to go out. We can represent the differences in the intensity of these impulses as follows:

Husband: Home Home Home Home Out Out Out
Wife: Home Home Home Out   Out Out Out

Now suppose the wife asks the husband if he has any interest in going out. He says he would a little rather stay home. Each has expressed, very tentatively, his or her dominant feeling, which could be symbolized by crossing out a "Home" for the husband and an "Out" for the wife. If these expressions were delivered in a vacuum we would expect the minority impulse in both persons to make itself felt more strongly, since both impulses would now be equal within each person:

Husband: ~~Home~~ Home Home Home Out Out Out
Wife: Home Home Home Out   Out Out ~~Out~~

But these expressions do not occur in a vacuum. The husband *hears* the wife's choice, and she hears his. She has expressed her majority impulse, but *he* has expressed her *minority* impulse, and vice versa. The real situation is as follows:

Husband: ~~Home~~ Home Home Home Out Out ~~Out~~
Wife: ~~Home~~ Home Home Out   Out Out ~~Out~~

Already it has become difficult to avoid polarization since the majority impulse of each has become more securely entrenched (3 to 2 instead of 4 to 3). Unless they make a compulsive effort to retain awareness of their original ambivalence, they will tend to feel their majority impulse more firmly. (Anyone who has ever flipped a coin in a moment of indecision can understand this process—if the coin comes up heads, thus expressing one impulse, we immediately become aware of wanting its opposite. Husband and wife in this example play coin to each other.) Both, therefore, now express their dominant wish a little more forcefully. After a couple more exchanges the situation is:

> Husband: ~~Home Home Home~~ Home ~~Out Out Out~~
> Wife: ~~Home Home Home~~ Out   ~~Out Out Out~~

Each has forgotten the original ambivalence entirely. The husband is aware only of a strong desire to stay home, the wife of an equally strong wish to go out. Ambivalence has been nicely resolved for both, but now there is a conflict between them.

This is, in fact, the way all of us go about making decisions—conscious or unconscious—in at least some aspects of our lives. We clarify our internal state by enlisting others to express our minority impulses. This is particularly likely to occur with those impulses that arouse shame or guilt. In the example above the husband is free of responsibility for any desire to avoid an evening alone with his wife. She, on the other hand, cannot be accused of being a passive homebody. Whoever wins the argument also loses, for he or she will bear the responsibility for the other's hidden wishes. We use each other like prison walls to help convince ourselves that we really want to be free.

But what leads people to so distort themselves in the first place? The principal reason is economic: Specialization, up to a point, reduces the amount of energy that is needed to maintain the solidarity of a relationship. The more interaction is ritualized through specialization, the more predictable it becomes; and the more that skills are divided, the less competition will occur. If each spouse seeks rewards and approval in different areas, the relationship will flow smoothly and effortlessly.

But individual human beings cannot permanently shed their overlapping characteristics the way competing species do in evolution, but instead suppress them with difficulty. And if the difficulty is too great, the energy saved in the interactions *between* the couple may be spent in maintaining *internal* balances. Furthermore, we must not assume that specialization eliminates discord since a division of labor often produces ritualized conflict: The expressive wife complains that the controlled husband is too cold, while he complains that she is too temperamental. This kind of running quarrel derives in part from the strain each experiences in suppressing that part of his or her personality that is assigned to the other. Finally, we must remember that understanding is facilitated by similarity of experience and feeling—those who desire the same thing may compete, but may also share a sympathy and acceptance of one another.

Chapter 14

THE FISH COMMISSION
AND THE WATER PROBLEM

The reports of presidential commissions on "social problems" have a characteristic style. Since the style is essential to the form, it can't be transcended by the impressive intelligence, erudition, insight, and humanity that at least some of its members bring to it. The assumptions that create such commissions are typical of American social thinking. The first of these assumptions is that "social problems" can be defined in isolation. This is based on contemporary medical thinking, which in turn comes from the theory of auto repair. That is: One does not see the problem as an ailing system, one seeks a malfunctioning *part* which is then repaired or replaced. When the system continues to ail, another part is sought, and so on, ad infinitum. Although an inefficient and self-defeating approach, it is highly lucrative. The excessive cost of human and mechanical repair in our society is rooted in this peculiar approach to systems and wholes.

Calling a social symptom a "problem" is a symbolic power play. Instead of being caught *inside* a whirlpool of forces, by this device we imagine ourselves as having climbed outside and above them. "Problem" suggests an individual looking down on a piece of paper with some symbols on it. It is as if a group of stomach-lining cells got together to form a commission on the "ulcer problem." The feeling of power thus gained is comforting but illusory.

170

A second assumption has to do with objectivity. Commissions are supposed to be representative of the public and attempt to comprise a variety of viewpoints. To hide their fierce involvement, warring participants affect a cool detachment that no one feels. Commissions thus begin by having only one precious item of agreement—a shared distress—which is the first thing to be banished from their deliberations. Their mutual pain and anxiety is denied, along with their sense of being stranded together in the midst of a social typhoon. For this they substitute a shared pretense, that is, that the crisis is simply a technical problem that men of good will and tolerance can solve with a little ingenuity and tinkering—a pretense that insults the humanity of all parties and makes their personal experience and distress seem insignificant.

This pose of detachment leads to defining the "problem" too narrowly, to recreating the error involved in viewing it as a "problem" in the first place. This error is inextricably woven into another—equally pervasive in American social thinking—the tendency to psychologize social phenomena. If we define the problem too narrowly to see the whole system, we won't be able to understand what all the commotion is about. As long as we assume that our society is functioning satisfactorily, then specific crises become mysteries, just as a malfunctioning body organ is a mystery to the medical specialist who looks for the answer within the limited area of his competence. This bewilderment leads quickly to the assumption that some sort of irrationality is involved—"human error," a "morale problem," or "psychological factors." We are like a cameraman who zooms in on a panic-stricken crowd to search their faces for the causes of their fright, thereby excluding from vision the building about to collapse upon them. Unable to perceive the falling building, we turn our attention to "mob psychology."

These errors—detachment, narrowing, psychologizing—are found regularly in American social analysis: in commission reports, media "white papers," and "studies in depth." Once these errors have been made, the analyst can only conclude by saying that (a) the problem is complex, (b) there is some merit in all the positions taken, and (c) everyone must try harder to show tolerance and understanding—leaving everyone feeling intolerant, confused, and dissatisfied.

"Explaining" behavior in terms of motivations that seem hard to understand or feeble creates an atmosphere of intolerance. If one really believed in the 1960s that students occupied or burned buildings because they felt neglected by faculty spending so much time on research, it would have been difficult not to give hardhats the nod. The conservative assault on "permissiveness" in America owes much to the barrage of psychological explanations of social phenomena that we have endured in the past decade.

Every culture contains some basic contradictions between its ideals and the reality of the society, and devotes enormous energy to binding these contradictions in complex compartmentalizations. (See Chapter 13.) In a sense one could say that this frozen ambivalence *is* culture—gives it its unique character and stability. The discovery and exposure of such contradictions, then, is accompanied not only by a great unraveling but also by an extraordinary release of energy—what we usually call violence, social upheaval, or revolution. These fundamental contradictions in a culture are the value faults along which social earthquakes must of necessity take place. Asking questions like "What is wrong with our hospitals?" or "What do women want?" is like asking what was wrong with Vesuvius in 79 A.D., or what it "wanted."

Presidential commissions usually conclude that everyone is at fault, and while such a conclusion hardly seems worth the effort and expense that goes into such a report, it must be commended at least for sending an absurd premise into a blind alley. For if you begin an analysis of a social phenomenon with the assumption that a crime has been committed, it shows some progress to decide that everyone is guilty, even if it illuminates nothing.

The opposing reactionary position—that unrest is due simply to a generalized trend toward laxity in the culture and will end when authorities take stern punitive measures—has more to recommend it. It errs only in mistaking symptom (e.g., the fact that the police have become discredited) for cause. Once law enforcement agencies are viewed simply as the military agents of a partisan group, their severity has no more meaning than that of an occupying army. But it has one advantage over liberal thinking: It manages to make a connection between one event and another. The conservative view points out that respect for authority has declined everywhere—that there is a generalized loss of allegiance for the traditional values of the culture. It may be absurd of the rightists to imagine that they can discipline players who have already left the team, but it is far less absurd than to define a generalized social decay as a collection of discrete "problems."

It is this inability to understand wholes and the processes of systems that often leads to the general discrediting of the liberal view. The pigeonhole mind can be tolerated only so long as things are going well, or at least as long as people believe that a system is capable of curing its own ailments. A basically healthy child can withstand a great deal of mindless medical tinkering, for example, even today.

But in time of crisis liberals become an increasingly dangerous luxury. The need for some sort of comprehensive theory about what is happening outstrips the desire for a safe, comfortable, undemanding approach to thinking about life. Polarization occurs in a society because both radicals and reactionaries have the capacity to come up with a comprehensive, interconnected vision of the world around them. The inability of liberals to recognize system properties—the stubborn clinging to piecemeal solutions in the face of infinite repetition and geometric reproduction—appears increasingly silly.

The theories of the right tend to be dualistic and conspiratorial, those of the left messianic and utopian; but almost any theory is better than none. People are slow to recognize this and seem surprised that although moderates express hostility and contempt toward militants, they often follow them in a crisis when the chips are down. In fact, moderates often despise their leaders as shrill and pretentious even in the very throes of the crisis. But militants provide something that liberal spokespersons are never able to offer—an awareness of the interrelationship between issues. Whether their particular framework is accepted or not, the radicals continually emphasize and dramatize the fact that the issues at hand cannot be isolated but are part of a more general problem. In times of crisis, however bizarre the theory and however unlovable its advocate, if it recognizes in any way the connection between institutions, it will gain adherents away from those who ignore that connection.

Chapter 15

PLEASURE, HEALING, AND CONFLICT

Talcott Parsons once remarked [1] that pleasure was the money of the body. I would have preferred him to say that money was the pleasure of the body politic, since pleasure existed before money, and since money and its institutions are modeled after the organization of pleasure in the body.

Both pleasure and money are organizing principles for the structures they serve. Pleasure is a kind of *lingua franca* for the body that, like money for a social system, translates a variety of *qualitatively* different stimuli into a single *quantitative* dimension of value. This enables us to organize a uniform hierarchy of value out of a heterogeneous chaos of unique experiences and events. Choice is thereby made easier, since priorities can be assigned according to a simple uniform principle. Action, therefore, is utterly dependent upon these organizing modes: Without pleasure, organisms would be inert; without money, formal organizations would be static.

Varying the distribution of these unifying principles performs many functions for the structure. In the organism, pleasure is attached to ego functions, just as a government imposes taxes in order to concentrate money in power centers. Indeed, the most interesting conceptual issues about pleasure and money concern their roles in increasing or decreasing the centralization of struc-

175

tures. At this point, however, analogies between the two principles become rather intricate, since societal structures are somewhat less centralized than the higher organisms. I would like,
therefore, to concentrate on pleasure in this chapter, although the
reader is invited to draw whatever analogies she finds amusing.

Sandor Ferenczi was fascinated with the role of the genitals in
maintaining centralized control over organ subsystems.[2] He was
concerned with the potentially distracting role that pleasure played
in instrumental functioning, and he envisioned an anarchic condition in which each organ system would be grooving chaotically on
its own activity rather than serving the needs of the total organism. The eye would be "absorbed in erotic looking," the skin would
forget its role as a "protective covering whose sensitiveness provides warning of danger," and so on. To prevent this, pleasurable
excitations are "turned aside" and stored in a "special reservoir
from which they are periodically tapped." The genital in
Ferenczi's model is thus a kind of central garbage collector, pick-
ing up all this diffuse joy and expelling it in an orgasm, thereby
allowing the various organs to get on with their instrumental tasks
for the good of the total organism. It was this anal, functional, and
fundamentally bureaucratic vision against which Norman Brown so
eloquently rebelled.[3]

This is not to say, however, that Ferenczi was incorrect. It
depends in part on whether you identify with the subsystems or
the organism as a whole. Individualistic ideology can easily confuse
us at this point, for we are, after all, total organisms, and the kind
of hedonistic rebellion with which we spontaneously (i.e., mechan-
ically, because of our cultural indoctrination) identify would, in this
case, lead to our own personal dissolution and death.

On the other hand, it's quite certain that substituting "organized" (i.e., genital) pleasure (a kind of circus for the subsystems)
for sensual "states' rights" amounts to some net loss in total
pleasure—just as there would be a net loss if we told a group of
people that they could not experience gratification unless all were
experiencing it simultaneously and in the same manner.
Synchrony is always, in this sense, entropic.

The tendency to identify with the part rather than the whole may derive from some vague awareness of what all this means at the societal level. For, at the present time, the societal equivalent of genital orgasm in the body is war. In war the total society prevents decentralization by the discharge of surplus wealth through destruction—a highly inelegant genital mechanism, it must be admitted.

Ferenczi was impressed with the role of pleasure as a distraction from the body's instrumental tasks. I'm impressed more by the likelihood that many of these tasks would never be performed at all were it not for their being linked to stimulation of the pleasure centers of the brain. How else could priorities be selected? Fear is only an emergency mechanism, signaling a shift to a set of crisis priorities, but what is a poor, indecisive organism to do when no danger threatens? The world is filled with infinite possibility: Shall it put its tail in the river, stuff leaves in its nose, climb a cliff, do somersaults?

Each activity has its appeal for some set of organ systems. How can they be mediated? How does an organism "choose" between two qualitatively different actions, each with its own unique set of appeals? How do I decide whether it's "better" to go dancing or go to a movie? Pleasure is a unitary concept, reducing all these unique events to a single quantitative standard, thus permitting the organism to "choose" whichever activity gets the highest applause rating on the pleasure meter.

That's one way of looking at it—reducing qualitative differences to quantitative ones. But part of that qualitative difference comes from the fact that different activities appeal to different organ systems. It's hard to compare dancing with moviegoing because in part it's my eyes that want to see a movie and my musculature that wants to dance. The pleasure centers adjudicate all these claims and render an automatic, bureaucratic verdict. Everything has its pleasure quotient, just as, in the body politic, everything has its price. Any uniform standard can produce grotesque absurdities and irrelevancies, but the everyday usefulness of such a system is evident.

Ferenczi's model of the organism, however, is too simple. He sees each organ giving up its eroticism to the whole, specializing in task functions for the general good and the general pleasure. Pleasure itself is largely given over to a specialized release organ, while only the germ cells retain totipotentiality and erotic anarchy.

But even if we ignore the genitals, eroticism is by no means evenly distributed throughout the organism. A foundation stone of psychoanalytic theory, in fact, is that it tends to be centered in certain bodily functions, and if we pursue this thought a little further we find that eroticism tends to be concentrated at points of transition—at boundaries and gateways: the orifices, the skin, the senses. Pleasure, then, is piled up at change nodes, just as money is concentrated in the social system at energy sources, or where change is sought.

Pleasure is not energy (nor is money); it is a control principle for the *distribution* of energy, just as appetite is not food. To overcome inertia, special investments of energy are always needed. Hence points of transition—boundaries, exchange centers, places of fusion and defusion—must be eroticized. The pleasure centers facilitate change by motivating the accumulation of energy at these points.

Hunger alone, for example, is not enough to motivate eating, any more than it is enough to motivate hunting and killing in a carnivore. There must be pleasure in the act *itself*, over and above mere tension-reduction. The problem with tension-reduction as a motivator is, as we shall see, that it lends itself too easily to overkill.

Both stimulation of the pleasure centers and tension-reduction suffer from being too generalized. An organism could hypothetically short-circuit the specific response and go for the main switch. But the main switch in the case of the pleasure centers is inaccessible to the organism. If we could find a way to stimulate our brains directly, it is true, we would do so and starve to death. Experimental studies affirm this. Fortunately, without a complex laboratory setup we simply can't do it.

The main switch for tension-reduction is unconsciousness or suicide, and this *is* accessible. If eating were not in itself a pleasurable act, even *without* hunger (and who should know better than

Americans that hunger is unnecessary to pleasurable eating), an organism in an extreme hunger state might perfectly reasonably elect to die rather than poke about for food.

The fact that eating, defecating, urinating, and so on are to some extent eroticized ensures survival by attaching pleasure to *specific* acts, while making the source of all this pleasure hidden. This attachment is what Freudians call "libido."

Reproduction is the most highly eroticized of all bodily functions. For, biologically, the survival of the individual organism is trivial, except as a vehicle for transmitting the genetic code. Reproduction is ensured by its being hooked to a pleasurable stimulation and release mechanism. Procreation is parasitic on eroticism.

Pleasure, then, has a fundamental role in maintaining the integrity of the organism and the commitment of the parts to the whole. Therefore, questions of healing are inseparable from matters of pleasure.

Healing is a process brought into play when parts of a system become disconnected from one another or from other systems, or when the system falls into a state of imbalance. The cruder forms of healing, such as most of Western medicine and some of the more degenerate forms of primitive medicine, operate on the simple assumption that all sickness arises from a defect in the organism's input-output system. Either something is inside that should not be inside—a germ, a tumor, anxiety, a demon, a poison—or something is not inside that should be inside—vitamins, corpuscles of one kind or another, antibiotics, the soul, analgesics. Treatment consists of putting things in and taking things out.

More subtle forms of healing, such as acupuncture, chiropraxis, and bioenergetics, concern themselves with adjusting internal balances independently of input and output; of reintegrating the organism by reacquainting the parts with each other through internal communication. For when we get right down to it, such internal communication is the difference between life and death. A living structure is one in which the parts communicate. A dead structure is one in which the parts have ceased to communicate. A mechanism is a dead structure in which the communication system is supplied and programmed by some external agency. And a diseased structure is one in which internal communication is garbled.

Disease itself occurs through adaptation. That is, the organism adapts itself to an external condition in such a way as to throw its own internal relationships out of balance. Disease is adaptation to a bad environment. Healing is a matter of restoring the balance that adaption has tilted.

In most forms of disease the burden of adaptation falls disproportionately on certain subsegments of the organism: Adaptation to nicotine falls on the lung, adaptation to competition falls on the heart, adaptation to stoicism falls on the jaw, adaptation to alcohol falls on the liver, and so on. A family's adaptation to a bad environment similarly tends to fall on one member, called by family therapists the "identified patient."

In many cases the distress falling on the subsegment by virtue of the system's adaptation is so great that there is conflict within the system as to whether to reintegrate the subsegment or slough it. If I am forced to sit in an uncomfortable position for a long time so that my back aches or my foot goes to sleep, I can easily reintegrate the injured party by paying special attention to it when I'm able to move again. But if my foot becomes gangrenous from a wound, my survival as a total organism may depend upon sloughing it, the way a lizard or a chipmunk sloughs its tail if caught.

"Autotomy" is the term usually applied to this sloughing. Most surgery is a form of autotomy, as is placing a child in a mental hospital, or an elderly family member in a nursing home. The alternative to autotomy for the system is the resocialization of the injured part, of which I shall say more in a moment.

In the most extreme case, the system may fragment itself altogether, through group dissolution, individual suicide, or certain kinds of psychoses. Ferenczi suggests [4] three advantages of such a maneuver common among lower animals "subjected to excessive stimulation": (1) creating a more extended surface allows increased discharge of tension; (2) giving up unified perception diffuses pain; and (3) the fragments have much greater adaptability. Ferenczi was fascinated by the bird that flies into the eagle's claws as if the tension were no longer to be borne. Unconsciousness is also a kind of fragmentation, permitting, Ferenczi suggested, a relaxed autonomy to the musculature. All these forms of fragmentation—unconsciousness, psychosis, and suicide—are in some sense a sloughing of the ego that has led the organism into such pain and distress—much like the disordered flight of an army that loses confidence in its blundering officers in the midst of a disastrous battle (*"Sauve qui peut!"*).

The more common way of dealing with disaffection in the organism's ranks, however, is what I would call "renurture." And this is where pleasure comes into the picture.

What impresses me about most healing is that it recapitulates early childrearing. A subsegment of a system is persuaded to stay in the system the same way an infant is persuaded to remain alive and join human society—by a kind of nurturant seduction. The double meaning of the verb "to nurse" is no accident. "Nursing back to health" is seducing the organ into belonging to the organism, and the organism as a whole to the community. The ending of Henry James' *The Turn of the Screw* describes the failure of such an attempt.

But we not only mother sick people, we also mother our own injured subsegments. When people hurt themselves they involuntarily make a nurturant gesture toward the injured part. If I hurt my hand I hold it very tenderly, or rub it, or bring it to my mouth to lick or kiss. Animals, of course, do the same thing. Children, who are more in touch with their real needs, will typically ask a parent to "kiss it" when something hurts, but as hard-bitten adults we must perform these services for ourselves.

Bathing, dressing with ointments, bandaging a wound are part of the same process. Heaven knows how much they help on a purely mechanical basis, but they certainly recapitulate primary nurturance. A bandage is like a shelter: It signifies that the subsegment is to be granted a protected status. In the same way, we allow adults who are sick to spend all their time in bed, like infants. To be "sick in bed" is a special status symbolizing nonresponsibility. In the same way we say an animal "favors" its injured leg. The injured subsegment is the "favorite" until it returns to the fold—normal work is not required of it. The message to the injured subsegment is clear. It says, "Don't leave, it's all right; stay here—it's not dangerous to be a part of this organism." This is the real message of the parable of the Prodigal Son.

The same process occurs in groups. Initiation ceremonies in clubs, secret societies, and so on follow a fairly strict formula. Frightening, intimidating, and disorienting rituals reduce the neophyte to the status of child, following which there is usually some nurturant-accepting behavior to signify his or her entrance into the group. Disaffection is subsequently handled either by re-seduction through nurturance or by ostracism or exile.

Encounter groups use the interesting device of getting a collection of people together who want to be healed—pretending to be an organic group with disaffected members—and then reintegrating each member in turn. When the group becomes whole, it dissolves, and the individuals take away whatever healing they received in the process of the bogus group's mending of itself.

I once tested this theory on myself. I had been reading David Bakan's brilliant book, *Disease, Pain, and Sacrifice,*[5] and thinking about healing. I had a thumb that for several years had been covered with a mass of warts. It was very ugly. I had recently asked a doctor how to get rid of them and he said they would have to be burned off. I asked if they ever cleared up spontaneously and he said no.

I decided to heal the thumb in accordance with the disaffection theory. Heretofore I had felt irritated with the growth and careless of my hands in general. I began to alter my attitude toward it. I took very good care of it—thought about it, put a bandage on to "protect" it, held it, kissed it often, and was generally very nice to it. In a week the growth was completely gone and has never returned. A friend of mine, working with yoga, saved himself a hernia operation in roughly the same way—concentrating energy on the place that needed attention.

Pain, then, is essentially like a baby's scream—a signal saying "love and nurture me, pay attention." Nursing a child, or caring for a sick person, is directing extra energy into them. The reason groups are so powerful as healing devices is simply that they bring such an intense focus of loving interest to bear on each person.

Yet obviously not all interest or energy or loving attention has a healing impact, any more than all pills are efficacious. Faith healers, licensed physicians, primitive witch doctors, friends, and relatives seem to do equally well and equally poorly with the everyday ailments that afflict humans. They all invest energy of one kind or another, and sometimes it seems to work and sometimes it doesn't.

I can only speak from my own experience with encounter groups, where the ailments are most often of the psychic variety, aside from the usual headaches, breathing difficulties, stomach symptoms, or occasional muscular stresses. It has become apparent to me over the years I've spent blundering about in a field to which I'm temperamentally rather unsuited, that my healing seems to occur more in response to a certain emotional state I sometimes find myself in than to anything else. Techniques, complete understanding of the problem, deep concern for the other person—all these are trivial in comparison.

The emotional state that seems important is one of intense but effortless alertness. Not the alertness of overcoming lethargy or concentrating on something—but an alertness that's simply there. It's marked by an almost total absence of thinking, not in the sense of mindlessness, but in the sense that action flows responsively and without consideration. The action, its source, and its reasons are self-evident. One can interpret them later (one is often asked to) but at the time they are intuitive, reflexive. In such a state (would that it occur more often!) I am unselfconscious, emotionally available, and unresponsive to social expectations or intellectual programs. I become unaware of anything except the person or persons before me—often to the point where I notice a subtle change in the light, such that everything in my visual background is obscured.

At one time I used to feel rather magical about this: If I was feeling right everything went right and I couldn't make a mistake. Then I realized that this was a false frame of reference, derived from *not* being in that state. In that tuned-in state there's no such thing as a mistake: You respond, it leads to something, you respond again. You don't think, "That's a dead end, let's try another tack," you're just in it, doing it, going where it goes, a *part* of it. The moment you become aware of yourself as a healer you're no longer in the condition that is healing.

But what *is* it that's healing about this state? For in my experience, both immediate and long-range feedback confirms that the most important healing takes place in response to it. It isn't just a matter of spontaneity—most spontaneity is neutral in its impact, and at times may be even negative. A healing intent, a focus is necessary, along with some understanding and skill, and a constancy of interest. But to a large degree the "internal dialogue"— Castaneda's nemesis—is silent, and there is no investment in any particular self-presentation, whether loving, brilliant, charismatic, selfless, spontaneous, or whatever. I usually feel an internal warmth and safety in such a state, and feelings of all kinds are very close to the surface.

The comfort I feel comes from a feeling of inclusion and belonging, and creates confidence that whatever is happening to me internally is generated by the situation and not dragged in from outside. Hence I'm much more likely to find myself "tuned in" in a marathon or residential setting than in a weekly meeting. It occurs when I feel totally involved and unaware of a life outside the setting.

What I'm suggesting is that the healing impact of being "tuned in" is simply a function of having all of oneself aboard the system. I am healing when I don't distinguish myself from the group of which I'm a part. My consciousness is roughly coterminous with its network. All my energy is available to the system, and I'm open to all emotional messages generated by that system. I'm a nerve ending for that system and *know* that I am. I act with the confidence that comes from knowing my reactions aren't totally idiosyncratic, and hence they're not.

This availability means that the situation is healing to me as well as vice versa: To be healing you have to have the capacity to *be* healed in this way, since the issue is one of connectedness, of revitalizing a damaged network of which you are yourself a part. All real healing, therefore, is self-healing, for the energy in the restored channels flows both ways.

People involve themselves in healing from a variety of motives, most of which obstruct the healing. They may be necessary and helpful in getting us *into* the situation of healing, but they interfere with the process itself, which requires abandoning oneself to a network that is irrelevant to ego needs. In other words, whatever being a healer means to me will attract me to the context in which that can happen, so that if I'm successful I'll feel good. But once I'm in the situation I must manage to lose myself, along with all such motives and needs. The only need remaining, ideally, will be the desire to participate in a healing process.

Hence, the most successful healers are those who are able to utilize the healing situation quickly for themselves—healing themselves so that they can be healers. They have the capacity to maximize the rapidity of the healing exchange. They define themselves into a position in which they can do what they're trying to define themselves as being. A gifted healer is one who can get the psychic economy rolling—swiftly acquiring some emotional spending money, spending it, getting it back and spending more.

The healing process, then, maintains the integrity of organic systems by seducing disaffected segments back into the fold. Pleasure counteracts centrifugal forces within the organism. It would be easy at this point to fall into the familiar posture of imagining Eros, the great social director, herding dissident campers into the dining hall while his enemy, Discord, lurks in the bushes outside.

But internal conflict is not merely a sign of ailing and imminent dissolution in organic systems. It is also the *origin* of such systems. The lack of internal ambivalence in an organism would obliterate it. Or at least dematerialize it.

Energy is movement. Matter is stasis. Matter is ambivalent energy. Matter is events that get stuck.

An entity occurs when a pair or set of opposing forces meet and balance each other sufficiently to cause an eddy in the flow of those forces. A hurricane for example, is an event to which we ascribe material form. A hurricane is a "thing." The same is true of a whirlpool. I'm suggesting that a whirlpool may be conceived as the core metaphor for all matter, as well as all forms and organizations of matter or even of symbols. A social institution, a human being, an atom, a marriage—all shapes, in fact, are created by ambivalence, brought into being by a collision of forces.

When the opposing forces are in balance any particles carried by or associated with them are forced to remain in orientation to one another. The particles themselves, of course, are similarly formed, and so on ad infinitum. Perfect balance equals perfect stability. A stable marriage, community, organism, or whatever, is one in which the ambivalence, the opposing forces, are in exquisite equipoise.

Motion is created, or recreated, when the opposing forces cease to be in balance. A human being can act, for example, only when a motivational imbalance occurs. Motion, then, requires imbalance, while integrity requires balance. Both balance and imbalance are essential to life, since life is both integrity and movement.

Unity is an enormously ambiguous, confused, and intricate concept, at least as it's conventionally used. First of all, it is clearly a mistake to talk as if the integrity of an organism were based on "unity" in the popular sense of an absence of conflict. Conflict, perfectly checked and balanced, is the essence of unity, as Eastern philosophy has always maintained.

Paradoxically, when we talk of an organism or a community or an organization as "unified" we often mean that it's sufficiently lopsided to permit it to act as a whole with some conviction at some particular moment in relation to some aspect of the environment. "Unambivalent" means unbalanced. Balance is conflict, imbalance is movement. We are concerned with unity under conditions of action, when it is problematic ("a unified thrust," for example, is a popular American cliché), hence we tend to overlook the negative relationship between balance and unity.

I like to think of material structures as energy with a hangup. The neurotic bind, the marital couple locked in chronic bickering but never separating, are for me the metaphor for matter, for organization. Ronald Laing's *Knots* [6] has the same symmetrical elegance as the yin-yang symbol: ambivalent forces locking each other into place by placing little mirrors of themselves inside each other.

We have difficulty understanding certain processes—especially those connected with change—because *we* are "hung up," merely by virtue of being complex organizations of matter. We often seek consistency, for example, and conflict-resolution, but ultimately such resolution, such consistency, would dissolve what we're trying to "unify." Families, societies, individuals—all are rooted in ambivalent stasis and inconsistency. The acceptance of such inconsistency in behavior and motivation maintains the balance that keeps the segments of the system in orientation to each other. Work and play, closeness and distance, anger and love, dominance and submission—both sides of each pair must achieve expression in some form or another, however covert, for the system to survive. The application of consistency and logic to organic systems can sometimes produce bursts of powerful movement, but it leads ultimately to dissolution. Consistency and conflict-resolution are in the last analysis entropic, if the Second Law has validity.

Ordered conflict, then, binds energy, and produces tension. Unraveling that conflict in any way releases tension and permits movement. Ambivalence is essential to the existence of life, since a balance of forces is what maintains the integrity of the organism. Yet to act, ambivalence must be unbalanced to permit the generation of motion.

But for action to be meaningful, some degree of consistency of motion is also necessary. Otherwise behavior would be mere oscillation. A perfectly stable, balanced system is capable only of oscillatory motion. Such oscillation is quite open and visible in small children at times; expressed refusal leads to acquiescence and back again. In adults it is more subtle and tortuous.

To go beyond oscillation, some way of binding motives must be developed. A self-concept is such a technique. It helps draw a boundary, and boundaries are a way of storing energy by insulating paired opposing forces against other forces that would unlock them. The dissolution of boundaries always releases an enormous amount of energy for this reason.

The knots that Laing portrays depend, for example, on a closed dyadic system. A couple, a person, a community often defines itself off from others: "I (we) am (are) special in this or that way, which is different from all others. I (we) always act in such-and-such a manner." This binds a lot of energy within the system, incidentally creating considerable tension. The success of the maneuver depends upon preventing access to the knot by other closely related systems. To take a simple example, a couple locked into and immobilized by a love-hate relationship can be temporarily released by an antagonistic third party; loving each other they can move aggressively outward. Similarly, a man who thinks of himself as strong and self-sufficient while being utterly dependent on his wife to take care of his physical needs may fall apart when her death prevents him from maintaining this self-deception.

But life is a good deal more complicated than this. Social scientists love bipolar dimensions, and the field is flooded with them, but somehow they never seem to lead to as much clarification as we expect.

Any bipolar dimension, for example, can be translated into two orthogonal dimensions with the same labels by a simple device: (a) first, posit an intensity-dimension orthogonal to the bipolar one; then (b) consider the intermediate vectors.

Two examples will serve to illustrate:

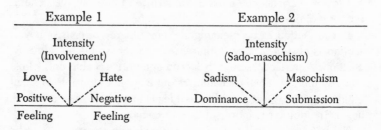

Example 1	Example 2
Intensity (Involvement)	Intensity (Sado-masochism)
Love　　　Hate	Sadism　　　Masochism
Positive　　　Negative	Dominance　　　Submission
Feeling　　　Feeling	

The first example simply expresses the familiar observation that love can be opposed either to hate or to indifference, the second that sadism and masochism, opposites in one sense, are joined in a higher (?) unity.

Intensity, in both these examples, can also be conceived as expressing a kind of "dimensional preference"—that is, a particular preoccupation with the theme that the bipolar dimension expresses, relative to other themes. In the first example, a person ranked high on the intensity-dimension would be one absorbed in issues of love and hate—less concerned, perhaps, with questions of respect, esteem, power, or whatever. In the second example, on the other hand, a person ranked high on the intensity-dimension would be preoccupied with questions of power in relationships, perhaps less interested in issues of love and hate. The intensity-dimensions, in other words, are in turn related to one another comparatively on a higher level of abstraction.

This can obviously be done with any pair of opposites. Jung divided the world into introverts and extraverts, and the term "ambivert" was thrown in to take care of people who seemed to fall on both ends in some way. But if there are ambiverts there are also "neutroverts"—people for whom the whole issue is simply irrelevant.

If we pay no attention to these higher order levels we will confuse ourselves no end. For every dimension that opposes x to y, we will find another that expresses the tendency to be hung up on xy questions more or less than ab questions, or some other dichotomy. Sometimes it seems less important to classify people on their degree of hostility or ambition or gregariousness, or whatever, than to classify them on the magnitude of the sine curve they weave around the midpoint of any one of these dimensions. That sine curve magnitude is the basis of the higher order dimension.

In my quantitative research years I was fascinated by the frequency, in factor analytic studies, of what I called "mirror factors." An analysis would generate a couple of pretty obvious-looking dimensions, and then, somewhere along the line, two more that looked just like the first two. In retrospect these mirror factors were probably the higher order dimensions I mentioned above.

I came to realize through all this that the notion of "independence" or "orthogonality" was probably just nonsense—a statistical artifact. Orthogonality simply expresses a balance of positive and negative relationships, as in the examples I gave. To say that love and hate, or sadism and masochism, have no relationship to each other is patently ridiculous, but perhaps no more so than other things revealed by statistics. Any time two variables are united at one level and opposed at another they will be ironed out by quantitative analysis into flat orthogonality. Conscious hate and unconscious hate, for example, might be positively related because both are hate, and negatively related because one is conscious, the other unconscious. If so, statistical analysis would reveal them as having no relation to each other. Thus the richness of a complex relationship is flattened into mere vacuity by rigorous analysis.

But this is only the beginning of dimensional complexity. It isn't just that an intensity-dimension can be discovered in the midst of any bipolar one. If we extend the intermediate vectors (love and hate in the first example) far enough, they begin to be difficult to distinguish. Both involve extreme tension aroused by the object, dependence upon and preoccupation with him or her, and so on. Tears accompany laughter, hysterical laughter accompanies grief. At the level of maximum intensity, emotions are as difficult to distinguish as they are when minimal. Intermediate levels maximize qualitative discriminations. *At peak intensity and at zero intensity all emotions seem to merge.*

I would suggest that this is true of all dichotomous extremes. It suggests that the notion of a dimension as a straight line is of limited utility—that, like most straight lines, they appear that way only because we see so small a segment of them, like the flatness of the earth. Extended infinitely, any dimension curves back upon itself and becomes a circle.

When we look at a coin edgewise it forms a short, thick line. Suppose we think of that line as a dimension of positive vs negative feeling, with the midpoint at complete neutrality. In actuality, the midpoint is nearest our eye, with the line bending away from us in both directions, but we can only tell this if we're up close and catch the light reflecting on the bending surface. If we now twist the coin sideways we suddenly realize that the apparent straight line is a circle, that negative feeling ultimately extends into what we call positive feeling, and vice versa.

All dimensions, it appears, have this character—that they all bend back upon themselves. Even size could be conceived in this way—supergalaxies becoming subatomic particles, with matter on one semicircle and anti-matter on the other.

The problem becomes further complicated if we consider the relation between dimensions over time. We generally examine the relationship between one dimension and another at a given point in time. If we study that relationship over time the orthogonality of two dimensions might be inconstant, becoming negative, positive or orthogonal at different times. Dimensions might collapse into each other at various times, forming the kinds of visions that people see during altered states of consciousness. But these are questions for another time, and another place.

Appendix A

This study was carried out with the aid of funds from the National Institute of Mental Health under grants MH-08128 and MH-10748. Ratings were made by Dori Appel Slater, Elizabeth Lozoff, and Marlene Hindley. The scales are fully described in Slater and Slater (1965) and *The Glory of Hera*. These results were presented in a paper to the American Sociological Association in Miami, Florida, in September 1966.

Two reliability tests were carried out for the scales. In the first test the author rated, for 30 societies, the notes on which the principal rater's ratings were based. Reliability was .85 for Militarism and .83 for Sadism. In the second test another rater studied the literature independently and made independent notes as well as her own ratings on 36 societies. Reliability was .75 and .70 for the two scales.

Militarism was correlated .76 with Simmons scale of "Prevalence of Warfare" (on the 32 overlapping societies); and .63 with Triandis's "Frequency of Warfare" (24 overlapping cases).[1]

Only those correlations significant at the .02 level or better were counted in the "fishnet" operation. Since this exploration was based on an early computer run, the total *n* was only 71. For any given correlation it was quite a bit less since for many societies there was incomplete information. Fisher's exact test was used whenever appropriate. I ignored correlations with other measures of warlike tendencies as well as with other "narcissism" scales, all of which were known to be highly intercorrelated. I also ignored many correlations that are essentially duplicates in Textor's analysis. The tabulations consist of chi-squares and phi coefficients based on

Table 1

CORRELATES OF MILITARISM AND SADISM (Textor)

Variables	Militarism		Sadism	
	p	n	p	n
1. Located in Africa	.02	68	—	—
2. Metal working present	.005	55	—	—
3. Class stratification, if present, based on hereditary aristocracy	.005 *	38	—	—
4. When stratification not present, craft specialization high	—	—	.02 *	11
5. Contracted debts present	—	—	.01 *	25
6. Incidence of personal crime high	.005 *	26	—	—
7. Incidence of theft high	.005 *	30	.02 *	30
8. Cousin marriage permitted	.01	67	—	—
9. Cousin terminology other than Eskimo or Hawaiian type	.01	65	—	—
10. Severe son's wife avoidance	.02 *	19	—	—
11. Sexual satisfaction low (children)	.01 *	34	—	—
12. Exclusive mother-son sleeping arrangements long	.02 *	31	—	—
13. Display of affection toward infant low	—	—	.01	44

four-fold contingency tables, but only the significance levels are shown in Table 1.

The number of statistically significant correlations is far greater than one would expect by chance at this level, particularly when we consider the clustering of results in the sexual and child-rearing spheres.

I also correlated the two scales with a variable not found in Textor's analysis: whether or not spouses customarily eat together, based on unpublished ratings by Whiting and his associates. On a sample of 65 cases for which sufficient data were available, there was a significant correlation between segregated eating and both Militarism and Sadism.

Variables	Militarism		Sadism	
14. Immediacy of reduction of infant's drives low	—	—	.02 *	38
15. Indulgence of child low	—	—	.005	50
16. Child's anxiety over performance of responsible behavior high	.02	46	—	—
17. Pressure on child for self-reliance high	.01	47	.01	48
18. Child's anxiety over nonperformance of achievement behavior high	.02	42	—	—
19. Child's anxiety over performance of achievement behavior high	.01 *	40	.02 *	40
20. Child's conflict over achievement high	—	—	.02 *	40
21. Child's conflict over obedient behavior high	—	—	.02	46
22. Extramarital coitus punished	.005 *	37	.01 *	36
23. "Castration anxiety" index high	—	—	.02 *	39

* Based on Fisher's exact test.

In William Eckhardt's study (1973), four scales were used. They were militarism, sadism, bellicosity, and the prevalence of warfare in the society. The four scales form a kind of continuum, from prevalence of warfare, which is devoid of psychological content, to sadism, which by definition implies a kind of surplus belligerence. Not too surprisingly, the more psychological measures of belligerence tend to be related to psychological variables, lending weight to a psychological interpretation of war, while the less psychological ones show more relation to structural variables like social class and technology.

Eckhardt groups his positive correlations somewhat differently than I did, putting all the child-rearing variables (unless specifically sexual) under the heading "Discipline," along with crime rates and belief in supernatural punishments. He finds the same kinds of relationships as those described earlier: All the military variables (sadism, especially) tend to be correlated with high crime rates and severe treatment of children.

The variables implying a weak marital bond and a strong mother-son bond included polygyny, extended exclusive mother-son sleeping arrangements, customs of men avoiding daughters-in-law and mothers-in-law, and a long postpartum sex taboo. [2] These were related primarily to militarism and bellicosity. On the other hand, sexual repression in infancy, adolescence, and adulthood was related to all four war scales.

The reason socioeconomic scales emerged so much more powerfully in Eckhardt's study seems to have been the addition of a nonpsychological measure, "prevalence of warfare," which correlated strongly with a number of socioeconomic variables, while sadism was related to very few. Only technological development was related to all four scales.

Eckhardt's emphasis on egoism requires some qualification at least insofar as it is based on "primitive" societies. He observes that the four military scales correlate with measures of "narcissism" more than with any other category, but he seems not to have taken into account that three of the four military scales are among the measures of "narcissism," thus considerably inflating the results. At the same time the independent measure "prevalence of warfare" correlates with as many of the "narcissism" scales as the other three, so his argument is not entirely invalid. Our initial study of narcissism [3] found all forms of militarism to be highly correlated with nonmilitary expressions of narcissism. It assumed that any *psychological* predilection toward warfare and violence was likely to be a subcategory of a more general narcissistic character, and this seemed indeed to be the case.

Appendix B

This study was made possible by two grants from the National Institute of Mental Health (MH-08128 and MH-10748). I would like to express my indebtedness to Dori A. Slater, who made all of the narcissism ratings, to Robert B. Textor, whose *Cross-Cultural Summary* was a major facilitating influence, and to John W. M. Whiting, William N. Stephens, and George Goethals for many useful suggestions.

The sample represents 58 of Murdock's 60 culture areas,[1] and all of the cultures are included in the "Ethnographic Atlas" sample, and in Textor's *Cross-Cultural Summary* (1965), on which much of the present analysis is founded. For any specific correlation the *n* will be reduced to the number of societies for which information is available on both of the variables concerned.

The measures of sexual restrictiveness were obtained as follows:

1. *The duration of the postpartum sex taboo (PPST)*. Here I followed Whiting, Kluckhohn, and Anthony (1958) and Stephens (1962) in capitalizing on the bimodal distribution of the length of the taboo by dichotomizing it. I also availed myself of those ratings included in column 36 of the *Ethnographic Atlas*,[2] and accepted the modifications of those ratings suggested by Whiting (1964). I use Whiting's cutting point of 11 months rather than the one-year point used in the atlas. A taboo of more than 11 months is rated "long"; all others are rated "short."

2. *Premarital sexual restrictions (PMSR)*. Ratings for this variable are based entirely on column 78 of the *Ethnographic Atlas*, which distinguishes between (1) complete permissiveness, (2) permissiveness as long as

197

pregnancy does not occur, (3) early marriage, (4) trial marriage, (5) prohibition weakly enforced, and (6) strongly enforced prohibition with emphasis on virginity. For our purposes the second, third, and fourth categories are combined since it is impossible to distinguish any important difference in restrictiveness among them. This leaves us with four degrees of restrictiveness.

3. *Extramarital sexual restrictions (EMSR).* For this measure I used two sets of ratings. The first was Simmons's rating of "postmarital sex restrictions on women," [3] and involves a three-point scale (dominant, intermediate, unimportant). The second was Ford and Beach's comparable rating of "punishment for extramarital coitus," which is also concerned primarily with women and is also trichotomous, with some societies punishing adultery seriously, others punishing it only in a token fashion, and still others entirely permissive.[4] Some 21 cases overlap the two studies, with perfect agreement in over half of them and complete disagreement in three. All cases involving any disagreement have been placed in the intermediate category.

4. *Restriction of sexual gratification in childhood.* For this I used Whiting and Child's rating of "initial sexual satisfaction" in early child training (1953).

5. *Restrictions on physical gratification in infancy.* For this more general measure I used the index of "overall indulgence in infancy" of Bacon, Barry and Child (1952), based on ratings of (1) display of affection toward the infant, (2) protection against environmental discomforts, (3) degree of drive reduction (hunger, thirst, etc.), (4) immediacy of drive reduction, (5) consistency of drive reduction, (6) constancy of presence of nurturing agent, (7) absence of pain from nurturing agent. This measure is closer to the broad psychoanalytic concept of libidinal gratification than the Whiting and Child measure but also lends itself moie easily to alternative theoretical interpretations.

These five types of restrictions only scratch the surface. There are other sexual taboos, such as pregnancy and menstrual taboos, avoidance patterns derived from the incest taboo, restrictions on nongenital and homosexual gratifications, generalized restrictions on body contact, patterns of *scheduling* bodily functions, such as eating, elimination, and copulation, a host of child-rearing patterns, such as early weaning and toilet training, having the child sleep alone, etc., and restrictions on various forms of tension discharge, such as laughter and physical play. The Puritans, with a true Freudian understanding of such matters, embraced almost all of these restrictions, including bans on laughter, dancing, and sports.

My measures of cultural complexity draw heavily on Murdock's work

(1964). Correlations between these variables and premarital sex restrictions, therefore, merely repeat his tables, except that my sample is smaller. The two measures of social complexity are both drawn from the *Ethnographic Atlas*. The first is the size of the local community (column 31), which the *Atlas* arranges on an 8-point scale, where 1 = less than 50 persons and 8 = one or more cities of 50,000. The second is the number of jurisdictional levels of social control beyond the local level (column 33), a variable adapted from Swanson (1960). The range for this variable is 0–4.[5]

My index of technological complexity is the least satisfactory, a small and rather haphazard sample of the immense realm of possible technological achievements. Nor does it escape contamination from a variety of climatic and other ecological factors. Its single advantage is that it is available for most of the cultures in the sample. The index is a composite of four variables drawn from the *Ethnographic Atlas:* metal working, weaving, pottery, and boat building (columns 42, 44, 48, and 50), each of which is scored in terms of presence or absence. (The *Atlas* also has ratings for two other variables, leather working and house building, but these proved useless, the former because it contained too many lacunae, the latter because it was invariant.) The first three variables in the index are highly loaded on Gouldner and Peterson's "Technology" Factor [6] and were selected in part for this reason. The fourth, boat building, was added to offset the apparent bias against peoples living in settings unsuitable for agriculture or husbandry. The composite index is computed by simply counting the number of "present" ratings on the four component variables and hence runs from 0–4.

"Narcissism" was measured by scores derived from a factorial analysis of seven cross-cultural ratings. These ratings, which have been described in detail elsewhere,[7] consisted of the following:

1. Sensitivity to insult (e.g., humiliations lead to suicide or homicide).

2. Invidious display of wealth (e.g., potlatch).

3. Pursuit of military glory (e.g., death in battle is seen as source of highest prestige).

4. Bellicosity (e.g., wars and raids are major occupation of adult males).

5. Bloodthirstiness (e.g., prisoners habitually tortured).

6. Institutionalized boasting (e.g., during feasts, after battles, during work activities).

7. Exhibitionistic dancing (e.g., individual skill is recognized and rewarded).

All 100 cultures used in the present study were coded on these variables, using the Human Relations Area Files whenever possible. When the first 71 had been coded, the seven ratings were intercorrelated and factor analyzed.[8] From this analysis two factors emerged, a general factor loaded on all seven scales and a bipolar one (ignored for the purposes of this analysis) that essentially opposed scales 3, 4, and 5 to scales 1, 2, and 7. A strong and factorially pure measure of the first factor could be obtained by simply adding all seven scales together, and when this was done, the scores on each factor were trichotomized to give, as nearly as possible, a rectangular distribution of high, medium, and low scores on each factor. Thomson's pooling square technique (1949) was used in constructing the factor tests.

Results were computed in two ways. Initially, the data were grouped into discrete categories and subjected to chi-square analysis, but in order to compare the linearity of the various relationships I switched to Pearson product-moment coefficients, as shown in Table 2. (Note that the correlations involving the two childhood-restriction variables are negative since these measures are expressed in terms of *lack* of restrictiveness.) Since all of the variables are, or can be conceived of as, continuous, it makes little difference which technique is used. The correlation coefficients are more sensitive and informative regarding linear relationships, while the chi-squares tell us a bit more about nonlinear ones. In actuality there are few differences in the results. Thirteen of the chi-squares are significant at the .05 level or better, 12 of the correlation coefficients. The significant correlations between narcissism and technological complexity, and between extramarital restrictions and jurisdictional levels, just fail to reach significance using chi-square; while significant chi-squares were obtained between (1) narcissism and jurisdictional levels, (2) overall indulgence and local size, and (3) overall indulgence and technological complexity, in part due to slight curvilinearities. In general, however, the differences merely reflect the fact that some combinations hover close to the arbitrary .05 level and fall above or below according to the test used.

The true sizes of the correlations for extramarital and childhood restrictions are probably greatly underestimated in Table 2 since most of the complex urban societies were not included in the samples from which these three ratings were drawn. At their height most of these societies are well known to have had strong extramarital restrictions and nonindulgent child-rearing practices, but it would hardly be appropriate to mix ad-hoc ratings of my own with those of previous authors.

The composite index of sexual restriction was constructed simply by converting each of the five measures to a five-point scale and adding up the scores. Thus, for PMSR, $V = 5$, $P = 4$, A, T, and $E = 2$, and $F = 1$. Since the PPST was originally coded by Whiting on a five-point scale, this was simply retained. For EMSR there are only three points: Severe punishment of adultery $= 5$, disapproval with few sanctions $= 3$, and permis-

Table 2

CORRELATION COEFFICIENTS BETWEEN SEXUAL
RESTRICTION, NARCISSISM, AND
COMPLEXITY VARIABLES

	Local Size	Jurisdictional Levels	Technological Complexity	Narcissism
Narcissism	.09	.14	.23 *	—
PMSR	.51 †	.37 †	.32 †	.19
PPST	.11	.04	.10	.26 *
EMSR	.41 †	.27 *	.62 †	.49 †
Sexual indulgence in childhood	−.33	.00	−.44 †	−.01
Overall indulgence in childhood	−.22	−.44 †	−.16	−.31 *
Composite sexual restriction index	.44 †	.31 †	.43 †	.43 †

* Significant at .05 level
† Significant at .01 level

siveness = 1. The Whiting and Child measure of sexual indulgence in childhood was broken down as follows: 6–9 = 5, 10–11 = 4, 12 = 3, 13–16 = 2, 17–20 = 1; and the Bacon, Barry, and Child scores on overall indulgence in infancy: 2–8 = 5, 9–10 = 4, 11 = 3, 12 = 2, 13–14 = 1. On these last two conversions an attempt was made to approximate a normal distribution as closely as possible. All blanks on all variables were assigned a score of 3. The resulting index is rather insensitive since over half of the societies contained two or more blanks, and a third contained three or more.

All the coefficients in Table 2 should probably be regarded as minimum estimates, given the crude nature of cross-cultural data (every case coming from a different ethnographer with a different baseline in his or her head) and the heavy dilution effect coming from the large amount of missing or uncoded data. This last limitation also limits the usefulness of computing partial correlations or undertaking multivariate analyses as a way of tackling the more basic questions.

Notes

(See Bibliography for full information on all references)

Chapter 1. Sex in America
1. Cuber and Harroff, 1965, pp. 172–80

Chapter 3. Identification: Personal and Positional
1. Freud, 1951, p. 62
2. Freud, 1933, p. 86
3. For references see Slater 1961b, p. 118, and 1962
4. Freud, Anna, 1946, p. 120
5. Sanford, 1955, pp. 112–14
6. Freud, 1951, pp. 110–11
7. Sanford, 1955, p. 110
8. Kagan, 1958, pp. 298–99
9. Fenichel, 1945, p. 104
10. See Slater, 1961b, p. 118, and 1962
11. Mowrer, 1950, p. 592
12. See Slater, 1961b, p. 119
13. See Slater, 1961b, pp. 119, 122–23
14. Parsons and Bales, 1955, pp. 91–94
15. See Slater, 1961b, p. 120
16. Freud, 1927, pp. 42–44
17. Fenichel, 1945, p. 335; Slater, 1961b, pp. 122–23; Symonds, 1949, p. 96; Brodbeck, 1954

Chapter 4. Parental Roles
1. Beaglehole, 1954, p. 161
2. Parsons and Bales, 1955, p. 80
3. Payne and Mussen, 1956, pp. 358–62

4. See Slater, 1961a, p. 300
5. See Slater, 1961a, pp. 301–302
6. Bott, 1960, p. 252
7. Bott, 1960, p. 439
8. Riesman and Roseborough, 1960, pp. 143–62
9. Scott, 1958, p. 187
10. LeVine, 1958, p. 358
11. Maccoby, 1960, pp. 528–29
12. Simmel, 1950, p. 129

Chapter 5.   Some Effects of Transience
1. Pierson, 1964, pp. 119 ff.
2. Riesman, 1955, pp. 37–38
3. Komarovsky, 1964; Young and Willmott, 1964; Slater, 1961a, pp. 296–308; Litwak, 1966, p. 14

Chapter 6.   Democracy and Grandparents
1. Patai, 1959, pp. 229–33; Guthrie, 1952, pp. 148–50
2. Simmons, 1945
3. Simmons, 1945, pp. 50–81, 234

Chapter 7.   Changing the Family
1. Goode, 1963, p. 355
2. Davis, 1964, pp. 276–320
3. Ryder, 1965, p. 852
4. Zborowski and Herzog, 1962, pp. 131–141, 223–32
5. Zborowski and Herzog, pp. 330–34
6. Zborowski and Herzog, 1962, pp. 142–51, 271
7. Mead, 1961, p. 22
8. Mead, 1953, pp. 14–16, 37–38, 55–61, 80–83, 99, 128–33
9. Mead, 1961, pp. 145 ff.
10. Mead, 1961, pp. 39, 51, 95, 103, 196, 352–54
11. Mead, 1961, pp. 374–77
12. Turner, 1921, p. 169
13. Calhoun, 1917, II, p. 198
14. Furstenberg, 1966, pp. 326–37
15. de Tocqueville, 1947, p. 386
16. Sunley, 1963, pp. 159–61; Calhoun, 1917, pp. 51–67, 131, 141–48, 152
17. Calhoun, 1917, pp. 132–44; Morgan, 1966, pp. 33 ff., 62–64, 77–78, 124–30, 171
18. Morgan, 1966, pp. 12, 18–19, 97–98
19. Morgan, 1966, pp. 20–21, 45–52, 65 ff., 77–78, 83–84, 87 ff., 106–108, 147–49
20. Morgan, 1966, pp. 30, 71–75, 83–86, 103–108

21. Ariès, 1962, pp. 378, 411–13
22. Mace, 1964, p. 307
23. Coser, 1964, pp. 527–8, 540
24. Coser, 1964, p. 527
25. Mace, 1964, p. 316
26. Coser, 1964, p. 539–40; Mace, 1964, p. 317
27. Goode, 1963, pp. 313–15
28. Diamond, 1964, pp. 430–31; Spiro, 1965, pp. 11 ff., 340, 384–88

Chapter 8. The Family in Ancient Greece

1. Gomme, 1937, pp. 90–102
2. For a more detailed discussion of this and other Greek patterns, see Slater, 1968, Chapter 1
3. Nye and Hoffman, 1963, pp. 215–30, 251–262, 282–305. Cf. also, Mace, 1964, pp. 92–116; Briffault, 1931, pp. 188–89, 248–49
4. Plutarch, IX, 752e–f, 753c–d
5. Kitto, 1960, p. 230; Xenophon, *Oeconomicus*, vii, 22–42
6. Ehrenberg, 1951, p. 207; Kitto, 1960, p. 228–229
7. Herodotus, vii, 84
8. Gundlach and Riess, 1966
9. See Slater, 1968, p. 12
10. Bettelheim, 1955, pp. 232–33; for a clinical case study on this theme see Slater, 1968, pp. 14–23
11. Freud, 1953, p. 106
12. Horney, 1932, pp. 349–353
13. Malinowski, 1929, pp. 299–300, 422–23
14. Ferenczi, 1952, p. 360
15. Stephens, 1962, pp. 80 ff., 124 ff.; Baruch, 1952
16. Ehrenberg, 1951, p. 193; Licht, 1963, p. 39; Fustel de Coulanges, 1956, p. 43; Blümner, n.d., p. 92
17. Semonides, in Lattimore, 1961, p. 11.
18. See Slater, 1968, pp. 25–26
19. Licht, 1963, p. 40
20. Blümner, n.d., p. 139
21. Licht, 1963, pp. 28–29
22. Finley, 1959, pp. 137–38
23. Bott, 1957, pp. 52–113
24. Gouldner, 1965, pp. 26, 60–64, 68–70; Plutarch, IX, 769
25. Ovid, VI, 613–22
26. Finley, 1959, pp. 128–29
27. Huizinga, 1955, p. 73
28. Aristotle, *Ethics*, 1.5; Gouldner, 1965, pp. 43–44, 58, 98, 108–11
29. Reich, 1960, pp. 222–27
30. Bateson, 1956, pp. 251 ff.
31. Horney, 1932, p. 360

32. Blümner, p. 88; Nilsson, 1961, p. 97; Rose, 1925, p. 95
33. Kerenyi, 1960, pp. 39–40; Lawson, 1964, pp. 172–76
34. Licht, 1963, p. 150–51
35. Licht, 1963, pp. 59, 345, 348
36. Licht, 1963, p. 427
37. Kitto, 1960, p. 18
38. Finley, 1959, p. 140
39. Euripides, *Orestes*, 251–52, 262–65, in Grene, 1959
40. Euripides, *Orestes*, 1590, in Grene, 1959
41. Euripides, *Orestes*, 932–37, in Grene, 1959

Chapter 9.   Traits of Warlike Cultures

1. Slater, 1968, Chapter 14
2. Slater, 1968, Chapter 14; Slater and Slater, 1965; Textor, 1965
3. In Textor's and my own previous studies this scale is called "Pursuit of Military Glory." For a more complete description, see Slater, 1968, Chapter 14 and Appendix
4. Grinnell, 1962, II, pp. 4–5
5. This scale, called "Bloodthirstiness" elsewhere, is described more fully in Slater, 1968, Chapter 14 and Appendix
6. Latcham, 1909; Cooper, 1946; Padden, 1957
7. For descriptions, see Textor, 1965; Whiting and Child, 1953; Stephens, 1962; Ford and Beach, 1951; Bacon, Barry, and Child, 1952
8. Eckhardt, 1973

Chapter 10.   Civilization, Narcissism, and Sexual Repression

1. Murdock, 1964, p. 399
2. Freud, 1953, p. 90. Note that the following quotations are drawn alternately from the Hogarth and Norton editions of *Civilization and Its Discontents*
3. Freud, 1962, p. 69
4. Freud, 1962, p. 59
5. Freud, 1953, pp. 79–81. cf. also Chapter 11 of this volume
6. Freud, 1953, pp. 91–92
7. Freud, 1953, p. 87
8. Freud, 1953, p. 143
9. Freud, 1953, p. 144
10. Freud, 1953, p. 51
11. Cf. Narroll, 1956; Freeman and Winch, 1957; Gouldner and Peterson, 1962
12. Freud, 1953, p. 44. I agree with Norman Brown (1959, pp. 137 ff.) that Freud never made a convincing case that sublimation was something other than repression. It seems to have just been applied to any example of repression that Freud approved of or thought was "worth it."
13. Stuart, 1955, pp. 34 ff., 86, 89, 107

14. Stuart, 1955, p. 45
15. Whiting, 1964; Whiting, Kluckhohn, and Anthony, 1958; Burton and Whiting, 1961; Stephens, 1962; Slater and Slater, 1965
16. Cf. Unwin, 1934, p. 322, 377, 604; Slater and Slater, 1965
17. Ryerson, 1960; cf. McLuhan, 1950; Mace and Mace, 1963, p. 80
18. For details on the sample, the measures used, and other aspects of methodology, see Appendix B.
19. Freud, 1962, p. 64
20. Freud, 1915, p. 321–22; Stuart, 1955, pp. 81 ff.
21. Freud, 1950, p. 56
22. Unwin, 1934; Sherfey, 1966
23. Gouldner and Peterson, 1962, pp. 24–27. The correlation between the narcissism index and the development of pottery is positive and significant at the .02 level of confidence.
24. Ryerson, 1960, pp. 68 ff., 145 ff.; Taylor, 1954, pp. 206, 221
25. Whiting, 1964
26. Bronfenbrenner, 1961; Mischel, 1958; Burton and Whiting, 1961; Hoffman, 1962; McClelland, 1961, pp. 328, 374–75
27. Ryerson, 1960
28. See Textor, 1965; Eckhardt, 1973
29. Weber of course argues that ascetic behavior was intended to demonstrate rather than solicit grace, but it has always seemed silly to me to base a massive change in popular behavior on an abstruse ideological detail. Most of the Protestant sects were sexually repressive and encouraged harsh child-rearing practices. Perhaps the emotional logic of the spirit of capitalism was a fusion: the asceticism designed to please the parent-deity, the financial success to demonstrate to peers the "fact" of having been chosen or favored over them (a little like the Biblical story of Joseph). Both themes constitute an appropriate response to a sudden new feeling of scarcity regarding parental love. Weber, 1930, pp. 52–53, 89, 104–107, 147, 152–53, 193
30. Weber, 1930, pp. 105, 106, 116, 119, 121, 149, 153–54, 157–59, 166; cf. Unwin, 1934, pp. 339–44, 381–82, 428
31. Unwin, 1934, p. 321
32. Taylor, 1954, p. 204; cf. also Watt, 1964, esp. pp. 281–82
33. Ryerson, 1960, pp. 75–129, 149–51; Whiting and Child, 1953, pp. 69–99. The findings regarding aggression are interesting in view of our own finding (Slater and Slater, 1965) that narcissism was positively correlated with early indulgence of aggression, negatively with the other four.
34. McClelland, 1961, pp. 133–51; Mace and Mace, 1964, pp. 60–91
35. Mace and Mace, 1964, pp. 80–85; McLuhan, 1951

Chapter 11. Short Circuits in Social Life
1. Freud, 1950, pp. 67–68. (Emphasis mine.)
2. Freud, 1951, pp. 92, 120–23

3. *The Boston Globe,* October 19, 1956
4. Murdock, 1949, pp. 4 ff.
5. Caplan, 1955, p. 63, 105–107
6. Caplan, 1955, pp. 108–109
7. Murdock, 1949, Chapter 10
8. Freud, 1953, Vol. IV, pp. 44–49; Caplan, 1955, pp. 81 ff.; Weinberg, 1955, p. 222
9. Murdock, 1949, Chapter 10
10. Mann, 1936, pp. 279–319

Chapter 12.   Emotional Priorities
1. Freud, 1949, pp. 23–24; Freud, 1953, Vol. II, pp. 114, 119; Vol. IV, pp. 33, 153
2. Freud, 1949, p. 79
3. Taylor, 1963, pp. 39–40
4. Taylor, 1963, p. 43
5. Olds, 1958
6. Freud, 1953, Vol. IV, pp. 157 ff.; cf. also Lindemann, 1944
7. Freud, 1953, Vol. IV, p. 154
8. Freud, 1953, Vol. V, pp. 343–45
9. Jung, 1924
10. Freud, 1953, Vol. IV, pp. 192–216
11. Freud, 1953, Vol. IV, p. 39
12. Spitz, 1945; 1946
13. Schaffner, 1955, pp. 27 ff.
14. Stuart, 1955
15. Parsons, n.d., p. 18
16. Freud, 1953, Vol. IV, p. 42
17. Cf. Szasz, 1957, pp. 191–221

Chapter 13.   Dualities
1. Mumford, 1949; Sjoberg, 1960
2. Marcus, 1966; Gouldner, 1965; Cleaver, 1968
3. Coser, 1956
4. Fromm, 1941; Redl, 1942; Schutz, 1958; Bennis and Shepard, 1956
5. Taylor, 1954, pp. 271–74
6. Mead, 1950, p. 211
7. Vogel and Bell, 1960, pp. 382–97
8. Vogel and Bell, 1960, p. 389

Chapter 15.   Pleasure, Healing, and Conflict
1. Parsons, n.d., pp. 1 ff.
2. Ferenczi, 1938, p. 16
3. Brown, 1959
4. Ferenczi, 1955, p. 230

5. Bakan, 1971
6. Laing, 1971

Appendix A
1. See Simmons, 1945; and Triandis, 1961
2. Cf. Stephens, 1962
3. Slater and Slater, 1965; Slater, 1968

Appendix B
1. Murdock, 1957, 1962
2. Murdock, 1962
3. Simmons, 1945
4. Ford and Beach, 1951, pp. 113–16; Textor, 1965
5. Cf. Murdock, 1964
6. 1962, pp. 25 ff.
7. Slater and Slater, 1965
8. See Slater and Slater, 1965

Bibliography

Ardrey, R. *The Territorial Imperative* (New York: Dell, 1968).

Ariès, P. *Centuries of Childhood* (New York: Knopf, 1962).

Aristotle. *Basic Works of Aristotle* (New York: Random House, 1941), translated by W. D. Ross.

Bacon, Margaret K., Barry, H. A., and Child, I. L. Unpublished ratings of socialization practices. Department of Psychology, Yale University, 1952.

Bakan, David. *Disease, Pain and Sacrifice* (Boston: Beacon Press, 1971).

Baruch, Dorothy. *One Little Boy* (New York: Julian Press, 1952).

Bateson, Gregory et al. "Toward a Theory of Schizophrenia." *Behavioral Science* 1 (1956): 251–64.

Beaglehole, Ernest and Pearl. "Personality Development in Pukapuka." In W. E. Martin and Celia Stendler (eds.) *Readings in Child Development* (New York: Harcourt, Brace & Co., 1954).

Bennis, W. G., and Shepard, H. A. "A Theory of Group Development." *Human Relations* 9 (1956): 415–37.

Bettleheim, B. *Symbolic Wounds* (London: Thames and Hudson, 1955).

Blümner, H. *Homelife of the Ancient Greeks* (New York: Funk and Wagnalls, n.d.).

Bott, E. "Conjugal Roles and Social Networks." In Bell and Vogel (eds.) *A Modern Introduction to the Family* (Glencoe, Ill.: Free Press, 1960).

————. *Family and Social Network* (London: Tavistock, 1957).

Briffault, R. *The Mothers* (New York: Macmillan, 1931).

Brodbeck, A. J. "Learning Theory and Identification: IV. Oedipal Motivation as a Determinant of Conscious Development." *Journal of Genetic Psychology* 84 (1954): 219–27.

Bronfenbrenner, U. "The Changing American Child: A Speculative Analysis." *Merrill-Palmer Quarterly* 7 (1961): 73–84.

Brown, Norman O. *Life against Death* (New York: Vintage, 1959).

Burton, R. V., and Whiting, J. W. M. "The Absent Father and Cross-sex Identity." *Merrill-Palmer Quarterly* 7 (1961): 85–95.

Calhoun, A. W. *A Social History of the American Family* (Cleveland: Arthur H. Clarke, 1917–19).

Caplan, Gerald. *Mental Health Aspects of Social Work in Public Welfare* (University of California School of Social Welfare, 1955).

Child, I. L. "Socialization." In G. Lindzey (ed.) *Handbook of Social Psychology. Vol. 2* (Reading, Mass.: Addison-Wesley, 1954): 655–92.

Cleaver, Eldridge. *Soul on Ice* (New York: McGraw-Hill, 1968).

Cooper, J. M. The Araucanians. *Bureau of American Ethnology Bulletin*, 143, vol. 2: 687–760 (Washington: Smithsonian Institute, 1946).

Coser, L. A. "The Case of the Soviet Family." In Rose Coser (ed.) *The Family: Its Structures and Functions* (New York: St. Martin's Press, 1964).

———. *The Functions of Social Conflict* (Glencoe, Ill.: Free Press, 1956).

Cuber, John, and Harroff, Peggy. *Sex and the Significant Americans* (Baltimore, Md.: Penguin Books, 1965).

Davis, Kingsley. "The Sociology of Parent-Youth Conflict." In Coser (ed.) *The Family: Its Structures and Functions* (New York: St. Martin's Press, 1964).

de Tocqueville, A. *Democracy in America* (New York: Oxford University Press, 1947).

Diamond, S. "Collective Child-Rearing: The Kibbutz." In Coser (ed.) *The Family: Its Structures and Functions* (New York: St. Martin's Press, 1964).

Dollard, J., Doob, L. W., Miller, N. E., Mowrer, O. H., and Sears, R. R. *Frustration and Aggression* (New Haven, Conn.: Yale University Press, 1939).

Eckhardt, W. "Anthropological Correlates of Primitive Militarism." *Peace Research* 5 (1973): 5–10.

Ehrenberg, V. *The People of Aristophanes* (Oxford: Basil Blackwell, 1951).

Erikson, K. *Wayward Puritans* (New York: Wiley, 1966).

Fenichel, O. *The Psychoanalytic Theory of the Neuroses.* (New York: W. W. Norton, 1945).

Ferenczi, S. *Further Contributions to the Theory and Technique of Psychoanalysis.* (New York: Basic Books, 1952).

———. *Final Contributions to the Problems and Methods of Psychoanalysis.* (New York: Basic Books, 1955).

———. *Thalassa* (New York: Psychoanalytic Quarterly, 1938).

Finley, M. I. *The World of Odysseus* (New York: Meridian, 1959).

Ford, C. S., and Beach, F. A. *Patterns of Sexual Behavior* (New York: Harper, 1951).

Foster, G. M. "Peasant Society and the Image of Limited Good." *American Anthropologist* 67 (1965): 293–315.

Freeman, L. C., and Winch, F. A. *Patterns of Sexual Behavior* (New York: Harper & Row, 1951).

Freud, Anna. *The Ego and the Mechanisms of Defense* (New York: International Universities Press, 1946).

Freud, Sigmund. *An Outline of Psychoanalysis* (New York: Norton, 1949).

———. *Beyond the Pleasure Principle* (New York: Liveright, 1950).

———. *Civilization and its Discontents* (New York: Norton, 1962) and (London: Hogarth Press, 1953).

———. *Collected Papers, Vol. II, IV, V* (London: Hogarth Press, 1953).

———. *The Ego and the Id* (London: Hogarth Press, 1927).

———. *Group Psychology and the Analysis of the Ego* (New York: Liveright, 1951).

———. *New Introductory Lectures in Psychoanalysis* (London: Hogarth Press, 1933).

Fromm, Erich. *Escape from Freedom* (New York: Rinehart, 1941).

Furstenberg, F. F. Jr. "Industrialization and the American Family." *American Sociological Review* 31 (1966): 326–37.

Fustel de Coulanges, N. D. *The Ancient City* (Garden City, N.Y.: Doubleday, 1956).

Goethals, G. "The Relationship between Family Esteem Patterns and Measures of Guilt, Identification and Aggression in a Group of Four-year Old Children." Unpublished doctoral dissertation, Harvard University, 1953.

Gomme, A. W. *Essays on Greek History and Literature* (Oxford: Basil Blackwell, 1937).

Goode, W. J. *World Revolution and Family Patterns* (New York: Free Press, 1963).

Gouldner, A. W. *Enter Plato* (New York: Basic Books, 1965).

——— and Peterson, R. A. *Notes on Technology and the Moral Order* (New York: Bobbs-Merrill, 1962).

Grene, D., and Lattimore, R. (eds.) *The Complete Greek Tragedies* (Chicago: University of Chicago Press, 1959).

Grinnell, G. B. *The Cheyenne Indians* (New York: Cooper Square, 1962).

Gundlach, R. H., and Riess, B. F. "Self and Sexual Identity in Men and Women in Relationship to Homosexuality." In L. Aronson and J. Rosenblatt (eds.) *Development and Evolution of Behavior* (New York: Freeman, 1966).

Guthrie, W. K. C. *Orpheus and Greek Religion* (London: Methuen, 1952).

Herodotus. *The Histories* (Baltimore: Penguin, 1954), translated by De Selincourt.

Hesiod. In *Hesiod, The Homeric Hymns and Homerica.* (Cambridge: Harvard University Press, 1959), translated by Evelyn-White.

Hoffman, Lois. "The Father's Role in the Family and the Child's Peer-group Adjustment." *Merrill-Palmer Quarterly* 7 (1961): 97–111.

Holmberg, A. R. *Nomads of the Long Bow* (Washington: U.S. Government Printing Office, 1950).

Horney, Karen. "The Dread of Women." *International Journal of Psychoanalysis* XIII (1932): 348–60.

Huizinga, J. *Homo Ludens* (Boston: Beacon Press, 1955).

Jung, C. G. *Psychological Types* (New York: Harcourt, 1924).

Kagan, J. "The Concept of Identification." *Psychological Review* 65 (1958): 296–305.

Kerenyi, K. *The Gods of the Greeks* (New York: Grove Press, 1960).

Kitto, H. D. F. *The Greeks* (Baltimore, Md.: Penguin, 1960).

Komarovsky, M. *Blue-Collar Marriage* (New York: Random House, 1964).

Laing, Ronald. *Knots* (New York: Pantheon Books, 1971).

Latcham, R. E. Ethnology of the Araucanos. *Journal of Royal Anthropology Institute* 39 (1909): 334–70.

Lattimore, R. *Greek Lyrics*. 2nd Edition. (Chicago: University of Chicago Press, 1961).

Lawson, John. *Modern Greek Folklore and Ancient Greek Religion* (New Hyde Park, N.Y.: University Books, 1964).

Lee, R. B., and DeVore, I. *Man the Hunter* (Chicago: Aldine House, 1968).

LeVine, R. A. "Social Control and Socialization among the Gusii." Unpublished doctoral dissertation, Harvard University, 1958.

Licht, H. *Sexual Life in Ancient Greece* (New York: Barnes and Noble, 1963).

Lindemann, E. "Symptomatology and Management of Acute Grief." *American Journal of Psychiatry* 101 (1944): 141–48.

Litwak, E. "Technological Innovation and Ideal Forms of Family Structure in an Industrial Democratic Society." Unpublished manuscript, University of Michigan School of Social Work, 1966).

Lorenz, K. Z. *On Aggression* (New York: Harcourt, 1966).

Mace, D., and Mace, V. *The Soviet Family* (Garden City, N.Y.: Doubleday, 1964).

Maccoby, Eleanor. "Effects upon Children of Their Mother's Outside Employment." In Bell and Vogel (eds.) *A Modern Introduction to the Family* (Glencoe, Ill.: Free Press, 1960).

Malinowski, B. *The Sexual Life of Savages* (New York: Harcourt, Brace, 1929).

Mann, Thomas. "Blood of the Walsungs." In *Stories of Three Decades,* (New York: Knopf, 1936) 279–319.

Marcus, S. *The Other Victorians* (New York: Basic Books, 1966).

Marcuse, H. *Eros and Civilization* (Boston: Beacon Press, 1955).

McClelland, D. C. *The Achieving Society* (Princeton, N.J.: Van Nostrand, 1961).

McGiffert, M. *The Character of Americans* (Homewood, Ill.: Dorsey, 1964).

McLuhan, H. M. *The Mechanical Bride* (New York: Vanguard, 1951).

Mead, G. H. *Mind, Self and Society* (University of Chicago Press, 1934).

Mead, M. *Growing Up in New Guinea* (New York: Mentor, 1953).

————. *New Lives for Old* (New York: Mentor, 1961).

————. *Sex and Temperament in Three Primitive Societies* (New York: Mentor, 1950).

Mischel, W. "Preference for Delayed Reinforcement: An Experimental Study of a Cultural Observation." *Journal of Abnormal Social Psychology* 56 (1958): 57–61.

Morgan, E. S. *The Puritan Family* (New York: Harper & Row, 1966).

Mowrer, O. H. *Learning Theory and Personality Dynamics.* (New York: Ronald Press, 1950).

Mumford, L. "The Fallacy of Systems." *Saturday Review of Literature* 32 (October 1949).

Murdock, George. *Social Structure* (New York: Macmillan, 1949).

————. "World Ethnographic Sample." *American Anthropologist* 59 (1957): 664–87.

————. Ethnographic atlas. *Ethnology*, 1962, 1, nos. 1–4.

————. "The Regulation of Premarital Sex Behavior." In Manners, R. A. (ed.) *Process and Pattern in Culture* (Chicago: Aldine, 1964).

Naroll, Raoul. "A Preliminary Index of Social Development." *American Anthropologist* 58 (1956): 687–715.

Nilsson, M. P. *Greek Folk Religion* (New York: Harper & Row, 1961).

Nye, F. I., and Hoffman, Lois. *The Employed Mother in America* (Chicago: Rand McNally, 1963).

Olds, J. "Self-stimulation of the Brain." *Science* 127 (1958): 315–24.

Orwell, George. *1984* (New York: Harcourt-Brace, 1949).

Ovid. *Metamorphoses* (Cambridge, Mass.: Harvard University Press, 1946), translated by F. J. Miller.

Padden, R. C. "Cultural Change and Military Resistance in Araucanian Chile, 1550–1730." *Southwestern Journal of Anthropology* 13 (1957): 103–21.

Parsons, T. "Some Reflections on the Problem of Psychosomatic Relationships in Health and Illness." Unpublished manuscript.

Parsons, T., and Bales, R. F. *Family, Socialization and Interaction Process* (Glencoe, Ill.: Free Press, 1955).

Patai, R. *Sex and the Family in the Bible and the Middle East* (New York: Doubleday, 1959).

Payne, D. E., and Mussen, P. H. "Parent-child Relations and Father Identification among Adolescent Boys." *Journal of Abnormal Social Psychology*, 52 (1956): 358–62.

Pierson, G. W. "The M-factor in American History." In M. McGiffert (ed.) *The Character of Americans.* (Homewood, Ill.: Dorsey, 1964).

Plutarch. *Moralia.* 15 vols. (Cambridge, Mass.: Harvard University Press, 1949), translated by F. C. Babbitt.

Redl, F. "Group Emotion and Leadership." *Psychiatry* 5 (1942): 573–96.

Reich, Annie. "Pathologic Forms of Self-Esteem Regulation." *Psychoanalytic Study of the Child* 15 (New York: International University Press, 1960).

Riesman, D., Glazer, N., and Denney, R. *The Lonely Crowd* (Garden City, N.Y.: Doubleday, 1955).

Riesman, David, and Roseborough, Howard. "Careers and Consumer Behavior." In Bell and Vogel (eds.) *A Modern Introduction to the Family* (Glencoe, Ill.: Free Press, 1960).

Rose, H. J. *Primitive Culture in Greece* (London: Methuen, 1925).

Rosen, J. N. *Direct Analysis* (New York: Grune and Stratton, 1953).

Ryder, N. B. "The Cohort in the Study of Social Change." *American Sociological Review* 30 (1965).

Ryerson, Alice. "Medical Advice on Child-rearing: 1550–1900." Unpublished doctoral dissertation, Harvard University Graduate School of Education, 1960.

Sahlins, M. *Stone Age Economics* (New York: Aldine, 1972).

Sanford, R. N. "The Dynamics of Identification." *Psychological Review* 62 (1955): 106–118.

Schaffner, B. (ed). *Group Processes, 1954* (New York: Macy Foundation, 1955).

Schutz, W. C. *FIRO: A Three-Dimensional Theory of Interpersonal Behavior* (New York: Holt, 1958).

Scott, J. P. *Animal Behavior* (Chicago: University of Chicago Press, 1958).

Sears, Pauline. "Child-rearing Factors Related to the Playing of Sex-typed Roles." *American Psychologist* 8 (1953): 431.

Sears, R. R., Macoby, Eleanor, and Levin, H. *Patterns of Child-Rearing* (Row, Peterson, 1957).

Selye, H. *The Stress of Life* (New York: McGraw-Hill, 1956).

Sherfey, M. J. "The Evolution and Nature of Female Sexuality in Relation to Psychoanalytic Theory." *Journal of American Psychoanalytic Association* (1966).

Simmel, Georg. The Sociology of ———. (Glencoe, Ill.: Free Press, 1950), translated by Kurt H. Wolff.

Simmons, L. *The Role of the Aged in Primitive Society* (New Haven, Conn.: Yale University Press, 1945).

Sjoberg, G. "Contradictory Functional Requirements and Social Systems." *Journal of Conflict Resolution*, 1960, 4.

Slater, P. E. "On Social Regression." *American Sociological Review* 28 (1963): 339–64.

———. "Parental Behavior and the Personality of the Child." *Journal of Genetic Psychology* 101 (1962): 58–68.

———. "Parental Role Differentiation." *American Journal of Sociology* LXVII (1961): 3.

———. "Prolegomena to a Psychoanalytic Theory of Aging and Death." In

Kastenbaum (ed.), *New Thoughts on Old Age* (New York: Springer, 1964).

———. "Psychological Factors in Role Specialization." Unpublished doctoral dissertation, Harvard University, 1955.

———. *The Glory of Hera* (Boston: Beacon Press, 1968).

———. "Toward a Dualistic Theory of Identification." *Merrill-Palmer Quarterly* VII (1961).

Slater, P. E., and Kastenbaum, R. "Paradoxical Reactions to Drugs: Some Personality and Ethnic Correlates." *Journal of American Geriatrics Society* 14 (1966): 1016–34.

———, Morimoto, K., and Hyde, R. W. "The Effects of LSD upon Group Interaction." *Archives of General Psychiatry* 8 (1963): 564–71.

———. "The Effect of Group Administration upon Symptom Formation under LSD." *Journal of Nervous and Mental Disease* 125 (1957): 312–15.

Slater, P. E., and Scarr, H. A. "Personality in Old Age." *Genetic Psychology Monographs* 70 (1964): 229–69.

———, and Slater, Dori A. "Maternal Ambivalence and Narcissism: A Cross-cultural Study." *Merrill-Palmer Quarterly* 11 (1965): 241–59.

Spiro, M. E. *Children of the Kibbutz* (New York: Schocken Books, 1965).

Spitz, R. A. "Hospitalism: An Inquiry into the Genesis of Psychiatric Conditions in Early Childhood." *The Psychoanalytic Study of the Child* I (1945): 53–74 (New York: International Universities Press).

———. "Hospitalism: A Follow-up Report." *The Psychoanalytic Study of the Child* II (1946): 113–17 (New York: International Universities Press).

Spock, Benjamin. *The Pocket Book of Baby and Child Care* (New York: Pocket Books, 1956).

Stephens, W. N. *The Oedipus Complex* (Glencoe, Ill.: Free Press, 1962).

Steward, J. H. *Theory of Culture Change* (Urbana, Ill.: University of Illinois Press, 1955).

Stuart, Grace. *Narcissus* (New York: Macmillan, 1955).

Sunley, R. "Early Nineteenth-century American Literature on Child Rearing." In Mead and Wolfenstein (eds.) *Childhood in Contemporary Cultures* (Chicago: University of Chicago Press, 1963).

Swanson, G. E. *The Birth of the Gods* (Ann Arbor, Mich.: University of Michigan Press, 1960).

Symonds, P. M. *The Dynamics of Parent-Child Relationships* (New York: Columbia University Press, 1949).

Szasz, T. S. *Pain and Pleasure* (London: Tavistock Publications, 1957).

Taylor, G. R. *Sex in History* (New York: Vanguard, 1954).

———. "The Age of the Androids." *Encounter* 21 (1963): 36–46.

Textor, R. B. *A Cross-Cultural Summary* (New Haven: HRAF Press, 1965).

Thomson, G. *The Factorial Analysis of Human Ability* (London: Houghton Mifflin, 1949).

Triandis, Leigh M., and Lambert, W. W. "Sources of Frustration and Targets of Aggression: A Cross-cultural Study." *Journal of Abnormal Social Psychology* 62 (1961): 640–48.

Turner, F. J. *The Frontier in American History* (New York: Holt, 1921).

Unwin, J. D. *Sex and Culture* (London: Oxford University Press, 1934).

Vogel, E. F., and Bell, N. W. "The Emotionally Disturbed Child as the Family Scapegoat." In Bell and Vogel (eds.) *A Modern Introduction to the Family* (Glencoe, Ill.: Free Press, 1960).

Watt, I. "The New Woman: Samuel Richardson's *Pamela*." In Coser (ed.) *The Family: Its Structures and Functions* (New York: St. Martin's Press, 1964), pp. 267–89.

Weber, M. *The Protestant Ethic and the Spirit of Capitalism* (New York: Scribner's, 1930).

Weinberg, K. *Incest Behavior* (Secaucus, N.J.: Citadel Press, 1955).

Weisman, Avery, and Hackett, Thomas. "Predilections to Death." *Psychosomatic Medicine* 23 (1961): 232–56.

Whiting, J. W. M., and Child, I. L. *Child Training and Personality: A Cross-Cultural Study* (New Haven, Conn.: Yale University Press, 1953).

Whiting, J. W. M. "Effects of Climate on Certain Cultural Practices." In Goodenough, W. H. (ed.) *Explorations in Cultural Anthropology* (New York.: McGraw-Hill, 1964).

———, Kluckhohn, R., and Anthony, A. S. "The Function of Male Initiation Ceremonies at Puberty." In Macoby, E. E., Newcombe, T. M., and Hartley, E. L. (eds.) *Readings in Social Psychology* (New York: Holt, 1958, pp. 359–70).

Xenophon. *Memorabilia and Oeconomicus* (Cambridge, Mass.: Harvard University Press, 1953), translated by E. C. Marchant.

Young, M., and Willmott, P. *Family and Kinship in East London* (Baltimore: Pelican, 1964).

Zborowski, M., and Herzog, E. *Life Is with People* (New York: Schocken Books, 1962).

INDEX

achievement behavior, 92, 93
adaptation, malfunctioning as, 180
addictive cycles, 102
"adequacy" in sex, 1, 10
adolescence, 124–126
Aeschylus, 86
aged, attitudes towards, 43–47
    denial in, 44
    determinants of, 44–46
    as function of performance, 45, 46
    Greek, 43, 44
    malevolency in, 47
    Middle Eastern, 43–44
    in "primitive" societies, 45, 46, 47
age segregation, 52–54, 60–61
aggression, 94–95, 195
    Freud on, 97–99
    restricted erotic gratification and, 100
    see also militarism; war
agriculture, development of, 105, 108
alertness, in healing, 183–184
Alexander, Franz, 153
ambivalence:

as creative force, 185–188
as culture, 172
    mechanism of, 35, 142–143, 144
    in mothers, 79, 80, 82–83, 85, 87, 90
    motivation in, 157–158, 167–168
anticipatory institutions, 116, 119
Araucanians, 91
Ardrey, R., 94
Ariès, Philippe, 60, 61
Aristophanes, 84
Aristotle, 81
Athena, 72, 73, 84, 86, 87
athletics, in Greece, 81
attractiveness:
    male vs. female views of, 2–3
    as social control, 124, 132–133
authoritarian family, myth of, 56–58
authoritarian parents, *see* parental authority
authoritarian personalities, 160
authoritarian societies:
    family systems in, 49, 55, 56–62, 65–66
    old age in, 45
"autotomy," 180

219

Bacon, M. K., 201
Bakan, David, 182
Barry, H. A., 201
Baruch, Dorothy, 74
Bateson, Gregory, 82
Beach, F. A., 197
belief systems, contradictory, 155–157
  ambivalence in, 159–160
  compartmentalization in, 156, 160–161
Bell, Norman, 165
bellicosity, militarism and, 94–95, 195
belligerence, 94, 195
Bettelheim, Bruno, 73
bioenergetics, 179
bipolar dimensions, 188–191
Blake, William, 175
"Blood of the Walsungs, The," 139–140
Blümmer, H., 75, 83
body odors, taboo of, 133
bogies, maternal, 83–85
Bott, Elizabeth, 30–31
boundaries, psychic, 153–154, 178, 187
brain, energy and, 141–142, 150
Brodbeck, A. J., 25
Brown, Norman O., 96, 176
Bunyan, John, 111

Calhoun, Arthur, 56, 57
"cargo cult," 53–54
Castaneda, Carlos, 184
celibacy, as crime, 75
change, personality, 164, 165
change, social and cultural:
  accidental theory of, 102
  analysis of, 111–112
  conflict and, 187
  contradictions and, 156–157
  democratic family and, 48–67
  in family and politics, 64–67

immigrant Jews as affected by, 50–52
Manus as affected by, 52–54
rapidity of, 35, 39, 49–50, 52, 62, 64
as response to social cost, 101
technology and, 62–63
theory of, 102
charismatic leaders, *see* narcissistic leaders
Cheyenne Indians, 91
Child, I. L., 112, 201
child-centered society, 61, 64
child-rearing, 92–93, 94, 95, 98, 109, 181
  as career, 13, 15, 41
  as community issue, 59–61
  as focus in social change, 111–112
  narcissistic withdrawal and, 119–120
children:
  "cult of," 57
  as innovators, 49, 52, 53, 56
  sexual gratification of, prohibited to, 103, 112–113
  status of, 48, 49, 60, 61
China, 63, 65, 66
civilization, sexuality and, 97–100
Civilization and Its Discontents, 104
class oppression, 95
clitoral stimulation, 2, 6
"close-knit networks," 30–31, 33
community life, 13–14, 17
  dyadic intimacy and, 122–140
  libido and, 115–140, 148–149
compartmentalization, 160–161, 172
competition:
  in Greece, 81
  orgasm as, 7
compromises, societal, 155–156
conflict:
  as creative force, 185–188
  see also tension reduction

conservatives, social contradictions and, 172–173
constancy, perceptual, 157
contradictions, in societies, 38, 155–169, 172
Coser, Lewis, 65
cross-cultural scales, 90–93, 103, 193–196
Cross-Cultural Summary, 90, 92, 197
Cuber, John, 5
cultural complexity, 96–97, 103, 104, 105–113, 198–199
  narcissism and, 107–110
  see also civilization; social complexity; technological complexity

dates, adolescent, 125, 126
death:
  as dyadic withdrawal in love-tragedies, 135–136
  fantasy, 11
  as libido withdrawal, 117–118, 136
  social integration activated by, 150
  tension reduction and, 151–153
death instinct, 151
decisiveness, 158
de-eroticization of sexual life, 124
definitions, effect of, 2, 3, 7
Demeter-Kore myth, 78
democratic family, 48–67
  American family as, 54–63
  economic factors in, 55
  historical forces and, 54–62
  state and, 63–64
  technological change and, 62–63, 64
democratic societies, old age and, 45–46
dependency needs:
  vs. independence, 159–160

socialization and, 117, 118, 119, 120, 127–128, 136
dimensions, bipolar, 188–191
Dionysus, 83
disaffection theory, 182
disease, as adaptation, 180
Disease, Pain, and Sacrifice, 182
distancing mechanisms, 34–35, 39, 44, 165
  between parent and child, 48, 49–50
"double bind," 82
"Dread of Woman, The," 73
dualities, in systems, 155–169
dyadic intimacy and withdrawal, 116, 121–140, 187–188

Eckhardt, William, 94–95, 195
"economic man," 119
Ego and the Id, The, 25
egoism, *see* narcissism
ego strength, 118, 121–122
encounter groups, 39, 182, 183
energy:
  in healing, 178, 185–188
  libidinal, 121–122, 141–142, 147
  see also gratification, delayed; narcissistic withdrawal; priority systems, emotional
eroticism:
  bodily functions and, 176–179
  as goal, 153–154
  sublimation of, 5
  as task-free, 10
  as women's domain, 5, 9
Euripides, 86
"experiential chasms," 50, 54, 55, 62, 63
extramarital dyads, 135–136
extramarital intrusion, 131–134
  impermanency of, 133
  prohibition of, 103, 105, 110
  romantic stylization in, 133–134
  time-space constriction in, 134
extroversion, 144, 189

family:
  American, 54–63
  contradictory roles in, 165–169
  extended, 30–33, 85
  in Greece, 68–89
  libidinal withdrawal and, 116,
    137–139
  nuclear, 30–33
  participation and power in, 70
  patriarchal, 26, 34–35, 68, 105
fantasy:
  about matriarchs, 68
  oedipal, 146, 151
  positional, 24–26
  in sexuality, 9, 11
female infanticide, 78
feminine ideal, 16
  historical view of, 3
  as non-sexual, 6
  as obsessional, 4
Fenichel, Otto, 23
Ferenczi, Sandor, 74, 153, 176,
  177, 180–181
Finley, M. I., 77, 85
flirtation, adulterous, 131
Ford, C. S., 198
fragmentation, in disease, 180–181
Franklin, Benjamin, 111
Freud, Anna, 21
Freud, Sigmund, 21, 22, 25, 57, 73,
  74, 94, 95, 96, 121, 124, 138,
  141, 143, 144, 146, 151, 152
  on civilization and sexuality,
    97–100, 104, 108, 110
friendships, 17, 18
frontier, as democratizing, 56
frustration, 104–113
funeral rituals, 117–118
future, orientation toward, 49,
  53–54, 56, 59, 60, 61, 63, 65,
  67

genitals:
  as central control, 176, 178
  fear of, 73–74, 82

female, 6, 10, 73–74, 82
  male, 1, 82
Glory of Hera, The, 193
Goethals, George, 197
Gomme, Arnold, 69
Goode, William J., 49, 66
Gouldner, Alvin W., 81, 107–108,
  199
gratification, delayed:
  culture creation and, 104–113
  emotional hierarchy and, 145–
    146
  libido diffusion and, 114–115
  see also infant gratification; sexual
    restrictions
Greece, classical:
  ambivalence of mothers in, 79,
    80, 82–83, 85, 87, 90
  domesticity in, 70–71
  drama of, 71, 78
  fear of women in, 72–74, 83–85,
    86–88
  homosexuality in, 72, 75, 80
  madness in, 81, 82–83
  marriage trauma in, 74–77
  myths of, 79, 81–83, 85
  narcissism in, 79, 80–83, 90
  old age in, 43, 44
  Olympian gods of, 71–72
  as patriarchal, 26, 69
  as warlike, 90
  women's status in, 69–72, 78–79
Grinnell, G. B., 91
guilt:
  as control, 110, 111, 119
  libido withdrawal and, 116
Gusii, 32

Harroff, Peggy, 5
healing:
  alertness and, 183–184
  pleasure and, 179, 185
  practice of, 185
  renurturing in, 181–183
Hebrews, old age and, 44

Hera, 72, 73, 83, 84–85
Herodotus, 71
hierarchy, emotional, *see* priority systems, emotional
Hindley, Marlene, 193
Hitler, Adolf, 34
Homer, 77
homosexuality, 25, 72, 75, 80
honeymoon pranks, 130
Horney, Karen, 73
hospitalization, magical thinking and, 47
Huizinga, J., 81
Human Relations Area Files, 199
Hume, David, 96

identification:
    cross-sex parental, 23–26
    personal, 20–26, 29–35
    positional, 20–26
    psychoanalytic vs. social psychological, 21–22
    with same-sex parent, 23–26, 27–35
    specialization and, 28–35
Immigration, Great, 61–62
incest taboo, 102, 114–115, 116, 138–139, 151
individualism, 45, 111
    as social artifact, 37–38
infant gratification:
    pain and, 147–149
    restrictions on, 93, 100–101, 103, 142–146
inner-direction, 40
instrumental tasks, 176–178
internalization, 20–24, 32–33, 35, 40, 111
intimacy, 19
    child-parent, 35
    in extramarital dyads, 132–135
    in marriage, 40
introversion, 144–146, 189
isolation, domestic, 15, 19
Isomachus, 71

James, Henry, 181
Japan, child-rearing in, 49
Jewish immigrants, 50–52
Johnson, Virginia, 6
Jung, Carl, 144, 189
jurisdictional levels, 201

Kagan, Jerome, 22
kibbutzim, 59, 66
Kitto, H. D. F., 84
Knots, 186, 187

Laing, Ronald, 186, 187
Lawrence, D. H., 7
learning, ideal of, 50, 51
"level" people, 144–145
liberals, 172–173
libido:
    "adhesiveness of," 144
    blocked, 102
    "borrowing" of, 97, 98, 102
    diffusion and withdrawal of, 114–116, 136–137, 139, 141, 149, 151
    displacement of, 102, 103, 104–105, 113, 133
    energy of, 121–122, 141–142, 147
    nature of, 114, 179
    pain and, 146–151, 152
    tension and, 151–153
"loose-knit networks," 30–33
Lorenz, K. Z., 94
love, political aspects of, 5
lovemaking, nonorgasmic, 10
Lozoff, Elizabeth, 193

Maccoby, Eleanor, 33
Mace, David and Vera, 64, 113
McLuhan, H. M., 113
Mailer, Norman, 7
male bonding, 110
Mann, Thomas, 139–140
Manus, 52–54
Marcuse, Herbert, 96

marriage:
    bond, 77, 85, 110, 122
    careers and, 41–42
    child as intrusion in, 131
    clergy's role in, 128
    contradictory roles in, 165–169
    dyadic withdrawal and, 116, 122,
        124, 125–131
    extramarital dyads and, 131–134
    fear of, 12
    God's role in, 128
    in Greece, 74–77
    honeymoon and, 129–130
    labor division in, 30–31, 71
    mobility and, 40–41
    polarization in, 166–167
    ritual, 127–128
    specialization in, 168–169
    as unequal contract, 17
Masters, William, 6
maternal mediator, 34, 35
matriarchs:
    fantasies about, 68
    sexual equality and, 105
Mead, Margaret, 52, 53, 54, 164
medical advice, child-rearing prac-
        tices and, 112
Medusa's head, 73, 74
men:
    fear of women in, 88–89, 110
    feminine ideals of, 2–4, 6
    sexual threats to, 4–5, 7
militarism:
    correlates of, 92, 93, 95, 99,
        194–195
    scale for, 90–91, 92, 193, 195, 196
Milton, John, 106, 109, 119
mobility, 27, 33, 36, 62, 84
models, modeling, 22, 32, 63, 71,
        164
money, pleasure and, 150, 151–
        152, 175–176
moral patterns, flexibility of, 39–40
Morgan, Edmund, 59
mother-daughter bond, 78

mothers, working, 41, 71
mother-son relationships, 74, 77–
        79, 81, 83–85, 86–88, 93,
        138–139, 145–146
mourning, hallucinating in, 143
Mowrer, O. H., 23
Murdock, George, 96–97, 139, 197,
        198–199

narcissism:
    in Greece, 79, 80–83, 90
    in innovation, 121, 136, 139
    levels of, 106
    libido diffusion and contraction
        in, 114–116, 136–137, 139,
        141, 149, 151
    restricted sexual gratification
        and, 101–110, 150
    rewards of, 120–121, 135, 136
    role models and, 106–107
    scales and studies of, 193, 196,
        197, 199, 201
narcissistic leaders, 120–121,
        129–130, 135, 139
narcissistic withdrawal:
    illness and, 148
    psychosis and, 117
    self-interest and, 118–121
    socialization and, 116, 117, 135,
        149
Nazi Germany, 65
neolithic revolution, 105, 108
1984, 123, 128
nursing, eroticism in, 147–150,
        181–183

obedience behavior, 92, 93
"object choice," 21
oedipal situation, 93, 95, 110, 145
oedipus complex, 145–146
    identification in, 25
Old Testament, 86, 87
Orestes, 86, 87
Orestes, myth of, 85–87

orgasm:
    "adequacy" and, 1–2
    as pleasure, 1, 7
    as release from tension, 5, 8–10,
      150, 152, 176, 178
    as technology, 1, 7
    as unit of lovemaking, 8
    war compared with, 177
orthogonality, 189–191
Orwell, George, 123, 128
other-direction, 40
Ovid, 79

pain, 143, 182
    libido and, 146–151, 152
parental authority, 48, 49, 50, 55,
    56–62, 65–66
Parsons, Talcott, 24, 29, 149–150,
    175
passivity, as female ideal, 3–4
peer groups, adolescent, 124–125
Peterson, R. A., 107–108, 199
"phantom limb," 143
Pierson, George, 36
Plato, 96
pleasure:
    as body's currency, 150, 151–152,
      175–176
    as central control, 175–179
    drive toward, 152–153
    healing and, 179, 185
    orgasm as, 1, 7
pleasure centers, in brain, 142, 177,
    178
Plutarch, 70, 77
polarization:
    marital, 166–167
    social, 173
pool maiden, myth of, 73
postpartum dyads, 136–137
    socialization in, 137
pottery, 107–108
power relations, between sexes, 68,
    70, 71, 88
pregnancy, narcissism in, 136

pride, sin of, 119
primitive peoples, 27–28, 32, 47,
    52–54, 73, 118, 123, 126, 138,
    148, 162, 179
    studies of, 90–95
primogeniture, 49
priority systems, emotional, 141–
    154, 177
"problem child," as familial role,
    165
Protestant ethic, 8, 104–105, 111,
    127
psychoses, as autotomy, 180–181
pubic hair, shaving of, 73–74
Pukapuka Island, 26
punishment, 21, 23, 29, 32, 33
Puritanism, 55, 66, 109, 110, 112
    family dilemma in, 58–61, 66
    orgasm and, 7–8, 10

quarantine, childhood as, 61, 63

radicals, 173
reactionaries, 173
rebellious personalities, 160
Reisman, David, 31, 40
"renurturing," 181–183
repression, sexual:
    achievement and, 112
    culture and, 92, 95, 96–113
ridicule, as social control, 125, 133,
    164
roles:
    child's, changes in, 60
    contradictory, 162–169
    culturally defined, 16, 18
    male social, 5
    parental, 27–35
    specialization in, 27–35, 37–39,
      40, 41
    traditional, 50–51, 58
Roseborough, Howard, 31
Ryder, Norman, 50
Ryerson, Alice, 102, 110, 112

sadism:
  correlates of, 92, 93, 99, 194–195
  scale for, 91–92, 193, 195, 196
sadomasochism, 9
Sanford, Nevitt, 22
schizophrenia, 82
Scott, J. P., 31
seduction, in infancy, 149–150, 181
self-concepts, 187
Semonides of Amorgos, 75
settlers, American, 55–56
sex antagonism, 76, 78–79, 86, 88, 102, 110, 125
sex-killers, 86
sex roles, contradictions in, 164–165
sexuality:
  in folklore, 3, 6–7
  in Greek myths, 79, 81, 82, 83, 85
  mother's, 84, 148, 150
  political use of, 5–7, 9
  promiscuous, dyad intimacy and, 123
  in social interaction, 149–150
  vs. work, 5
sexual restrictions:
  effects of, 97, 99–101, 104–113
  premarital, 102, 103, 105, 109, 110
  quantitative factor in, 109
  studies of, 103, 197–198, 201
  of women, 6–7
sexual segregation, 26, 31, 40, 51, 76, 78, 85
Shakespeare, William, 104, 120, 123
shame, as control, 110
Sherfey, Mary Jane, 105
Simmel, Georg, 34
Simmons, Leo, 45, 193, 198
Sjoberg, Gideon, 155–156
Slater, Dori Appel, 90, 193, 197
sleep, as libidinal withdrawal, 152
social anxiety, 115–116, 117–119, 120, 125–126, 130, 135, 151

social complexity:
  measures of, 100–101, 102, 103
  narcissism and, 108–109, 113
social cost, 41, 94, 98, 101, 107, 108
social phenomena, psychologizing of, 171–172
social problems, definition of, 170–171
social systems, contradictory, 157, 160–161, 172
  compartmentalization in, 160–161, 172
  concept of role in, 162–163
  family roles in, 165–169
  processes confused in, 173–174
  sex and age roles in, 164
Socrates, 76
Sophocles, 84
sorcery, 46–47, 73, 83
Soviet Union, 63, 65
specialization, role, 40
  collaborative, 28
  cost of, 37–39
  in marriage, 41
  parental, 27–35
Spitz, R. A., 149
"steep" people, 144–145
Stephens, W. N., 74, 197
Stuart, Grace, 100, 104, 150
suicide, 118, 123, 178, 180
Swanson, G. E., 199
Symonds, P. M., 216
syphilis, 110

taboos, 130, 133
  postpartum, 101–102, 103, 109, 110
  theories of, 101–103
  see also incest taboos
Taylor, G. R., 112, 141
technological change, in democratization, 62–63, 64
technological complexity: measures and studies of, 100–101, 102, 103, 107–108, 199, 201

narcissism and, 107, 113
as phallic pride, 107
tension reduction:
death and, 151–153
as motivator, 178
threshold effect in, 152
Textor, R. B., 90, 92, 94, 193, 194, 197
Tocqueville, Alexis de, 56
transference, mechanism of, 142–143, 144–146, 151
transience, effects of, 39–41
Triandis, L. M., 193
Trobriand Islanders, 73
tuned-in state, 183–184
Turner, Frederick Jackson, 56

unconsciousness, 180–181
uniformity, 38
unity, concept of, 186–187
Unwin, J. D., 97, 105, 112

vacations, eroticism and, 5
vaginas, "hairy," 73
Victorian society, 28, 55, 77, 131, 164
villains, as heroes, 119, 120, 135
virginity, 3, 76, 84
as nonthreatening, 87
Vogel, Ezra, 165

war:
narcissism and, 108, 110
orgasm compared with, 177
restricted sexual gratification and, 100
scales, 195, 196
see also militarism
Weber, Max, 111
Whiting, John W. M., 101, 112, 194, 197, 201
women:
equality and, 41
genitals of, 6, 10, 73–74, 82
in Greece, 69–88
masculine strivings of, 79
men's fear of, 88–89, 110
oppression of, 88
sexuality of, psychoanalytically defined, 6–7, 10
social position vs. psychological influence of, 70–71
sorcery and, 73, 83
unity among, 16
see also mother-daughter bond; mothers, working; mother-son relationships
Women's Liberation groups, 18

Xanthippe, 76

yoga, 182
youth-worship, 44, 46